D0787410

THE DUEL

*De Gaulle
and Pompidou*

THE DUEL

De Gaulle
and Pompidou

BY

PHILIPPE ALEXANDRE

TRANSLATED BY
ELAINE P. HALPERIN

HOUGHTON MIFFLIN COMPANY BOSTON

1972

First Printing   c

Copyright © 1972 by Houghton Mifflin Company.
All rights reserved. No part of this work may be reproduced
or transmitted in any form by any means, electronic or
mechanical, including photocopying and recording, or by
any information storage or retrieval system, without
permission in writing from the publisher.

Originally published in French under the title *Le Duel:
De Gaulle–Pompidou.* © Editions Bernard Grasset, 1970.

ISBN: 0–395–13640–7
Library of Congress Catalog Card Number: 72–177450
Printed in the United States of America

320.944
A382d

192311

To Nathalie,
to Nino.

Mills College Library
Withdrawn

MILLS COLLEGE
LIBRARY

Contents

Author's Note

To A FRIEND who was planning to write a book about him, de Gaulle once said in all seriousness: "To write about de Gaulle is no easy task."

The difficulty is twofold. To tell the story of the partnership between General de Gaulle and Georges Pompidou, to recount the relationship between two very dissimilar men that lasted for a quarter of a century, to explore their differences as well as their friendship — all this seemed risky but also rewarding. Moreover, we have lost the habit of explaining history in terms of the reactions of those who make it. And yet moods as well as selfish motives are often at the root of historic decisions.

From their first encounter until their last farewell, the two men engaged in a lengthy tête-à-tête. Seeking to reconstruct their dialogue meticulously, I was very careful not to fill unavoidable gaps with flights of imagination.

In dealing with General de Gaulle, I was reluctant to record all his words as they were recounted to me. The general was often moody, and so he was quite capable of contradicting something he had said only a moment before. He also liked to elicit a response from his listener, if need be by concealing his own feelings. Eminently equivocal, de Gaulle often took unrestrained pleasure in passionate but contradictory statements. Therefore, I had to make a selection. I limited myself to those thoughts that de Gaulle expressed to many people and that reflected his considered opinions. At times I had to deny myself the pleasure of reproducing for my readers the pungent remarks that the general so often enjoyed making. The reader will in any case understand that I could not reproduce anything that I myself had not carefully verified.

As for Georges Pompidou, he has always remained exceedingly discreet about his relations with Charles de Gaulle — at least until now. Here again I decided to omit any reaction of his that seemed excessive or ephemeral. I have recorded only those things that, in my judgment, really left their mark on the man. I deliberately omitted passing resentments or manifestations of pettiness that were probably due to weariness.

The reader will perhaps notice that certain important areas — France's foreign policy, for example — have been passed over in silence. I was not attempting to write the history of the Fifth Republic nor that of Gaullism. Consequently, I omitted everything that had no direct bearing on the relations between de Gaulle and Pompidou.

I would like to express my deep gratitude to the ninety persons who, from September 1969 to July 1970, helped me reconstruct these events. I am particularly indebted to those people in high places who gave me so much of their valuable time. The reader will certainly understand why I cannot name them. However, I would like everyone who helped me in the governmental hierarchy to know how very grateful I am.

The Cast of Characters

CHARLES DE GAULLE: Born in 1890, he became an historical figure at the age of fifty by undertaking the kind of unreasoning venture Frenchmen are so fond of. He belonged to that lesser provincial nobility whose only asset is the possession of certain virtues. Its members serve God and country — sometimes both. Of Irish ancestry, de Gaulle had three children. One, a defective daughter, died in 1946. Living in the shadow of the great man, his wife, Yvonne Vendroux, managed to make herself inconspicuous. The rest cannot be told in a few lines.

GEORGES POMPIDOU: His relatives, country schoolteachers, liked to boast of him as a professor in Paris. A succession of happy coincidences plus General de Gaulle's sponsorship — the "great man" distrusted professional politicians — brought him to the center of the political stage. Born in 1911, he comes from a region of France, the Auvergne, that gave France shrewd politicians and equally shrewd cattle merchants. His son, Alain, is a doctor; his wife, Claude, belongs to the fashionable set in Paris. Pompidou likes poetry and entertains literary ambitions; he also enjoys fine French cooking and the company of VIPs.

MAURICE COUVE DE MURVILLE: A professional diplomat, he has held all the major posts, from Bonn to Washington. De Gaulle made him a minister because he was one of the country's highest-ranking ambassadors. A perfect executive, secretive and haughty, he has a British sense of humor. Political ambition came to him quite late in his career, after six years as foreign minister. Born in 1907, he is a Protestant, a golfer — not a very good one, however — and a student of modern painting, as is his wife. His is perhaps the most one-track mind in French politics.

JEAN-MARCEL JEANNENEY: Father of a large family, son of the man who presided over the Senate during the thirties, he is a professor of law. He entered the political arena at the invitation of his childhood friend Michel Debré; but ever since May 1968, the two men have not been on good terms. Jeanneney served as a minister in several of de Gaulle's cabinets. Architect of the fateful 1969 referendum, after Pompidou's election he became a member of the opposition. He is known for his bow ties.

ANDRÉ MALRAUX: One of the great French writers, Malraux began his career by fighting on the side of the communists in the Spanish civil war; he ended it as one of General de Gaulle's ministers from 1958 to 1969. His was the great romantic voice of Gaullism. An adventurer eager to escape boredom, he quit politics when de Gaulle resigned and went back to his writing. But was he ever really a politician? Everything he did had a poetic quality. Born in 1901, he has a tormented look, facial tics, and a swarthy jaw.

JACQUES CHABAN-DELMAS: The luckiest of Gaullists. A general in 1944 at the age of 29, he helped liberate Paris. His triumphs have been varied: sports (tennis), women, politics (mayor of Bordeaux for the past twenty-five years), innumerable friends. But for eleven years de Gaulle relegated him to purely honorary functions (as President of the National Assembly), which he performed with a certain elegance. Is he too handsome to be taken seriously? Yet he played a major role in the Algiers conspiracy that brought de Gaulle to power in 1958. And he bore up well under the king's ingratitude. In 1969 Georges Pompidou appointed him premier. He hates to work, he says somewhat flippantly.

FRANÇOIS MITTERAND: A friend of Chaban-Delmas's and leader of the opposition, he was regarded with contempt by General de Gaulle and the Gaullists. He ran against the general in the 1965 presidential elections. From 1948 to 1958 he held several ministerial posts. "A Florentine prince," say his enemies. A seductive-looking man (he has a Roman profile), he is one of France's finest political orators. But occasionally, notably in May 1968, his own machinations proved his undoing. Married and father of two sons, he has friends in fashionable Parisian circles. A Catholic and a socialist, he favors cooperation with the communists. He likes to play golf and read, and enjoys the attentions of a small but appreciative circle. One of his brothers is a general and a Gaullist.

RENÉ CAPITANT: More Gaullist, people used to say, than de Gaulle himself, his association with the general began before the war, when de Gaulle was a colonel. Capitant was always fond of de Gaulle and served him with tremendous ardor. He is the author of Gaullism's social doctrine. But he hoped to bring de Gaulle closer to Marx and Trotsky. When Pompidou was a banker, Capitant was on bad terms with him. He died in 1970, a few months before the general. He was 69.

ROGER FREY: Sporting gray, wavy hair, and an affected smile, he collects red roses and revolvers. Young and poor when he first embraced Gaullism, by 1958, when he was 45, he had become one of France's most powerful politicians. Founder of the Gaullist party, the Union for a New Republic (U.N.R.), he served as Minister of the Interior for five years, turning the police loose against all of de Gaulle's enemies. Very little is known about his origins or his early youth, but de Gaulle used to say: "Frey? He has his baccalaureate."

JACQUES FOCCART: If Frey's background is obscure, Foccart's is even more so. No one even knows his real name. De Gaulle's personal informer, he headed the secret police and all the Gaullist commandos. Many conspiracies were naturally attributed to him. His appearance jibes with the stories about him: he has a glacial look that takes in everything — an impassive face. He was responsible for the addition of the word "barbouze" to the French vocabulary. Today it means secret agent.

OLIVIER GUICHARD: One of the Gaullist barons, he really is a baron. During the war his father served under Marshal Pétain. Perhaps to atone for this sin, Guichard at a very young age offered his services to General de Gaulle. In 1958 he thought that his discreet loyalty would be rewarded; but he had to wait eight years for a ministerial promotion. The general felt that Guichard's personal life was not above reproach and that he had too many questionable connections. Inured to ingratitude, he was 49 when his friend Pompidou, upon becoming president, gave him the coveted post of Minister of National Education. Tall, massive and calm, he always looks tired. And perhaps he really is tired after so many years spent in the service of Gaullism.

LÉON DELBECQUE: A native of northern France like de Gaulle, he is a friend of Chaban-Delmas's. In 1957, when Chaban-Delmas was Minister of War in the socialist government, Delbecque served as his adviser. He was active in the movements and conspiracies in Algeria that brought de Gaulle to power in 1958. But the general, ungrateful like all monarchs, thought the young man a nuisance. A fierce champion of French Algeria, and hostile to the general's peaceful policy, he was excluded from the Gaullist family. In 1968 Chaban-Delmas tried in vain to persuade de Gaulle to pardon Delbecque.

RENÉ COTY: In 1953, at the age of 71, he was elected President of the French Republic in the thirteenth round of balloting because he was the least well known of all the French politicians. His wife soon became very popular. A president without power, he was forced in the spring of 1958 to appeal to de Gaulle in order to avert civil war. Showing little gratitude for this, the general took Coty's place six months later. Forgotten by the Gaullists, Coty died in his native city of Le Havre. De Gaulle's speech at Coty's grave consisted of no more than a few cold, trite remarks.

MICHEL DEBRÉ: Son of a famous doctor, grandson of a rabbi, he is the most ardent, the most uncompromising, and the most quick-tempered of all the Gaullists. Nicknamed "Saint John the Baptist," he was a passionate champion of French Algeria. Nevertheless, because of his devotion to de Gaulle, it was he who carried out the policy that culminated in Algerian independence. But his mental anguish only annoyed de Gaulle. In 1962 the general removed Debré from the premiership and replaced him with Georges Pompidou. For a long time Debré was on bad terms with Pompidou — the two men are very unlike — yet as soon as the general departed, Debré offered Pompidou his services. He has four sons, a brother who paints, a house in Touraine and a single religion: Gaullism. He claims to be its grandfather.

GEOFFROY DE COURCEL: In June 1940 he was the general's principal collaborator in London. Diplomacy is his profession. Silent and distinguished-looking, he again served under de Gaulle in 1959. His reward came three years later when he was appointed French ambassador to London, a position his grandfather had held in 1885 and one he hopes to keep until the end of his days.

CHRISTIAN FOUCHET: He joined de Gaulle on June 19, 1940, twenty-four hours after the general's famous appeal from London. Fouchet was 29 at the time; a tough man, he was ready and eager to embark on any mission de Gaulle might have in mind for him. A high functionary in Algiers at the time of Algerian independence, he was later appointed Minister of National Education and entrusted with student reform. As such, he was responsible for the maintenance of order during the May 1968 riots. Tall, white-haired, possessor of a powerful voice, he quarreled with Pompidou in 1970, accusing him of betraying Gaullism.

RAOUL SALAN: A general who commanded French troops in Indochina and Algeria, and the most political of all French military leaders, it was he who shouted "Vive de Gaulle" in Algiers in 1958, thus paving the way for the general's return to power. But de Gaulle, who distrusted military men — especially those who had ideas of their own — retired Salan in 1960 at the age of 60. A year later, Salan took his revenge by organizing the Algiers putsch with the help of army men and *pieds-noirs*.° Sentenced to death, he went into hiding in Algeria and organized the *Armée secrète* (O.A.S.). Captured, he was sentenced to life imprisonment, although de Gaulle wanted him executed. He remained in prison for seven years before being pardoned.

EDMUND JOUHAUD: Born in Oran, he was a general in Algeria and an ardent champion of French Algeria. Less political than his friend Salan, he quit the army in 1960 and retired to his native city. A year later he took part in the Algiers putsch. Less fortunate than Salan, he was captured and sentenced to die, though he was later reprieved. After the events of May 1968 he was released from prison and became the head of an organization for repatriated Algerians.

GASTON MONNERVILLE: A black lawyer born in French Guiana, he carved out a political career in the Lot, where Pompidou has a country house. For twenty-one years, from 1947 to 1968, he gracefully presided over the Senate. But in 1962 de Gaulle deprived the Senate of its principal function: election of the President of the Republic. Thereupon Monnerville became a fierce opponent of Gaullism and de Gaulle. The general told all his ministers that they were never again to speak to Monnerville. Yet he was the man who, according to the constitution, was to replace the President of the Republic in case of need.

VALÉRY GISCARD D'ESTAING: France, too, has her eggheads. Giscard d'Estaing, a disciple of Kennedy and Galbraith, is one of them. Reared in the expectation that he would one day become President of the Republic, in 1962 at the age of 36, he was appointed Minister of Finance. He appeared to be on his way. But less than four years later he was dismissed from the post by Pompidou. D'Estaing struck back by criticizing the general, uttering his famous "Yes, but . . ." After de Gaulle departed in 1969 he entertained the hope of becoming president, but his aspirations proved short-lived. Realizing he was still too young, he finally decided to support Pompidou. The new president rewarded Giscard by reinstalling him as Minister of Finance. Slender, elegant and prematurely bald like so many brilliant intellectuals, he likes to ski and hunt wild game in Africa. His wife and daughters are all named after flowers.

° Translator's note: The *pieds-noirs* were the European Algerians.

BERNARD TRICOT: Allergic to the game of politics, Tricot is a cold, silent functionary. For invaluable service to de Gaulle during the war in Algeria, he was recompensed in 1967 by being named the general's principal adviser. After de Gaulle's departure, Tricot continued as a conscientious functionary, his days and nights spent poring over legal documents.

PIERRE JUILLET: In 1951, at the age of 30, he was already a Gaullist. But he was primarily Pompidou's personal friend and adviser. He dislikes seeing his name in print. In addition to being a public official, he works for a few commercial enterprises.

MICHEL JOBERT: A small, thin man with a twinkle in his eye and an ironic smile, he served as adviser to several politicians, including both Gaullists and non-Gaullists. In 1963 he became Pompidou's adviser. Some people claim that he is the real head of the government. He is rarely seen in public and his voice is seldom heard. In 1969, when he was 48, he moved into the office next to the president's, on the first floor of the Elysée Palace. He stated at that time that his only ambition was to remain at this post.

DAVID ROUSSET: Writer, philosopher, Trotskyite, he is a typical leftist intellectual, although he looks like a plump gourmet. He became a Gaullist in May 1968 and won election as a deputy, a fact that surprised many Frenchmen. But it is unlikely that he will remain for long a member of the Gaullist majority; in his opinion, Pompidou is not revolutionary enough.

FRANÇOIS-XAVIER ORTOLI: This Corsican happened to be born in Indochina. A civil servant, he was appointed minister in 1967 when Pompidou was fed up with professional politicians. But his career as a minister has been marked by several defeats: first during the monetary crisis of 1968 — he was the Minister of Finance at the time — and again in 1970 during the Franco-Algerian schism. Pompidou nonetheless appreciates both his devotion and discretion.

JOËL LE THEULE: In 1958, when only 28, he was the youngest Gaullist deputy. But it took de Gaulle ten years to make him a member of his cabinet. Formerly a professor of geography in a military school for noncommissioned officers, he is a bachelor.

RAYMOND MARCELLIN: Since 1948 he has been a minister many times in many different cabinets. Consequently, it took a miracle to induce de Gaulle to appoint such an old-time politician to his cabinet. The miracle was the May 1968 crisis, after which Marcellin became Minister of the Interior. A bachelor, he spends all his days and a good part of his nights in his office issuing military orders to the police, pursuing leftist students, Maoists and Castroites with unflagging zeal. The very opposite of an intellectual, he was elected deputy for a constituency in Brittany; and he has all the traits of a man from Brittany: tenacity, a feeling for law and order — and a bad disposition. The French police consider him a perfect leader whose moods never prevent him from sleeping peacefully at night.

EDGAR FAURE: Universally regarded as France's most brilliant politician, he is a gifted speaker with a talent for coining ambiguous phrases and winning elections. He joined General de Gaulle in 1966, when the Algerian tragedy had been forgotten. Minister of National Education from 1968 to 1969, he was cashiered by Pompidou. Frenchmen are waiting to see what form his revenge will take. Bald, a pipe smoker, a talented writer, lawyer and law professor, he finds no task distasteful. Ever since 1969 he has been carrying in his breast pocket a letter of praise from de Gaulle — "my boss," as Faure refers to him. His wife, Lucie, writes novels and runs an anti-Gaullist review. He is very much influenced by her. Everyone calls him by his first name. Although born in 1908, he will always entertain the ambitions of a young man.

THE DUEL

*De Gaulle
and Pompidou*

Introduction

GENERAL DE GAULLE had retired from the world.

He was working in a small study he had furnished on the ground floor of the tower in his house at Colombey. His desk was piled high with pamphlets, newspapers and sheets of paper covered with writing in his own hand. There were countless deletions and all the signs of punctilious labor. Each word was carefully chosen. "I'm scribbling," the general would say.

Beneath the lowering Champagne sky, the window directly in front of him opened onto a stretch of grass and centuries-old trees. Beyond, on the other side of the wall enclosing his property, two policemen needlessly kept guard. There was no noise of any kind. De Gaulle was concentrating. Relentlessly, he pursued his task. It was to occupy six, perhaps seven of the remaining years of his life — the time span of a presidential term.

He worried about the time he still needed to complete his task. The same anxiety had haunted him earlier, at the Elysée. Once a week, three assistants brought him notes and documents from Paris. He worked long hours each day in his eagerness to finish the job. That autumn, in the year 1970, he would be eighty years old.

"May heaven allow him to write the whole truth," Madame de Gaulle sighed. "That's his only purpose, his unique obligation to himself as well as to France. There are so many lies, myths, and stories to stamp out. May God give him the necessary strength!"

Jealously, the general preserved his secrecy. In the summer of 1969, he decided to withhold publication until after his death.

Then he changed his mind.   With some relish, he confided to those near him: "To be sure, there are many things still to be said. But I will also discuss a few men. I'll add a little gossip here and there."

What things? What men? May 1968? Pompidou? The rupture? His exile? In Paris, the general's companions indulged in canny speculations. Some thought the general would use his pen to avenge himself, to denounce those who had deserted him. History was a long skein of betrayals, of treachery and ingratitude. For thirty years, in heart and mind, de Gaulle had suffered deeply because of such occurrences. Now, in "the evening of his life," he saw a chance to draw his own portrait as it would go down in history: alone, friendless, surrounded by envy, by enemies. His followers devoured by ambition and he, de Gaulle, carrying in his own arms a nation so often discouraged and dispiriting.

"Frenchmen are tired of climbing to the summit," the general said after his departure. "They long to return to the valley where they can dangle their feet in the streams and go fishing in peace."

His memory never faltered. Awesome, it was also without pity.

. .

At peace now, Pompidou took over his legacy. He had been second in command; now he was first. This ascent had not taken him by surprise. He was loath to imitate the general, to "ape" him, as he put it, or to be haunted by his image. His days were devoid of anguish, his nights empty of nightmare. There were many changes at the Elysée Palace: furnishings, pictures, habits, faces. But whenever questions arose that had to do with France — the state, power — Pompidou instinctively followed the path of his predecessor.

His debonair countenance on occasion gave way and he would thunder exactly like the general: "Let no one be under any misapprehensions about the republic!"

De Gaulle was a man for tempests. He sought them and exploited them; they fed his ardor. Pompidou avoided storms. To a former Gaullist minister he admitted: "I'm not an historic personage. I represent no personal equation. I have my own style, my own manner, my own methods — and there's the difference. But in all essential matters I will not deviate an inch: all that counts is the independence of France, her role in Europe, and her position in the world. Little by little, day by day, I will see to it that she gets her proper share of things, without fanfare or drama. But I will see to it."

Solitude weighed upon Pompidou. Three hundred feet from the Champs-Elysées with all its hubbub, the Elysée Palace was an island of silence. Sometimes Pompidou would stop in front of a window for a moment and gaze at the sunlit park. He would sigh: "To think that I can't even go for a short walk about Paris!"

He knew how the general used to organize his time, separating basic problems from secondary ones. How often had he sat in the armchair facing the desk that was now his! At every turn he came up against the past, but he tried not to dwell on it. De Gaulle was far away, living but invisible, present but silent. The tie had been severed forever. It was better that way.

"There can be no meeting, no contact between de Gaulle and myself," he said. "He would be tempted to give me advice and I not to follow it. It is enough for me to know that I am profoundly Gaullist. This is what guides me and determines my actions."

. .

The silence between the two men was not an empty one. For years they had shared disappointments and ambitions. Pompidou was the admirer, de Gaulle the benefactor. All in all it spelled affection, a friendship of sorts, compounded of reservations, anger, clashes, resentment — all the vicissitudes of complicity.

What happened between them? Neither would say. The general took this mystery with him to Colombey. At the Elysée, Pompidou was bound by discretion and respect.

Most of the Gaullists closed their eyes. De Gaulle had left, "the Dauphin" remained — that was all. At least for the time being. "Let's not question the past. It's still too near," they said.

But now and then an imprudent witness interrupted the silence. Facts, episodes, details cropped up and the "friendship" took on the changing colors of life.

"Goodness," said one of the ministers, "it's much too difficult. We'll never know. Pompidou is an enigma. And the general resorts to allusions, as if he were challenging his interlocutor to react. To be realistic, one can only say that the two of them worked side by side and together lived through fair and foul weather. Then they parted."

Henceforward, in speaking of the men who were now in charge of the affairs of France, the general employed an icy plural: "they." To the old companions who came to visit him in his retreat, he refused to say a word about his impressions of what was going on "there," in Paris. "To reproach no one, either publicly or privately" — such was the rule he finally imposed upon himself.

His former ministers — Couve de Murville, Jean-Marcel Jean-neney, André Malraux, all of whom had retired from public life — went regularly to Colombey. De Gaulle talked to them of the changing seasons, the condition of the highways, the nearby forests, even of the soft, runny cheeses he liked so much. And he spoke of France — the France of Louis XIV, of Napoleon, of the year 2000. He never mentioned the France of Mr. Pompidou. Then he would accompany each guest to his car, repeating one last time, as he always did to Malraux: "I'm far from it all, very far. And so I will remain. That's all you can say publicly about me."

The ministers, who were now Pompidou's ministers, sent him cards on his birthday, on New Year's day, on June 18, or merely to assure him of their constancy. Sometimes he answered in his own hand, sometimes the replies were written by his secretary. Always, he limited himself to polite phrases and thanks. Among the Gaullists a friendly rivalry developed in regard to the messages each had received from the general. The old faithful watched for the mail from Champagne, hoping de Gaulle would give them a sign of life. But in vain. To men who were not involved in politics, especially military men, the general wrote somewhat longer letters. But he was always careful to make no allusion whatsoever to his successor. A soldier himself, he had learned to keep quiet at Saint-Cyr.

Silence, thus cultivated, became a gesture.

. .

But during the first few months of exile the general readily gave way to bitterness and rancor. At that time he seemed to find it excessively painful to remain silent. In talking about Pompidou to his intimates, de Gaulle uttered vengeful imprecations. One of his listeners summed it all up by saying, "He was just plain nasty."

"But, after all, we all had to take a lot of malicious remarks. We didn't break off with him on account of it," another minister commented.

In the summer of 1969, in letters and in confidential conversations, the general deplored the fact that Frenchmen had failed to follow his lead. He predicted a troubled future. He claimed that the country, governed as it was by timid or weak men, would soon flounder in inactivity. He foresaw a return to the ridiculous political games at which parties, groups and factions had become past masters. He underscored the inevitable cheating, the jockeying — the "soup," as he put it — and the triumph of special over national interests. Now, as in 1946, he was back in Colombey, an impotent spectator, a man without power.

He did approve certain initiatives. In July, when his brother-in-law, Deputy Jacques Vendroux came to spend a few days at Colombey, de Gaulle discreetly encouraged the establishment of a parliamentary society called Présence et Action du Gaullisme. "We have to be able to sound the alarm, should it become necessary," the general said. To a former minister he spoke more explicitly: "It can be the yeast that will cause the dough to rise."

People muttered that he would not be long in coming back to the capital once a week to stay in the town flat that had been furnished for him on the Avenue de Breteuil — just as he once used to go to the Rue de Solférino during "the crossing of the wilderness."

The general, however, had laid aside his anger and his chagrin.

His wounds no longer bled. He had found serenity and happiness of a kind. Never had visitors seen de Gaulle so tranquil, so intimate. When he welcomed them to his squat country house, he worried about the difficulties of the trip, very touched that people had come 280 kilometers to see him. In the drawing room, the only signs of past grandeur were a few gifts offered to the former president and scattered here and there on old pieces of family furniture. De Gaulle would stir up the fire in the hearth and serve the apéritifs himself. When his guests were seated around the table, he would talk about what he had seen on television. He would ask banal questions and listen courteously to his guests.

When he was not working at his desk, he would go for walks in the nearby forests he loved so much. On Sundays he sometimes went on a picnic. Charging up the stairs of his house, he was satisfied to know that his strength was still with him. "The general is happy now," Madame de Gaulle would say fondly.

He had triumphed over the last act of his epic — his departure. That which had been, all things considered, a defeat, a pitiable flight, he had turned into a work of art worthy of history. There was no little satisfaction in this. The general had left power "morally intact," as he put it (the hundreds of letters he received were proof of this); and he was physically intact as well. The essentials had been preserved: history would not be blighted by the image of a fallen, aging, diminished sovereign. "In all his actions, a man must be picturesque," he remarked on one occasion.

His curtain call had done no damage to the preceding acts.

. .

At the Elysée, too, people looked to Colombey. Pompidou heard the men around him speak of the general's so-called plans. He could already visualize the string of old grumblers, lining up to see de Gaulle and hear his words, then returning to Paris to spread venom and spite. The chief of state was being watched and this annoyed him. And the name of Charles de Gaulle resounded in his ears like an awesome warning.

People were waiting for some solemn, incontrovertible proof of his loyalty. A few weeks after his inauguration at the Elysée, as he was welcoming to dinner the Gaullist leaders who had come to unburden themselves, Pompidou lost his temper: "Rubbish! Rubbish!" he said.

Repeatedly he reminded his listeners that he had worked with de Gaulle for a quarter of a century, that he had received from the general innumerable evidences of confidence, gratitude and friendship. Gaullist he had been and Gaullist he would remain. That should be enough. Who but Pompidou could have led the army to success after the sorry failure of April 27, 1969? Had everybody forgotten Malraux's somber prophesy that it would be impossible to build "a victory for Gaullism upon the defeat of the general"?

A Gaullist whom Pompidou did not like had anathematized Pompidou, publicly calling him a Sancho Panza of malfeasance at the expense of Don Quixote. Pompidou had immediately replied by insisting that the rebel be excluded from the Gaullist party within twelve hours. This was done without delay.

For its part, Présence et Action du Gaullisme announced that it would keep watch on the new chief of state. These words were a slap in the face for Pompidou. "Vigilance is directed at someone who has been guilty of treason. Whom have I betrayed?" he asked. The premier, Jacques Chaban-Delmas, advised serenity for the Gaullists. "As for myself," he said, "when I hand on the torch, it will be with the immense satisfaction of having done what I should do so that the general will be able to say — oh, without telling me directly, it will be enough to know that he is thinking it — 'Well done, Chaban.' "

One must rid oneself of memories that can become as painful as remorse. That is what Pompidou said to a former minister of the general's who expressed his intentions of writing his own memoirs: "Do you want to write about May nineteen sixty-eight? About the general's departure? You don't have the right to do so, do you hear? You don't have the right."

The general's successor could relax. Time was his ally. The present silence would last several years, perhaps seven. To one of his old companions, de Gaulle said: "I will intervene only if 'they' go completely off the tracks."

Pompidou had only to pursue the general's grand design, especially in foreign policy, a domain in which Pompidou had had little experience. For the rest, in everything that was less important, the new chief of state was free to impose his will.

He lost little time in speaking more openly. And if he remained extremely discreet in matters touching General de Gaulle — as he had been for twenty-five years — the reason was not so much vague apprehension as habit. A pact had been concluded: "My successor will not do as I did," the general had predicted in 1965. "He'll do as he pleases. He'll do the best he can. He won't do the same things."

. .

Charles de Gaulle and Georges Pompidou — "They're a couple," a minister said. A couple that liked one another, first a little, then a lot, then tired of one another, quarreled and separated — an ill-matched couple, like so many. A quirk of fate had thrown together two men who had little in common. One, a monarch of another age, his head in the clouds, counted the days as centuries and dreamt of his France. The other, one among fifty million Frenchmen, a man from the Auvergne, a peasant, observant of the changing seasons, welcomed the dazzling gifts of Providence as though they were his due.

The secrets of this couple belong to the state. De Gaulle and Pompidou, separated from one another, remain nonetheless linked by a common duty; their moods, their feelings, their passions have merged into a chapter of history. They will leave behind them only a myth and an image. They cannot themselves recount the slow succession of moments, in war and peace, in sunshine and tempests, that forged their adventure.

Part I

THE ENCOUNTER

There is a tide in the affairs of men
Which taken at the flood leads on to fortune;
Omitted, all the voyage of their life
Is bound in shallows and in miseries.

Julius Caesar, *act 4, scene 3*

CHAPTER 1

The Keys to Fate

OLD AGE was something de Gaulle had had occasion to observe. "I saw Pétain die before nineteen thirty," he said. Churchill had declined gradually. And Adenauer was booted from office by an ungrateful people.

Now, all of a sudden, at the age of seventy-four, the general in turn was condemned to the miseries of aging. He was ashamed, almost afraid. From the fifteenth to the twenty-fourth of March, 1964, he visited Mexico and the Antilles under a leaden sky; everywhere he was acclaimed, and his palms were bruised by handshakes. No one knew that he made this trip with a catheter in his suitcase, submitting to a painful medical treatment every evening of the tour. His aide-de-camp, a devoted colonel, witnessed his silent calvary. If the general refused to talk about his sufferings, the reason was neither pride nor reserve. Age had intervened and was crossing his strategy.

When he returned to Paris he accepted the humiliating verdict of the doctors: a prostatectomy was necessary and urgent. It was a routine operation and the disorder subsequently was found to be benign. But at a moment when several candidates were eager to succeed him, Frenchmen would suddenly realize that the general was mortal.

Two or three of his closest collaborators and members of his family were informed. So was the premier, Georges Pompidou. With great secrecy a plan was mapped out. A trip to Picardy was canceled on the pretext that peasant demonstrations were feared.

De Gaulle spent several days alone in his Elysée office. Interviews were cut to a minimum. The general was considering the question of succession. Until now he had scarcely revealed either his intentions or his wishes. There had been too many other problems of a more urgent nature. In conversation he had of course spoken confidentially now and then — often, however, during an outburst of ill humor — or else he had questioned people. In the early days of the Fifth Republic, he had occasionally touched upon the subject with one of his ministers, an old companion of the early days.

"When I am gone," he had said, "well, France should have someone who is known throughout the world, who is morally respected, a man of intellectual prestige. Above all, above all, he should be a man who is not the slave of any particular party or political ideology."

But as soon as the question of names came up the conversation would end abruptly. It was soon apparent that de Gaulle had no successor. This perhaps did not displease him.

At the moment the new republic was still too fragile and the French people too susceptible to their old bugaboos. The general could not leave the fate of the country to chance.

Finally, he made up his mind. On April 16, 1964, just before he left for the hospital, he delivered a speech that was a farewell of sorts. First he drew up a balance sheet: "Having been careful during the past five years to keep the books myself, I can be explicit about our situation."

To prove to himself that even if his body were vulnerable, at least his mind was unimpaired, the general used the occasion to test his memory. He juggled figures as he had never done before.

On the same day, the general handed a sealed envelope to a member of his cabinet; it contained his instructions. Furthermore, he confirmed them orally. If disaster should befall him, the premier must take up the torch. A few Gaullist dignitaries, especially André Malraux, were summoned to the Elysée and informed. It was no ordinary interim government that was thus being entrusted to

Pompidou, but rather a legacy, something partaking of legitimacy.

Ten years earlier, in 1954, the general had penned another last testament: instructions in regard to his burial, the ceremony to be very simple, no flowers, no pomp, exactly like the burial of his young ailing daughter, Anne. De Gaulle had made three copies of the document in his own hand, two for members of his family and one for his chief of staff, Georges Pompidou. Ever since then, he had stubbornly refused to change a single comma of his will. It was a family, not a political testament, written at a time when de Gaulle had ceased to have any connections with the state.

But in 1964 the general had other obligations, not to his family, but rather sacred ones to France.

. .

Pompidou had been premier for two years and a few days. Until now he had only dreamed about his future. He had never dared to say anything about these dreams in public or in the presence of de Gaulle. He had merely endeavored to remain at his post, that of second in command.

The general's instructions converted his dreams into ambitions. Pompidou had been given the right to preside over the Council of Ministers. The President of the Senate, Gaston Monnerville, was the individual to whom the constitution assigned the position of interim chief of state in the event of a power vacuum, yet he was not informed. Like everyone else, he learned about the general's operation seven hours after it had been performed.

Naturally, Pompidou did not allow himself to become too excited over the ephemeral possibility of assuming the presidency. But since de Gaulle had chosen him as his successor, he would prove himself worthy of the honor, just as he had done after every previous promotion.

Within a few days he was metamorphosed. He showed where his true talents lay. Yesterday so timid, the neophyte disclosed at the tribune of the Assembly that he could beat at his own game a politician as experienced as François Mitterand. "On the peaceful banks of the opposition, like the emigrés of the Old Regime on the shores of England, you impatiently await the hour when you will return to the government, having learned or forgotten nothing" — such was his opening attack on Mitterand. Then, so that all of France would know, Pompidou added: "But the future is not yours; it is not for ghosts!"

In his small room at the Cochin Hospital, the echo of this voice with all its youthful vigor reached de Gaulle. Upon his return to the Elysée he retracted the will in the sealed envelope. There was never to be another.

He had left behind an assistant only to find a Dauphin, the title now bestowed upon Pompidou by the press. The general did not take offense. Rather, he offered Pompidou advice: "Show yourself. Do what you must in order to make people talk about you. Go here and there."

As for himself, he queried his physicians.

At first Pompidou did not take the general's advice too literally. He remained prudent. But from time to time he dropped a pregnant phrase. On one occasion, he said to a deputy: "Now I understand the tragedy that befell my predecessor, Michel Debré. But what can you do when you have held this post with all its responsibilities for a long time? It is impossible to go back to being a mere minister again!"

He exhibited his own brand of nobility — twenty years spent close to de Gaulle, many of them in the shadows, in obscurity. Twenty years of patient loyalty.

"And, I believe," he added, "twenty years of affection."

.   .

In 1944 the government was in the hands of heroes: members of the Resistance, Free French, socialists, communists, Gaullists — and even military men still wearing their uniforms. But Georges Pompidou had no glorious titles to brandish when he first hatched his schemes in the wings, offstage. He had only diplomas. He was thirty-three. Men of his age had just lived through epic times. He had spent the war years teaching literature to schoolboys. The Liberation found him engaged in writing a critical study of Racine's *Britannicus.*

He had always remained aloof from the rough and tumble. At the Ecole Normale Supérieure, where his classmates were divided into rightists and leftists, Pompidou showed a superb indifference to political passions. While residing in Marseille around 1936, at the time of the Popular Front and Nazism, when mounting dangers everywhere inspired either hope or fear, catapulting intellectuals and workers into the streets, our young professor was delighted to discover the city's small artistic circles and the drawing rooms of Protestant socialites.

He was, after all, a provincial. He was still a provincial in Paris at the moment of the Liberation, in a Paris that had recovered none of its prewar elegance.

Contacted by a university friend who had said: "The general is looking for someone who knows how to write," Pompidou had his opening. At the general's headquarters on the Rue Saint-Dominique, Pompidou began a lowly apprenticeship. He was naturally put in charge of school and university problems. These were not burning issues for the general. The leading minister was René Capitant, already one of the great Gaullist figures; he was forty-three, a professor of law, and since 1943 he had enjoyed the general's trust and confidence.

Occasionally Pompidou would knock on the door of the forbidding Capitant to express an opinion. The minister would get rid of the young man in cavalier fashion: "I settle the serious matters with the general," Capitant told him. "And if there is any criticism to be made, he will make it himself and in a voice that can be heard."

Twenty-seven years later, shortly before his death, Capitant remarked with a certain malevolence: "Pompidou's influence at the time could not have been very great or I would have noticed it."

This was true. Pompidou was not a very active cabinet member. He was really an assistant. But little by little he was given new tasks: notes to draft, reports on the press to prepare from scratch.

He attracted the attention of de Gaulle's chief of staff, who said: "A good recruit, that Pompidou."

This compliment was subsequently to embellish the Pompidou legend.

Long weeks passed before Pompidou was to find himself in the presence of General de Gaulle — the boss, the symbol. This was an event that Pompidou often recounted. De Gaulle thundered; Pompidou trembled. But the young attaché afterward discovered — or so he said — that this historic personage was not as intimidating as he at first seemed to be.

But who wouldn't have been dazzled by the de Gaulle of 1944, the man of mystery, whose voice was to reecho for years in everyone's memory? Even Malraux had reacted strongly to the great man, so why wouldn't this young man from Auvergne — without a fortune, a name or a past — have been dazzled? The young Captain de Gaulle had at least shared certain affinities and loyalties with Marshal Pétain. Georges Pompidou, still steeped in literature and Romanticism, suddenly found himself in the presence of history — living history. He knew nothing of the general's small cares and preoccupations, the trivial, power-related intrigues, the jockeyings for political position. In Charles de Gaulle he saw only majesty.

As for the general, he had no precise recollection of this initial encounter.

.   .

His future? Pompidou never dreamt for a moment of returning to teaching. He had already learned all he needed to know about the profession. From the time he first taught, Pompidou had decided that he would not vegetate as a professor until the age of retirement. The Ecole Normale Supérieure with all its polish can lead to anything. To his friends in Marseille and Paris, the young man confided his dreams. But he showed no impatience. He would await his chance.

Being a member of the general's cabinet brought no change in his daily life. He continued to have the familiar problem of making ends meet. He still received his professor's salary, plus a quasi-symbolic indemnity. Not enough of course to enable him to kick up his heels. The Pompidous and their two-year-old son lived in a three-room apartment behind the Ecole Militaire. He often walked to the Rue Saint-Dominique. His wife did her own marketing and cooking, and traveled about by metro. The young cabinet attaché did not expect a great fortune.

After a few months someone suggested appointing Pompidou to the Council of State. This was not a passport or even an exceptional favor from the general, who cared little about the comfort of his colleagues. It was a natural promotion for a graduate of the Ecole Normale Supérieure, who, moreover, was a political scientist and had had some experience with public affairs. Besides, the appointment would not become effective until a few months later. When one of his friends came to congratulate Pompidou, the new appointee replied: "Please, I beg you, don't speak about it. It's not much of a promotion. I'll earn about as much as when I taught at the Lycée Henri-Quatre."

For the moment, Pompidou remained in the general's cabinet. On the Rue Saint-Dominique, he occupied the small office of a campaign headquarters. There had been no time as yet to roll out the red carpets of the ministry. Even the furniture smelled of the war.

Pompidou made a few friends, or rather acquaintances. But mainly he had found his vocation: not power but the closest thing to it — government service, or, as the general said, "public affairs."

. .

"I'm getting the hell out of here!"

On January 14, 1946, after having battled the political parties for weeks, de Gaulle announced his decision to his chief of staff. At the Rue Saint-Dominique rumors were rife. Many believed this was just a maneuver or a fit of bad temper. The chief of staff said nothing to the other cabinet members. All anyone knew was that the general was very excited. But, after all, de Gaulle had often experienced worse things.

Three days later, on the 17th, the general repeated: "This time I'm leaving."

He said this to his aide-de-camp and to two other collaborators. These men did not consider the news worth repeating. The general's fits of depression were well known.

On January 20, a Sunday, the general assembled his ministers at noon sharp in the Salle des Armures on the Rue Saint-Dominique. It all happened very quickly. The general's work table and the drawers of his desk had been emptied by an aide-de-camp. In uniform, de Gaulle appeared before the ministers, shook their hands, made a four-minute speech, shook their hands again and left.

A few seconds later, after having put his documents away in an office on the first floor, the general descended the front steps and entered his car. "I don't want to see anyone," he declared.

Just as he was to do twenty-three years later, de Gaulle left unceremoniously, without pomp or protocol, without any grandstanding. After a few hours — the time it took to recover from the shock — his chief of staff called all the cabinet members into his office, made the general's excuses, thanked them on his behalf, and asked them to empty their desk drawers. He wanted to leave the place in order.

The general was convinced that he would be recalled before a week had gone by. "My departure is no more than a misadventure," he said.

The weeks passed but his hope persisted. His companions were also convinced that France could not get along without her liberator. But Georges Pompidou was quick to face reality. Shortly after the general's departure he wrote to one of his friends: "The general is now a legend. He will probably not reemerge."

But a departure as theatrical as the general's, without a gesture, was also a form of art. Pompidou, the specialist in Racine's tragedies was to remember it for a long time — especially in 1965 and again on May 29, 1968.

But for the moment he had to make his way alone.

CHAPTER 2

A Companion in Solitude

COLOMBEY: a squat, completely remodeled house, furnishings that revealed something of the family, a park of centuries-old trees. In Paris people were dueling for power. The general, for his part, was marking time. He was watching for the moment when France would fall into his waiting arms. He sensed the conflicts, the scenes, the impending battles. All this was familiar terrain.

The general's collaborators had found niches — in a ministry, an embassy, an administrative council — the "soup," as he called them. He had no word of reproach for these men. They would be back as soon as he returned. He hadn't slammed the door. With mounting impatience, he kept abreast of the news.

The general had just enough to live on, no more. From an ungrateful nation he would accept nothing. In any case, the funds for the Anne de Gaulle Foundation were safe.

The general and Madame de Gaulle had named this charitable organization for handicapped children after their sickly daughter who was buried there in Colombey. Few have appreciated the tremendous place which this dead child occupied in the general's heart. Little Anne was his greatest sorrow. In England, in Algeria, during the darkest hours of the war, de Gaulle would interrupt his work at the close of each day to sit with his daughter while she had her dinner. If he failed to come, she refused to eat. He would return to his work after she had fallen peacefully asleep.

The general himself carried his daughter to her grave. Then silent, stoical, unmindful of the tears that flowed freely down his cheeks, he returned to his house.

Thus the Anne de Gaulle Foundation was not an ordinary charity. Until recently Madame de Gaulle had run it with the help of one of the general's discreet collaborators. But he had taken a post in Tunis and had named Pompidou to succeed him as chief administrator of the foundation. He sent Pompidou to Madame de Gaulle.

Pompidou, the former professor, had equipped himself perfectly for the task. In Madame de Gaulle's opinion, he possessed that cardinal virtue, discretion. Pompidou thus acquired the habit of going to Colombey at regular intervals to discuss the foundation's budget. Whenever he came, the general, impatiently cooling his heels, would question him. The conversations centered on France, on the world. Pompidou brought with him something of the aura of Paris. De Gaulle was not resigned to being a country gentleman indefinitely.

· ·

Colombey again, and again, winter. De Gaulle, in the presence of Pompidou, was indulging in the sport of character assassination: all the leaders of the Fourth Republic fell prey to his sarcasm. This was the game of politics as seen from the vantage point of Colombey-les-Deux-Eglises. But what about Frenchmen generally? They were cold, hungry, afraid — afraid of war, of having to go without butter, of the communists and social revolution.

"And what about you? What are you doing?" the general asked. Pompidou answered reluctantly. He didn't like to talk about himself. There was really nothing to tell. But the general insisted. Pompidou was a member of the family.

Yes, Pompidou had at last become a member of the Council of State. He was even entrusted with a few files. He was learning his new trade. In addition, he headed the state tourist commission. This didn't take too much of his time. Traveling was something reserved for the privileged few. His life? He didn't miss teaching and had no other ambitions. Thirty years in the Council of State? Why not? The work was pleasant, the corridors quiet — there were attentive bailiffs on every floor — and the windows overlooked a garden where children played under the benevolent eyes of Cocteau and Colette. And since his work afforded him a goodly amount of leisure, as a member of the Council why shouldn't he write something later on?

De Gaulle brooded over his boredom. To write, yes of course. But mainly to act. One day, when the general learned that André Malraux was hard at work on his *Museum without Walls*, he said with a sigh of envy: "How lucky Malraux is to go from one thing to another, from art to public affairs and from public affairs to art, without the slightest difficulty!"

De Gaulle, for his part, could no longer bear this premature retirement. He had no talent for it, he wasn't nearly old enough.

And so in his impatience he returned to the French people, or rather to France. It was good to return to history, even through the back door. Abandoning his village, the parish priest, the postman, the cabinetmaker, the august mayor, the general went off to the four corners of the country to spread his gospel. It was a veritable crusade. The Resistance fighters and the soldiers of Free France took their old campaign outfits out of moth balls and donned them before meeting him. The general's voice addressed all who would listen. Bayeux, Strasbourg, Paris — cities whose names spelled victory. In a country where Frenchmen voted socialist, M.R.P. (Popular Republican Movement) or Radical, where they allowed themselves to be governed by a skillful mix of political parties, many listened to the general.

Pompidou did not accompany de Gaulle. Fascinated, he followed these gatherings from a distance. When one had had the enormous good fortune of approaching intimacy with a great man, it was impossible to remain aloof or indifferent. While other Frenchmen, ministers and journalists, were tempted to shout "dictator" or to warn against the danger of fascism, Pompidou kept reiterating: "A great man."

Early in the spring of 1947 de Gaulle founded the Rassemblement du Peuple Français (R.P.F.) and launched his squadrons of volunteers. Officially, Pompidou remained on the sidelines. He was leery of getting politically involved. His sole loyalty was to the "great man." Besides, he had little confidence in the future of this spontaneous movement. When the fever subsided, de Gaulle would return to his solitude.

And to Pompidou, who didn't remain completely aloof. He had a foot in the door, an ear and eye on the R.P.F. Once or twice a week he visited the Rue de Solférino where the general, the powerful monarch, received his legions. More often he went to the Rue de l'Université, to a small office of the Gaullist party. There he wrote slogans, went over the manifestoes, offered his editorial services.

There too he was to supervise the drafting of the R.P.F.'s first bible, a collection of the general's speeches and quotations from his writings. It was designed to serve as an ideological manual. In it de Gaulle provided answers to all questions.

Indeed, writing was Pompidou's profession. But to ascend a platform and harangue the populace, no. There were others for that, professionals. It was better to observe and, if possible, to understand.

. .

The barons surfaced. There were three of them: Roger Frey, Jacques Foccart, and Olivier Guichard. We will encounter them throughout this entire story, maneuvering between de Gaulle and Pompidou. Although the fortunes of the others, the historic leaders of Gaullism, of the R.P.F., of the Fifth Republic, were to prove varied, these three would remain together, for better or for worse. Like Alexander Dumas's three musketeers, they followed in the wake of a fourth — d'Artagnon-Pompidou.

Only young men attended the birth of the Rassemblement. The barons remained in the background. Gaullism had its champions — Malraux and Debré — and its stars, men like Jacques Chaban-Delmas. The barons remained in the shadows. Two of them, Guichard and Frey, were R.P.F. deputies. Recruited by Jacques Soustelle, they were assigned lowly tasks: to travel through the provinces and check up on the local branches of the Rassemblement, their membership, finances and leadership. They were discreet. Of the three, Foccart alone plied a trade. He was in the export-import business, preoccupied with trivial affairs, as de Gaulle was to observe later. Frey and Guichard, on the other hand, were making a career of Gaullism. They were not overburdened by ready cash. This was the period when the barons arranged their first luncheon meetings: "We met regularly with Debré, Chaban-Delmas and Pompidou. We lunched in restaurants and talked about General de Gaulle and the Gaullists. On Sunday mornings we would often meet in Roger Frey's apartment to sum things up."

Other luncheons took place once a week, on Wednesdays, at the Latin American House. These included the princes, Malraux and Debré, as well as the barons.

It was during these repasts that the problems of the R.P.F. were really dealt with, without de Gaulle's knowledge. New recruits were added; others were replaced. The budget was discussed; the funds available were not enormous. Conversation often turned to nonpolitical subjects — the theater, books, the arts.

Georges Pompidou did not attend all of these luncheons. In general, he had little say about the affairs of the R.P.F. Early in 1948 he became the general's chief of staff, although he remained a member of the Council of State. And he still took care of the Anne de Gaulle Foundation, visiting Colombey at regular intervals. But he took no part in the intrigues of the R.P.F. His gray eyes kept a careful watch over the fallen sovereign's little court. Like a typical Ecole Normale Supérieure graduate, blasé, somewhat skeptical, he was a little lost among the members of this political camarilla, who dreamt of power.

But he kept the general informed about the trivial disputes that comprised the everyday life of the R.P.F. And de Gaulle took a certain delight in discovering that Pompidou shared his contempt for human frailties.

"Oh, the Gaullists," he was to say one day, "apparently there are lots of busybodies among them." And the general would gesture vaguely, as if sweeping away specks of dust.

Endowed with an excellent memory, Pompidou was to recall these early years of Gaullism.

.　.

In spite of everything, the Rassemblement gave rise to grandiose aspirations — in de Gaulle as well as among the Gaullists. Legislative elections were in the offing. Preparations had to be made; the elections had to be won; power was there for the asking. There was no dearth of volunteers, militants or candidates. The R.P.F. sought methodically to canvass all of France.

The general, however, had no intention of making personal appearances during the preelection campaign: "Can you see me," he said, "putting my hat in a little cubbyhole in the checkroom of the Palais-Bourbon?"

Nor could Pompidou see himself engaged in a parliamentary career. And so he took no part in the planning of the electoral campaign or in any of the work at the party's headquarters.

At that time the general and his friends were preoccupied with prosaic matters. The exchequer of the Rassemblement was empty. All sorts of activities had been carried on — there were more than a thousand meetings during the month of February 1949 alone — and these cost money. New subsidies had to be found before the campaign began. André Malraux hit upon an idea — a typical one for a poet. He suggested the dissemination of stamps throughout the country so that citizens would be able to contribute financially to the public welfare which de Gaulle symbolized.

On this occasion, an R.P.F. leader related how Pompidou emerged from the shadows: "The stamp campaign was prepared by a financial committee of sorts. We had one initial meeting. Pompidou was seated next to a director of the Rothschild Bank, who must have held some position such as treasurer of the R.P.F. It seemed to me that the two men were working together to promote this enterprise. At subsequent meetings, whenever the treasurer was absent,

Pompidou took his place. He did a good job. The stamp campaign proved a great success."

After these legislative elections, Pompidou was once again put in charge of the R.P.F.'s financial committee. His job was to find the money to pay the expenses incurred during the campaign.

This was no accident. Ever since he took over the Anne de Gaulle Foundation, Pompidou had come to epitomize, in the eyes of de Gaulle, financial and administrative expertise. No more and no less. There was no dearth of thinkers, politicians or strategists in the general's entourage. Besides, he himself was all these things.

De Gaulle was grateful to Pompidou for having taken on a thankless task for the R.P.F., a modest but indispensable one. The general had no intention of lending a hand in such matters. But he certainly didn't deprecate the stewardship of others.

The files of the Council of State, plus the financial problems of the R.P.F. hardly gave a man time for frivolity. Pompidou was forty years old. Only one favor was granted him: a flat on the Rue Charlemagne in one of those Parisian apartment buildings at the edge of the Marais. He entertained a little, but quite modestly. His cuisine was of indifferent quality — Madame Pompidou was not one to spend hours at her stove — but people went to the Pompidous' for good company rather than for good food.

His confidential tasks with the R.P.F. won him de Gaulle's notice. Pompidou gave no sign of entertaining political ambitions. In de Gaulle's eyes this was tangible proof of purity of heart. The Rassemblement was a complicated seraglio in which men, groups, federations and cells were constantly waging a muffled war. De Gaulle seemed to grant his favors now to one group, now to another. He appreciated the neutrality of his chief of staff, even if it sprang exclusively from the Auvergnat's prudent nature.

The finance minister of the R.P.F., like his opposite number in the government, had his say. At regular intervals, Pompidou sent the general brief notes that were not restricted to financial matters.

The 1951 elections placed 120 R.P.F. deputies in the Palais-Bourbon. This was a goodly number but obviously not large enough to bring de Gaulle back to power. Rumor had it that Pompidou, in a note to the general, described the outcome as "disastrous." Thereafter Pompidou clearly foresaw that the R.P.F. would suffer because of this failure to achieve its unique objective.

Delicate, painful discussions and even disagreements ensued. De Gaulle was viscerally hostile to the regime established by the Fourth Republic, to all its political parties, combines, "dirty tricks." Even his silence disclosed his rejecting attitude. The R.P.F. deputies found it increasingly difficult to put up with the general's intransigence. "The smell of the soup," the general jeered.

From a certain distance, Pompidou witnessed the tragedy of the Rassemblement. He kept himself informed. He listened to the general's diatribes against "those" deputies. Not being the target, Pompidou approved.

On March 5, 1952, when Antoine Pinay was invited to form a new government, the leaders of the R.P.F. gathered around the general in a room near the Rue Saint-Dominique where for a few months de Gaulle reigned. According to one of the participants, the meeting took place in "an atmosphere that was charged with drama: one could sense that the general had already decided to dump the R.P.F. I've always thought, although I don't know why, that Georges Pompidou, who naturally did not attend the gathering, had been consulted."

. .

It took the Rassemblement more than a year to meet its demise. During this interval, the general's "finance minister" was faced with a desperate situation. The R.P.F. did not have a cent. Debts had accumulated and the bailiff was frequently seen delivering a blue envelope to Colombey, to General de Gaulle, President of the R.P.F. This was when Pompidou and a few loyal businessmen went to see all their acquaintances in an effort to raise money. But most employers no longer believed in de Gaulle. They preferred to donate secretly to those who were then in power.

On May 6, 1953, in a communiqué that Georges Pompidou handed to the press, de Gaulle announced his withdrawal from the R.P.F.: "This marks the end of our illusions," the general declared. "We must make ready in case we are needed."

Once again he returned to solitude. As for the Rassemblement, it was virtually dead. Its final phase proved painful. A bailiff even came to the Rue de Solférino, the headquarters of the movement, threatening to seize the furniture.

Georges Pompidou was to assume the task of disposing of the movement's unfinished business. The R.P.F.'s militants were left to their own devices. Some had no jobs and virtually no means of livelihood. Often Pompidou himself received them in the Rue de Solférino and attempted to find employment for them. These companions of de Gaulle's — obscure, ordinary citizens — were to be eternally grateful to him.

As for the first-rank Gaullists, who likewise had been orphaned, they tried to make the best of their new situation. Once a week, when de Gaulle came to Paris — and Pompidou was always in the adjacent study on the Rue de Solférino — they came to see the general. But the future was bleak and held no hope.

De Gaulle indulged in bitter imprecations, but his was a voice crying out in the wilderness. Colombey was all that was left to him, particularly the small study set up on the ground floor of the tower. Here, surrounded by books, using a plain working table and a solid armchair, the general intended to write his war memoirs, to scribble away and thereby seek to launch a final appeal. Little by little he found consolation in the pleasure of writing, of covering sheets of paper with sentences and paragraphs, searching patiently for a certain phrase and endlessly emending his work. With all the enthusiasm of a young man, he was discovering a fresh source of joy.

Pompidou too was busy: the Council of State, lectures at the Institut des Sciences Politiques, tidying up the R.P.F. Out of loyalty, respect and a tender devotion, he remained at the general's beck and call. His heart had gone out to this prematurely aging, worn-

out, defeated man, a man still convinced that he was invested with a
sublime mission.

. .

The Gaullists harbored no illusions. Their future was not tied to
de Gaulle. The adventure was over; it had died quietly. Fifteen
years later, Pompidou himself admitted: "I thought the general
didn't have a chance because of the political atmosphere, the public
indifference to Gaullism."

Alone with his memories, his past, de Gaulle contemplated history, the history he had created. His trips to Paris were becoming
less frequent. With somber satisfaction, he allowed his name to sink
into oblivion. Former collaborators, especially Pompidou, kept him
abreast of what was going on, what people were saying. Everything
was subjected to his sarcasm. More and more was being tossed into
"the soup" while France was dying. He, de Gaulle, was perhaps
"the last of the French" — so he described himself to a friend.

His war memoirs progressed rapidly. By the start of 1954 he had
completed a definitive text, typed by his daughter Elisabeth, reread
and revised. Fine. He called in Pompidou, the financier, and naturally asked him to take care of the practical details. He knew he
could count on the discretion and clear-mindedness of his chief of
staff. The book was the general's final appeal to France. It was not
to be handled like an ordinary manuscript.

Pompidou took the manuscript and prepared to negotiate. He
began by ceremoniously inviting to his home editors of France's
three largest publishing houses. He allowed each editor a few hours
to read the precious text which, he said, "must not leave my apartment." Then the three editors called on de Gaulle in Paris and
were asked to suggest how to launch the book.

The general gave his verdict. Pompidou labored over a contract.
Then, once all the various provisions had been agreed upon, the
general signed the contract and offered his editor a glass of champagne. Once again, Pompidou proved to be the model agent.

At this point, the former professor revealed his own preoccupations: de Gaulle had afforded him an opportunity of doing so. With all the delicacy of a reigning monarch, the general had expressed an interest in the lives of his men. The Gaullists were free to do as they pleased. A few of them were politicians, but not Pompidou. Once again the former professor was seeking a suitable position.

Pompidou told de Gaulle that Baron Guy de Rothschild, whose acquaintance he had made, had offered him a position. The general approved. After all, what is more fitting for a financier than to join a very prestigious bank?

The chief of staff had thought of everything. He had even found someone to take his place: Olivier Guichard, one of the barons.

"All right," said the general, "let it be Guichard," even though, in de Gaulle's opinion, he was a bit young. "He has tact but I'll have to keep a close watch over him."

Pompidou assured the general that despite his work at the bank he would have time to keep an eye on his successor. And he himself would remain as before at the disposal of de Gaulle for any important mission.

The general knew of course that no important mission was in the offing.

.   .

Thus, with the blessings of the general, at peace with his own conscience, now that Guichard was taking over, Georges Pompidou devoted himself to his new profession, his third. Once again he was the neophyte, for the finances of the Rothschild barons were quite different from those of the R.P.F. Once again he found himself launched in an alien world. Being neither impatient nor impetuous, he thought that this was where he would probably remain permanently. In fact, he was almost certain.

Pompidou treasured memories. Moreover, as everyone knew, he was one of the last faithful. To have observed and listened to a man like de Gaulle, to have witnessed his rise and decline was something entirely different from negotiating on behalf of the oil interests of Baron Guy de Rothschild. But a man had to live, even without de Gaulle.

"During those years," one of the general's aides-de-camp has recounted, "we scarcely saw Pompidou at Colombey. I don't remember that he lunched there even once. The bank took up a good deal of his time."

After his swan song on the plan for a European army, de Gaulle resumed his silence. Almost no one visited Colombey. Those who did were for the most part former companions who had time to hark back to the good old days. To keep one foot in the Paris camp, the general continued to drive the 280 kilometers from Colombey to the capital in his old Citroën, the car of his days of glory. Ingeniously, as old men do, he padded his schedule with visitors, playing the comedy of a man of power.

Pompidou was still fascinated by de Gaulle. Not for a single instant did he imagine that the general would ever again be the leader of France. But he remained under de Gaulle's spell.

Whenever the general came to Paris, accompanied by Madame de Gaulle and his aide-de-camp, Pompidou left the bank and hastened to the Rue de Solférino or the Hôtel La Pérouse. To be there, close to the "great man," to hear what he had to say, to follow his thinking — this was enough to satisfy Pompidou. It must be said that Pompidou was in no way self-seeking. Perhaps it was merely his need for an exclusive friendship with the "great man" that brought him to his side.

"In those days, when I came to the Rue de Solférino," a loyal disciple of the general's relates, "I had first to see Guichard and Pompidou. Often, citing one reason or another, I would ask to see the general. Pompidou would try to ascertain the real object of my visit. He would question me shrewdly, attempting to discover what I knew or thought or might have heard. Then he would urge me not to take too much of the general's time. Finally, after my audience with the general, I was again stopped by Guichard or Pompidou. I was asked to give all the details of what I had said, what the general had answered. And the general's state of mind. Oh, the general's state of mind was the most important of all."

Our informant added: "Moreover, even when the general wasn't there, Pompidou often came to the Rue de Solférino, either during the lunch hour or at the end of the day. He would remain there for a few minutes talking with Olivier Guichard or Jacques Foccart. He would settle some practical problem — there still were some — or concern himself with the pecuniary difficulties of a momentarily embarrassed militant, and then he would leave."

Whenever de Gaulle traveled to a foreign country or to the colonies, it was Pompidou once again who took care of the practical details. In 1956 he organized the general's voyage throughout the French empire, contacted the government through Chaban-Delmas, who was a minister at that time, arranged for the use of a ship, the *Caledonia*, as well as for a military escort, and dealt with the delicate questions of protocol.

By now Pompidou had made many new and varied contacts. He dined in town at fashionable restaurants, rubbing shoulders with prominent Parisians. Everyone knew him. But above all, because of his position with the Rothschilds, he became acquainted with industrialists, financiers, employers, and politicians then in office, none of whom were Gaullists.

Listening carefully, he relayed to the general whatever the VIPs of the moment were talking about. In de Gaulle's eyes, Pompidou was no longer the discreet administrator but a man well informed about many things, including affairs of state.

"The general had two informants at that time," one of his aides-de-camp relates, "Foccart and Pompidou. In Foccart he had a listening post among former members of the Resistance, veterans, Africans, and even certain trade union leaders. As for Pompidou, he was the businessman, representing the industrial world, the bourgeoisie and the Parisians. Besides, the two men, Foccart and Pompidou, got along beautifully. Their friendship was to last fifteen long years, until nineteen sixty-nine."

.   .

The meetings of the barons and the luncheons at the Latin America House continued to take place regularly. Present were Michel Debré, who periodically announced his resignation as deputy, and also, of course, Frey, Foccart and Guichard — sometimes Malraux. Pompidou did not share the political fervor which, in the absence of the general, pitted these men against one another on all sorts of questions.

"He intervened rarely," one of de Gaulle's visitors relates. "However, I remember that in nineteen fifty-seven, he ardently advocated the construction of an atomic plant that France was hoping to put in the works. He said it was the key to our independence. But at these meetings we mainly discussed the constitution, the 'system,' to use the general's word."

.   .

On Wednesdays the general would arrive at 5, Rue de Solférino, an ordinary building with an imposing stairway supported by a cement pillar and a bronze banister. The general would greet Foccart, Guichard and a few others who happened to be there — half office boys, half guerrilla fighters.

On the first floor there were two doors, one of which was padded. Behind them was "his" study, with two tall windows overlooking the street, white walls, waxed oak moldings and doorways. Made of oak, too, were the large, cumbersome desk and the armchairs with square feet placed at angles near the doors. A metal model of the Lockheed the general had used during the war stood in the opposite corner.

The study closely resembled the office of a bourgeois notary public from northern France. Nothing was lovely or even comfortable; nothing appealed to the eye.

Seated at his desk, the general would turn his back to the light in order to spare his ailing eyes. Then the ritual would begin: the newspapers, the mail, talks with collaborators, interviews. An immutable routine that lasted more than ten years. No noise, no telephones ringing — the chill, the half light of a church.

The "house" was at its least numerous. Olivier Guichard had had a week to prepare for this Wednesday, to establish, with the help of the aide-de-camp, the order of visitors and to select from among the plethora of newspapers, reviews and documents of all kinds whatever might be of interest to the "great man" — this was how the faithful referred to him. The all but invisible secretary, a former navy officer, had slipped the various letters addressed to the general between the pink pages of a large book. In one pile were those that required a personal answer, in another those which the secretary would himself attend to.

Nothing changed from one Wednesday to the next save the names of the visitors.

. .

France had just begun her Algerian calvary. The general discouraged curiosity. Removed though he was from power, mystery still continued to be his rule. He said: "Algeria, Algeria! That is a far vaster problem."

Even when the words "French Algeria" or "independence" were uttered in his presence, he remained silent. He never tipped his hand.

Through the good offices of Guichard he even went so far as to publish a communiqué contradicting in advance all the remarks on the subject that could be attributed to him.

Nor did Georges Pompidou venture an opinion on such an explosive subject. All he said was that the problem could remain unresolved for many years.

"Algeria," he confided to one of de Gaulle's companions, "has been put on ice. And for a long time." Another time, at a Gaullist luncheon, he confessed, "Algeria, I really know nothing about it."

In the course of time he became a full-fledged banker, a kind of general manager of the Rothschild Bank, going from one item of business to another, from oil to nickel, from transportation to construction. He was the contact man, paving the way for negotiations. The profession demanded discretion. A chance remark could affect the Rothschilds personally. Pompidou, too, was practiced in the exercise of secrecy.

Having finally become well-to-do, he moved to the Quai de Béthune where the Ile Saint-Louis forms an angle. His windows opened onto the Seine. There was nothing bohemian about his apartment: a huge drawing room, many fine pictures, conventional furniture. In the bedroom, one painting, the work of Pompidou's son, Alain.

Lunches, dinners, little restaurants, fashionable nightclubs, theater, women in the social swim, actors, singers, painters; all the well-known journalists, preferably editors of big newspapers; charity balls, evening parties where catty remarks were exchanged — all these figure in the official biographies of Monsieur Pompidou.

Amid these diverse activities, politics continued to hold a considerable place. The Rothschilds' right-hand man conferred with deputies, ministers, presidents, people of all kinds save communists. He naturally preferred the general's companions and saw to it that a place was preserved for him among the barons. Olivier Guichard, promoted to chief of staff thanks to Pompidou, scrupulously kept him abreast of everything that was being said within the Gaullist family.

CHAPTER 3

Second Floor, 5, Rue de Solférino

A THOUSAND SMALL SIGNS heralded the coming storm. A cabinet fell. An identical one took its place. No longer did the general feel even tempted to indulge in sarcasm. In November 1957 the Gaullists met, planned, organized. Many Frenchmen who ignored or even hated the general nonetheless joined the Gaullists. The Rue de Solférino had come to life. Guichard and de Gaulle's aide-de-camp now had a good deal to do, deciding whom they would favor by arranging interviews for them with the general.

But de Gaulle discouraged his companions and friends: "I shall never be called back." The barons, and Pompidou too, believed him implicitly. "The system prefers anything whatsoever to de Gaulle," the general said, "even chaos, even the fall of France."

After All Saints' Day, de Gaulle received the good Léon Delbecque, a man who proved his worth as a member of the R.P.F. Delbecque had just become a member of Chaban-Delmas's staff. Chaban-Delmas was Minister of War at the Rue Saint-Dominique, a post close to the heart of de Gaulle. Delbecque wanted to take advantage of his privileged position to preach Gaullism, especially among the military. Full of enthusiasm, he confided his plans to the general. But de Gaulle interrupted him: "You'll be wasting your time. It's all over. There's nothing doing, believe me. Besides, Frenchmen don't give a hoot about Algeria. As for the *pieds-noirs,* yes, maybe they'll get out in the streets — between two drinks of anisette."

Nevertheless, de Gaulle allowed Delbecque and many others to

MILLS COLLEGE
LIBRARY

waste their time. Within two months groups and workshops were formed in many parts of France and Algeria — this caricature of the early Resistance movement was hastily dubbed "the 1958 conspiracy." In the Rue de Solférino, Olivier Guichard tried to keep abreast of what was happening. It wasn't easy. And he in turn informed the general and Pompidou, both equally silent. Léon Delbecque, the *franc-tireur,* was in almost constant contact with the barons. He would go to see one, then another, or meet them in bistros.

As early as February, he informed de Gaulle that he had managed to obtain precise, detailed reports. "The army and the population," he said, "are just about to revolt."

But the general obstinately refused to believe it. Then, as Delbecque enumerated the many distressing indications, de Gaulle, suddenly animated, stretched out both arms and said: "Well, yes, Delbecque, you can see how things are. If we had a regime, a government, a state, the problem would be resolved in two shakes of a lamb's tail. The *pieds-noirs?* They are Mediterraneans, Mediterraneans through and through. They don't understand anything. And the army? Oh, the army! It is busy with promotions, leaves. Besides, it obeys."

The general stood up and accompanied his visitor to the door. Before leaving, Delbecque managed to add a few words: "My general, believe me, I am sure of Algeria. I know it is ready. It's the apathy of the metropolis that scares me."

But the interview was over. De Gaulle answered rapidly: "Well, if you want to, talk it over with Debré. You and he can see whether it will be possible to accelerate the course of events."

. .

The work of Penelope, accomplished by Delbecque and a few other collaborators, bore fruit. At long last the French began to listen. A public opinion poll placed de Gaulle at the top of a list of

French political figures. But only 13 per cent of the population had been polled.

Many people queued up every Wednesday in the Rue de Solférino — former friends, recently rediscovered, plus some new ones and a few strangers. The general still seemed as indifferent as ever, but he was only putting on a prodigious show.

Pompidou, because of his inexperience, could not believe in the success of these small-scale clandestine machinations. "At the moment there is a trend in your favor," he told de Gaulle. "But I am afraid that it will come to nothing."

"That is also my opinion," the general answered.

.   .

By March it was clear that an explosion impended. No one could say where it would lead. The barons and Delbecque decided to form a committee for the collection of information on everything that was going on. It was a gigantic task. "We met secretly," Delbecque has recounted. "Sometimes in one person's house, sometimes in another's."

Delbecque paid a second visit to the Rue de Solférino. For once the general was willing to let him have a glimpse of what he secretly planned to do if he were invited to take over once again. First, rather reluctantly, he said: "By the time they call upon me, everything will be razed or burned. Nothing will be left. Algeria will cease to exist. But when the communists begin to frighten the wives of the capitalists, then, yes, I'll be sent for."

Finally, after Delbecque named all the men of good will who were holding themselves in readiness — "We have to tell them something," he urged — the general uttered the long-awaited words: "A presidential regime? You don't impose a regime on a country, and especially not on France, a land with a personality of its own. But we shall have to move in that direction, introducing at the same time a large amount of regional autonomy."

This was what Delbecque had been waiting for. After notifying the barons, he flew to Algeria. On April 25, 1958, the first disciplined, methodically organized demonstration took place in Algiers. It was a dress rehearsal.

"This parade of twenty-five thousand people was obviously a victory for me," Delbecque said. "I said to the general, 'See, when the time comes, the *pieds-noirs* will forget their anisette!' De Gaulle merely shrugged his shoulders: 'They'll take anyone, don't you see? Anyone except me.' By now, I think my nerves were on edge: 'Well, but if it *did* happen? What if the explosion did take place and a national referee was needed? Would you accept then?' Answering me gravely, for the first time in ten years he called me by my first name: 'Yes. I'm at France's disposal, Léon.' "

Delbecque went on: "Pompidou happened to be in the Rue de Solférino, having moved back into the first-floor study opposite the stairway. When I left the general, Pompidou asked me to come into his office. He was alone. He asked me many questions and I answered all of them without any hesitation. I noticed, but this didn't surprise me, that he knew everything, even the most confidential plans. Our conversation lasted a long time. I remember I also suggested that Pompidou send his own men to Algiers."

Either Pompidou failed to understand or else he didn't care to tip his hand. A few days later he sadly confided to an old associate: "The general has never been farther from power."

Perhaps Pompidou really believed this, after all. Among the barons only the heavy eyes of Foccart expressed a slight enthusiasm.

. .

May 13, 1958. History was being enacted in Algiers. In Paris the future heroes had not yet packed their bags. They had decided to wait a day or two before crossing the Mediterranean — the Rubicon.

As for Pompidou, his habitual routine remained unchanged. While the radio transmitted the cries of the people of Algiers, he dined on the banks of the Seine at the home of a friend in the company of three enemies of Gaullism. He was the only one to finish his dessert. Such sang-froid impressed the others. Actually, Pompidou knew the timetable of the planned operations in Algiers. But whereas his dinner companions were alarmed, he maintained that this flare-up would not amount to very much.

That evening the barons did not yet realize that the victory so long dreamt about was now a possibility. That lovely spring evening Chaban-Delmas, who had just lost his ministerial post, remarked to a Gaullist leader: "This is all nonsense. De Gaulle will never return. Let's go home. Let's go to sleep. Let's not give people a chance to talk about us."

What about de Gaulle? Tomorrow, as usual, he would be at his appointed place.

The next day was a Wednesday, May 14. The customary little rituals in the Rue de Solférino took place: the general shook hands with a few people; his aide-de-camp carried a black briefcase that appeared to be empty. The entire day would be spent as usual. No surprises. Pompidou came to hear the news. There wasn't any. The editor of the house that was publishing the *Memoirs* was in the office of the "great man." De Gaulle was finalizing things. He had completed his sixth chapter. There were to be seven in all. The third volume of the *Memoirs* would be ready on August 15 and was expected to appear toward the end of October. When the editor mentioned "events which, after all, could . . ." the general took off his glasses and in all sincerity asked: "What events?"

But just the same, a little later he advised Georges Pompidou to remain prudent, calm, and available.

It was Guichard who did most of the work. He handled the crowd of journalists the following day, distributing a brief statement the general composed. Guichard had mimeographed it on the rusty old R.P.F. machine. At the same time, he contacted the new head of the government, or at least one of his advisers. That evening, after de Gaulle had gone back to Colombey and its sweet silence, Pompidou dined with Frey and Guichard. The intermission was over. Pompidou announced that he would resume his functions on the Rue de Solférino. The general had asked him to do so. That was explanation enough.

. .

Thereupon events followed one another in rapid succession. A marvelous surprise! The barons couldn't believe their eyes. On May 19, in the rococo Palais d'Orsay, the general met with journalists — people he had forgotten who were now full of curiosity. Close on their heels were throngs of Frenchmen. The press conference proved most amiable, and soon after, de Gaulle returned to Colombey. This tiny village in Haute-Marne, over which squadrons were flying and where policemen were cooling their heels, had now become the capital of France. Today de Gaulle could master his impatience: people were coming to him.

A meeting with the premier having brought no results, de Gaulle, skipping the intermediate stages, announced in a world-shattering communiqué that he was entering the fray. Pierre Pflimlin's government, which lacked the courage to protest, succumbed to panic. The ministers were no longer in command. The police no longer obeyed. An announcement was made that in Algiers paratroopers were making ready to land in Paris and seize the city.

The barons were busily at work and Pompidou was giving them instructions. He had no letter of credit, no title, no power. But the Gaullist machine, in spite of its cliques and rivalries, obeyed him. The French had scarcely heard his name mentioned, although it was a reassuring one. Throughout this storm of activity, of desires and fears, Georges Pompidou managed to avoid committing the slightest faux pas. Others assumed the right to invoke Nation, Country, People. Pompidou had but one god, de Gaulle, but one tactic, silence.

The general appreciated this.

. .

Georges Pompidou was once again de Gaulle's chief of staff. He had no time to wonder about his own future. The days were still filled with uncertainty and drama. The former professor of literature discovered in the midst of the tempest the de Gaulle of the great days, the historic de Gaulle, a man whose conduct he knew about only from others, through hearsay. Neither during the war nor even at the time of the Liberation, had he been close to the general. But May 1958 brought him magnificent consolation. At that moment not a single one of the historic Gaullists was as close to the general as this discreet, amiable, calm banker. In granting first place to an amateur Gaullist, de Gaulle took his revenge on all those who had professed their loyalty and who had neglected or betrayed him during the last twelve years.

On May 27 an aide-de-camp rang up the Quai de Béthune and invited Pompidou to lunch at Colombey on the following day. Many months had elapsed since the director of the Rothschild Bank had had occasion to make the trip to Colombey. The luncheon on the 28th, however, was not a social occasion but a work session.

The game was not yet over. The Fourth Republic was still breathing its last. That very evening the Pflimlin government resigned. Hours passed and de Gaulle was not invited to take charge. In Algiers, impatient army officers were preparing their final offensive: the paratroopers were ready to descend upon Paris.

A cigarette in his mouth, Pompidou drove along the road to Colombey. He was alone.

Meanwhile, in utmost secrecy, de Gaulle had received at his country home some emissaries from the headquarters in Algiers — two colonels and General Dulac. This was strictly a meeting of professionals — the Ecole de Guerre was examining the revolution.

As later reported by one of the visitors, "the interview centered on three points: first, the continued unwillingness of the political parties to turn to de Gaulle; second, the 'resurrection plan' drafted by the military leaders in Algiers, which considered the idea of landing paratroopers in the streets of Paris (de Gaulle demanded additional manpower and materiel); third, immediate implementation of this plan if the political parties remained hostile to de Gaulle."

What the general neglected to mention to the three army officers was his hope that he would not be forced to resort to such extreme measures. Legality was far preferable to a pronunciamento, especially for someone like Charles de Gaulle.

It so happened that Pompidou was bringing encouraging news. He arrived at noon, shortly after the departure of the three army officers. During the last few hours he had gathered a good deal of information, especially from non-Gaullist circles. The general questioned him. He alluded to Pompidou's "contacts," but was less caustic than usual.

At one o'clock they sat down to lunch. Contrary to custom, de Gaulle continued the discussion during the meal. Time was of the essence. The composition of the new government was a matter of concern. Pompidou exhibited optimism, sure that the general would achieve his object: the appointment of four ministers of state, representing the political parties of the Fourth Republic. For all the rest, specialists could be called in. The new government, however, would last only for a limited time; France must be "put back on the right path."

The interview ended around three in the afternoon. It was now time for Pompidou to drive back to Paris, where he could be very useful. In a few words, the general told him that he was counting on him to insure some sort of continuity. Pompidou accepted the honor and responsibility but, as he said in passing, that too would be for a limited time only. Once the initial phase of the general's activities had ended, he would return to the bank. He had no desire to hold a high administrative office again — that would mean a step backward — and even less did he aspire to a political career.

Pompidou drove back to Paris satisfied. Not for a second did it occur to him that the general's return would lead to violence. He was happy at the prospect of working closely with the general once again, of being for a while at least the major domo of the man he most admired. He was also pleased at the thought of serving an apprenticeship in government and returning to the Rothschild Bank with new trumps in his hand — experience in negotiation and decision-making, the establishment of important contacts, the acquisition of additional prestige. "Former Director of the President's Council" was an enviable title in the business world, especially when the president was Charles de Gaulle. It would be the best kind of apprenticeship, an unhoped-for chance for the one-time professor of literature, who certainly had been a jack-of-all-trades.

Was he just lucky? Not at all: he was a man of quality. One thing was certain: the general never chose his collaborators haphazardly. After May 28, 1958, Pompidou was justified in believing that luck had played but a modest role in his destiny.

.   .

Only one step remained, the step that would bring the general to power. And this would be due not to Providence but to the inexorable march of history. A few days to wait, at the most; a few days of work for Pompidou.

The rest, however, occurred swiftly. Once back at the Quai de Béthune, Pompidou learned what all of France already knew: the general was to arrive that night to meet with the presidents of the Assemblies. At Saint-Cloud. The rendezvous was to take place at ten that night.

The meeting at Saint-Cloud marked the official debut of the chief of staff. Things went badly. The presidents arrived one hour late, an hour during which Pompidou tried to calm the irate general, albeit with little success. The seventy-minute interview that ensued between de Gaulle and the two dignitaries of the republic was stormy. In an adjacent drawing room, Pompidou, Foccart, and de Gaulle's aide-de-camp stared fixedly at the closed door behind which the general was waging battle.

As soon as de Gaulle appeared, their worst fears were confirmed. The general "collected" the aide-de-camp on his way out. "To Colombey!"

Pompidou and Foccart were left to their own devices; they looked at one another in consternation. History, alas, seemed to have chosen between parliament and the "paratroopers."

The following day brought fresh drama. The general was not to remain long in Colombey brooding over his "disappointment" — or nursing his fury. The President of the Republic, René Coty, publicly invited him to come to the Elysée at seven-thirty in the evening.

Naturally there were no witnesses at the meeting between Coty and de Gaulle. Once again, Pompidou waited in an adjacent room. He scarcely had time to notice the gold moldings of the Elysée, the the rococo interior that bespoke the monarchy, the empire and the republic. He was already at work, having spent the day drawing up a list of the people he would like to take with him to Hôtel de Matignon, the premier's official residence — those who would make up the general's cabinet. Such was Pompidou's prerogative. But far more difficult was the task of actually forming a government in which yesterday's enemies could work side by side and cooperate. Pompidou had thought of many names to suggest to the general. This, too, was part of his assignment.

In leaving the Elysée, he accompanied de Gaulle to the Hôtel La Pérouse. After dinner, he returned to work.

In Algiers the "resurrection plan" was canceled. The paratroopers unpacked their bags.

The month of May 1958, curiously enough, has been stricken from Pompidou's biographies. According to legend, the erstwhile professor does not appear on stage until May 29, at precisely eight in the evening. The entire drama, however, had been enacted in the wings. And among all the actors, Pompidou played an important role. He filled in the general at every moment, followed the various phases of the "conspiracy," contained the eagerness of some while stirring up that of others — all this without ever putting in an appearance.

The Gaullists were not fooled. Throughout the life of the Fifth Republic, a mysterious tie was to unite de Gaulle, Pompidou and the barons, whose association sprang not from the Resistance nor the "crossing of the wilderness" but from this desperate yet victorious battle.

CHAPTER 4

The First Separation

AFTER ALL KINDS OF PLOTS, both civil and military, France was on the verge of civil war. The legal government had abdicated and called for a savior, a "providential man." And de Gaulle quickly took hold of a power which had not so much to be won as assumed. For five days history unfolded in a modest two-room suite at the Hôtel La Pérouse. While de Gaulle held court, listening to all of the country's politicians, Pompidou, once again in an adjacent room, issued summonses, consulted and assigned the pawns of the new system. As always, he remained invisible. While most of the Gaullists were delirious with joy at having felled the Fourth Republic, Pompidou quietly reestablished contact with the defeated politicians.

During these last days of May 1958 he quickly developed his new personality. For many politicians there was something of the devil about de Gaulle, the head of the R.P.F., whom they had fought for twelve years. They were not about to open their hearts to him. But between them and the general was this chief of staff whom they had met at dinner long ago and who seemed amiable and accommodating. He engineered the transition that de Gaulle insisted must be peaceful, interposing himself when necessary. Not for nothing had the general called to his side a man who already had contacts in the enemy camp.

A few irreconcilables remained — François Mitterand in particular — but one by one all the others succumbed to the general's charm.

In the next room, Pompidou soothed and advised. "Don't talk to 'him' about that today. The general is entirely disposed to accept your views but he detests conditions, anything that smacks of an ultimatum. Rest assured; I can promise you that everything will be arranged within forty-eight hours."

You came to the general worried, nervous, perhaps feeling somewhat aggressive. You left with a smile. And there was Pompidou in the doorway, saying: "Well, has the general told you of his plans? Did he tell you that he is counting on you? And naturally you didn't mention the problem that annoys him so. Believe me, all will go well."

He settled all the details — questions of protocol, of security; a political adviser, he was also a major domo. And a self-effacing one.

On June 1 the general went to the Assembly. He returned the next day, then repeated the gesture for the last time on June 3, before moving into the Matignon. He was about to leave the Hôtel La Pérouse when Léon Delbecque arrived from Algiers.

"Foccart made me go up the back stairs," Delbecque has related. "He accompanied me to de Gaulle's room. On entering the living room, I saw Madame de Gaulle and Pompidou. They were packing up. I went into the adjoining room where de Gaulle greeted me with outstretched arms: 'Bravo, Delbecque. You played your hand well.' He added: 'You'll have to admit that I didn't play my hand badly either.' He told me that he would be in Algiers within three days, that he had already selected his ministers. I began to say that the people of Algiers were worried about the composition of the government. He interrupted me: 'That, well, that's my business. It's up to me to decide.' "

. .

Before de Gaulle there was nothing: the general was not an ordinary premier. To underscore the distance that separated him and poor Pflimlin, de Gaulle did not wish to receive the reins of government from the hands of his predecessor. He was welcomed to the Matignon by a functionary who, although young, bore a great name:

Prince Michel Poniatowski. When the drawers of all the chests were empty, the general settled into his new quarters. From the dying Fourth Republic he retained only those regulations and customs that suited him.

De Gaulle was to improvise the new regime as he went along. A statesman of historic dimensions, he walked in the footsteps of Louis XIV, Bonaparte, Napoleon III.

Formerly, when premiers arrived at the Matignon, they inherited professional advisers who had zealously served socialists, radicals or independents. These men insured continuity. De Gaulle, however, wanted no part of this traditional practice. His team of technical advisers and envoys consisted largely of Gaullist cavalry officers of tender years and modest pedigrees. It was directed by a banker from the private sector.

Every morning at ten Pompidou convoked the general's entire cabinet in his office on the first floor of the Matignon. He would call upon each of these men in turn. He had known them all for the past ten years and knew them to be experts, people of experience — Pompidou himself had chosen them. His sharp eyes, now gentle and mocking, now hard, observed them closely. At times, when the reading of a report seemed to go on forever, Pompidou, gazing out on the Matignon's classical courtyard, would become lost in reverie. He detested ponderous explanations. His nimble mind grasped problems quickly; this he knew about himself.

Before the advent of Pompidou, a premier's chief of staff had never picked up the phone to call a minister. Pompidou owed this privilege to the general, who never telephoned but instead summoned people and then lectured them. From his very first days at the Matignon, Pompidou set himself up as the general's confidential agent. Everyone accepted this arrangement without bothering to check. Surprisingly enough, professional politicians who had enjoyed the highest responsibilities and had known only underlings as departmental chiefs of staff, were now willing to put up with this general overseer. From his observation post, Pompidou followed the affairs of the various ministries, offered advice, issued orders, at times even made decisions. Non-Gaullist ministers allowed this up-start whom the monarch had chosen to ennoble to conduct himself as their equal.

"He makes quick decisions," Malraux said. Actually, Pompidou was a good judge of men. Rarely did he modify initial impressions. He knew whom to handle with respect, whom to treat sharply. Above all, he knew how the general felt about Pierre, Antoine or Guy. And that was enough to give him self-assurance. As for his own impressions, he kept them concealed behind his amiable exterior.

His great strength lay in his understanding of de Gaulle. "In the general's presence, Pompidou was like a crocodile, open-mouthed on the rug, ready to devour any victim his master might toss to him," one Gaullist dignitary has recalled.

In 1958 Georges Pompidou coped happily with all the problems de Gaulle chose to confide to him. And there were many. After twelve gloomy years in retirement the general was rediscovering the delights of power. But he was careful not to expose himself to petty annoyances. To be sure, he had aged since 1946. He was no longer the erect, stern Liberator clothed in all his glorious accouterments. Now he sometimes gave the impression of being as sanctimonious, as skeptical as any ordinary radical. Jupiter's lightning still struck, but only infrequently. Still the central figure, he was also his own audience. At eleven in the morning, at five in the afternoon, or at the very end of the day, he would summon Pompidou into his office and behave like a Greek tragedian, using his chief of staff as the classical confidant. Forever waiting in the wings, Pompidou was ready to lend an ear to the hero's monologues.

Power also entailed the performance of a thousand trivial unworthy tasks that preempted much of the day's work. Pompidou took care of these matters so unobtrusively that de Gaulle hardly realized that they were being attended to. Sometimes it was a minister whose ruffled feelings had to be soothed; at other times it was the price of milk or the discount rate. The general knew of course that these were his prerogatives, but he was quite content to let Pompidou handle them. This gave de Gaulle time to meditate, to concentrate on the essentials: Algeria, the constitution, foreign relations, the dismissal of the army officers who had raised him to power.

.   .

The Algerian affair was a cup overflowing with bitterness as well as a training ground. As soon as he was installed in the Matignon, Pompidou decided to steer clear of the thorny problem. De Gaulle, he felt, was the man to cope with it. But to which camp did he himself belong? No one will ever know. The curious thing is that every politician thought Pompidou was on his side. The champions of a French Algeria saw Pompidou as the man who, for the past ten years, had regretted the abandonment of Morocco and Tunisia. But as an opponent of torture and colonialism, he seemed to be on the side of the liberals. Like de Gaulle, he was content to let the wolves howl.

How many careers have been swallowed up by the Algerian affair! Since the crisis promised to be a protracted one, Pompidou did not allow himself to be swept up by it. He left it to the general to sort out the maze of passions, self-serving interests and international ramifications. The situation was a complicated one.

Pompidou performed favors for people. As soon as the new government was installed, he was entrusted with the secret of a former premier's contacts with the Algerian rebels, established two years before.

An imprudent man might have exploited this information and become involved in machinations of his own. Pompidou merely handed the files over to de Gaulle, saying, "I know nothing about the matter." His experience at the Rothschild Bank had taught him to value the oil of the Sahara. This was the only aspect of the Algerian problem on which he was willing to express an opinion. But even here he limited himself exclusively to the economic and industrial facets of the question.

There were plenty of well-meaning men around de Gaulle. Each of them had his own panacea for peace. Each came to offer advice, vouchsafe information, suggest solutions. And each hoped in exchange to be taken into the general's confidence, a relationship that would have conferred invaluable advantages. But de Gaulle resolved to keep his own counsel as long as possible. He issued only vague and somewhat contradictory statements. Pompidou proved equally discreet. To be sure, the general did not conceal from Pompidou his private prognostications: "At best there would be an association with Algeria, ending in independence for her; at worst, the outcome would be immediate autonomy." But when Pompidou was questioned, he said nothing. "If you want to know what the general is planning to do about Algeria, go and ask him," he would say. This was perhaps the sort of thing that de Gaulle liked most about Pompidou.

.   .

Thirteen days after his return to power, the general officially addressed himself to the big problem: constitutional reform. He was always thinking about it — in fact he thought of little else. His views on the subject were very precise. And he remembered that it was the Fourth Republic, the "regime of political parties," that had led to his departure in 1946. He had not come back in 1958 to settle old accounts, but rather to restore the powers of the state and the principle of legitimacy. Ever since Vercingetorix, all the misfortunes of France — and it is not easy to tot them up — sprang from the degradation of the state. "We have just seen, when we were on the brink of disaster, what this leads to," he said.

To accomplish the task to which he assigned top priority, de Gaulle pressed into service ministers, functionaries and experts, to say nothing of Michel Debré. One couldn't have too many people working on the problem! Pompidou, too, was included. Despite his experience in the Council of State, he had little interest in juridical matters. But everyone followed de Gaulle's example, spending hours reading manuals of constitutional theory and practice and "working away at the law" — to use the general's expression.

The entire summer of 1958 was devoted to these juridical questions, which de Gaulle studied with meticulous attention. For weeks a battle had been raging over the role of the future President of the Republic. The idea of electing the chief of state by universal suffrage was under discussion.

"A national picnic, American style," de Gaulle commented. "Can you imagine what that would mean in France?"

De Gaulle wanted neither a figurehead who presided at flower shows nor an American-style chief of state. Agreement was finally reached on some vague formula that provoked a thousand arguments: the President of the Republic was to be the source of executive power.

De Gaulle himself pored over the articles of the proposed constitution. He edited them, deleted unnecessary commas, lovingly chose elegant prepositions — in short, he scribbled, as if he were still writing his *Memoirs*. Occasionally, he would come up against a complicated sentence and push the sheet of paper away. "But what does that mean?" he would say irritably to some collaborator more accustomed to legal jargon. Or, peremptorily, he would say: "That's idiotic!"

With passionate interest, Pompidou watched the general polish and repolish "his" constitution. Rarely did he intervene. His help was not indispensable. He left to Debré the task of coping with both the general and the political hacks.

For months and years the general was to repeat: "This constitution is good, even excellent. Besides, I drafted it. But it is really less important than the men who implement it."

Georges Pompidou scarcely realized that someday he would be one of these men.

. .

A lovely summer. After so many somber years, France at long last gave the impression of being governed. She had rediscovered her great magical voice. At meetings of the Council of Ministers, young government officials suddenly awarded honors and politicians astonished at having recovered some of their prestige vied against

one another with the old enthusiasm. Once a week the Council of
Ministers assembled in the Elysée, in the benevolent presence of
Monsieur Coty; cabinet meetings, on the other hand, took place at
the Matignon. Regardless of whether the items on the agenda comprised agriculture, education, commerce or public works, the general allowed his ministers complete freedom of initiative. But Pompidou kept an eye on everything.

De Gaulle and Pompidou occupied adjacent offices on the first
floor that were separated by a corridor. The general's office overlooked the park; Pompidou's faced the courtyard. Pompidou made
telephone calls, checked the files, summoned administrative
officials. De Gaulle granted interviews, listened, reflected, and
gradually disclosed his conception of France's destiny.

Pompidou prevented altercations, smoothed over the surface of
things and felt no need to display his talents. It was very pleasant
indeed for the general. Referring to a minister or an administrative
official, de Gaulle had only to say, "That Mr. X . . . I simply can't
stand him anymore." Thereupon Pompidou discreetly saw the culprit and matters were set straight. "Believe me, you're making a
mistake to oppose the general," he would counsel.

Among the host of people who bustled about, milled around, or
politicked, Pompidou represented the epitome of filial devotion.
And he was not doing this for his own advancement. Pompidou had
common sense and de Gaulle appreciated this quality. He liked to
be brought back to earth from time to time — by Madame de
Gaulle, for example.

"It's a difficult problem," he admitted one day. "I don't like
those blessed yes men and yet I can't stand opposition." Pompidou
was reassuring, even tempered. A genuine Auvergnat.

. .

Once the new constitution had been adopted and approved by 70
per cent of the people, the usual routine had to be resumed, the

groundwork for legislative elections laid. For a few months de Gaulle had ruled without parliament and without political parties. Those were golden days. Sometimes, to shock the people he was talking to, he would say: "Deputies? What for? After all, de Gaulle is here." Actually, however, he disliked what he called "the kitchen," perhaps because of the smell of "the soup."

For some weeks the "Gaullists" (the quotes were the general's) — the Freys, the Debrés, the Chaban-Delmases — had been creating a political party, the U.N.R. (Union for a New Republic). This reminded de Gaulle of the R.P.F., of defeat and betrayal and the bitterness they engendered. For a split second he considered the possibility of repudiating these children who claimed they were his. But to govern, he would need a majority. He had no intention, however, of becoming too involved. He wished merely to be kept informed about what was happening within the U.N.R. The task was entrusted to Pompidou.

Conscientiously, the chief of staff went to work. Very discreetly, Pompidou kept tabs on U.N.R. activities. Although he never appeared at party meetings, he was kept fully informed by Frey and Guichard. He gave advice — meaning orders. Doing what he had once done for the R.P.F., he kept the U.N.R. solvent and found money for electoral campaigns. This was something he of course knew how to do. Thanks to his experience at the Rothschild Bank, he knew precisely where to look to obtain contributions from business firms and industrialists.

But the general himself had no faith in the party. "It would be fine," he remarked sarcastically, "if the U.N.R. could come up with at least twenty deputies."

Pompidou was obviously more optimistic. The outcome proved him right: 212 deputies for the U.N.R. The chief of staff himself phoned the good news to de Gaulle that Sunday night in November. He forebore to add, "I told you so," but that was what he was thinking.

The general thus discovered that his devoted collaborator had a real flair, at least in handling elections and parliament. It was a good deal to expect from a chief of staff. The service so rendered was important, a detail worth noting.

. .

This dawn of a new regime brought fresh hope. In the shadow of the general, men were doing what was natural — planning their careers. Each dreamt of becoming an ambassador, a political leader, a minister — or else merely a member of the administrative council. Pompidou for his part indulged in the luxury of indifference. His own career was assured: after performing his current mission for seven months, he would resume his position in a famous bank, something no former minister would disdain.

This enabled him to judge somewhat harshly the obvious greed of his Gaullist companions. He was more than satisfied and said so. As early as July he confided to a close friend who marveled at his rapid advancement: "The general knows that in six months I'll be going back to the bank." And he repeated this from time to time to the ministers, the barons and all the general's advisers.

This position won him universal respect. He was safe from a sudden drop in the general's esteem or from a mere flare-up of the "great man's" temper. In the ferment of a newly emerging regime, Pompidou could remain calm and sure of himself. One of the general's aides-de-camp, who was particularly sensitive to his master's volatile humor and fearful of it despite twelve years of service, could not understand Pompidou.

"It's quite simple," Pompidou explained. "First I was a professor. Then I collaborated with the head of the government. After that I was a councilor of state and a banker. I don't want to spend the rest of my life learning a new trade. I'm forty-seven, too old to experiment. The bank suits me. It gives me latitude and time for my family."

"But the general . . ."

"I've worked for the general as much as anyone. He knows he can always count on me. It is the great honor and happiness of my life that I have been useful to him. But I'm sure he will find another fine chief of staff."

Later, he justified his behavior in the following terms: "Politics frightened me. I had no particular flair for banking. But I went back to the Rothschilds telling myself that once I was there, no one would come and fetch me back."

The general said nothing. Weeks passed and still he refrained from questioning Pompidou. Then, one day late in October, he asked Pompidou if he hadn't changed his mind. Without any self-consciousness, Pompidou replied that France would soon experience a definitive recovery. Salvation was around the corner.

"You're right," de Gaulle said. "Besides, in two years, once the Algerian affair has been settled, I will go back to Colombey."

And the general added: "One cannot rule the French for long. Better to leave before they grow tired of you. I will return to Colombey and they will return to their old games."

The December 31 deadline approached. De Gaulle was somewhat contemptuous. To leave the service of France in order to find a soft berth in the sun seemed rank betrayal to him. Besides, it was de Gaulle who did the dismissing, not the other way around. He would miss Pompidou — his skill, his contacts. He was a man you could count on, and he was never caught napping.

The general said to Guichard: "History will never know the tremendous role played by Pompidou in the establishment of the Fifth Republic."

But to Pompidou himself he addressed no compliments. Only a gesture that perhaps signified: "Well, be happy!"

The general summoned Geoffroy de Courcel, one of his oldest companions. In his most military manner, he said to him: "I need you."

Courcel could not understand. "Is Pompidou leaving you, my general?"

Concealing his disappointment, the general answered in a bantering tone: "Yes, he prefers to go off to the Rothschilds and make money. You will take his place."

Geoffrey de Courcel mentioned his health, which really was not very good. De Gaulle became impatient: "It's only a matter of two years. In two years the Algerian affair will be settled and you'll be free."

All the same, the general found it hard to resign himself to the departure of his confidential agent. One aide-de-camp, who knew de Gaulle as some know the gospel, later recounted: "Within six months de Gaulle had developed a fatherly affection for Pompidou. Beneath a tough exterior the general is extremely feeling. Often, for example, he would ask me if one of his aides-de-camp was happy; he worried about the health of "his" men. It was during the summer of nineteen fifty-eight that his affection for Pompidou took root."

By the end of the year the general had not given up hope. To his future premier, Michel Debré, he said: "Pompidou is a man of quality." Then, casually, "Try to convince him."

Naturally, Debré began by offering Pompidou the ministry of finance. Next, he invited Pompidou to become Minister of National Education, a post for which he was admirably suited. Politely, but firmly and definitively, Pompidou said no. De Gaulle, apprised of this, flew into a rage: "May God look after him!" — which can be interpreted to mean, "Let him go to the devil!"

On January 8, 1959, the first day of the Fifth Republic, Pompidou welcomed Michel Debré, the new premier, to the Matignon, just as Poniatowski had welcomed de Gaulle. Pompidou, looking grave, went into his office for the last time. There, standing erect, he transmitted his powers to Debré's assistant, a high-ranking official who bore the glorious name of Racine. He uttered three banal words. A single sheet of paper with a dozen typewritten lines on it lay on the table. The drawers, the wastepaper basket and the ashtrays were empty.

A short while before, at the Elysée on the other side of the Seine, the general had given Pompidou his freedom.

"We'll see each other again," de Gaulle had said.

Polite, meaningless words that de Gaulle used when conversing with friends as well as with enemies.

Earlier, the new chief of state had visited the Arc de Triomphe in an open car. Upon his return it was Pompidou who sat beside him as he drove down the Champs-Elysées in a small victory demonstration. There was de Gaulle, standing up, majestic, his arms raised. And who was that stranger to whom none of the cheers were addressed? Was this already a portent? No. The general stood alone. He alone epitomized the new legitimacy. He wanted no politician to accompany him, not even a Gaullist to whom the crowd might have attached a name . . .

Pompidou was the anonymous witness, the unidentifiable understudy.

Part II

THE CONTRACT

. . . for thee, thine uncles and myself
Have in our armours watch'd the winter's night,
Went all afoot in summer's scalding heat,
That thou mightst repossess the crown in peace:
And of our labours thou shalt reap the gain.

Henry VI, *Part III, act 5, scene 7*

CHAPTER 5

The Nocturnal Visitor

DE GAULLE AT THE ÉLYSÉE: at every step, at every glance, the general encountered mementos of another republic — Félix Faure; Emile Deschanel; Raymond Poincaré; Albert Lebrun. Far from fulfilling a mandate, de Gaulle was accomplishing a mission. André Malraux, that visionary minister, envisaged for his chief a setting in keeping with this renaissance: the Château de Vincennes. The general hesitated, thought about it, and then refused. "I would be charged with the folly of grandeur."

Thirteen years earlier de Gaulle had slammed the door behind him, leaving the French to rule themselves. Now he was determined to see things through to the end, to leave behind him a completed work.

His immediate concern was Algeria. The general alluded to Algeria as the "drama," the "affair"; at times he called it a "millstone." Fortified by the confidence reposed in him by the French, as well as by the Muslim foreign nations, he hoped to resolve this problem quickly so as to be free to attend to his country's internal affairs. Yet months passed and Algeria continued to occupy more and more of his time. It was a long, dark tunnel. The general improvised slogans and launched them in the hope of evoking a response. Peace was not yet in sight. To one of his intimates the general confided:

"With this millstone around her neck, France is paralyzed. She cannot take her proper place in the world. There is not enough time to wait patiently." Then he added: "I will not live forever."

The general refused to share his mission with anyone. To a collaborator who spoke about the government, he said roughly: "The government? I am the government."

"No, my general, if that were true, the parliament could overthrow you."

De Gaulle shrugged his shoulders. "The parliament! Your supposition is idiotic!"

On the other side of the Seine, at the Hôtel de Matignon, in the very same office de Gaulle had occupied the year before, the premier, Michel Debré, shouldered his share of the Algerian burden.

Debré went to work determined to do a good job. Everything was grist for his mill: not a single file, report or letter eluded his red pencil. His four sons romped up and down the marble staircase while the Republican Guards looked on and their father, seated beneath a portrait of Richelieu, tracked down traitors and incompetents. At seven in the morning the premier was at his desk reading newspapers — they aroused his indignation — and telegrams and dictating memos to each of his ministers. The very next day he would send each of them a reminder of the previous day's instructions. He allowed no respite for himself or his colleagues. One minister nicknamed him the "schoolmaster." Although they all admired and liked him, they found him hard to work for.

The general was pleased to note this feverish activity, this desire on the part of Debré to come to grips with everything, to check up on everyone. The premier managed to find time to go to the Elysée once a week, carrying a plan for reform under his arm. The general would hand it on to his assistant, Geoffroy de Courcel, saying, "To be filed."

Thus protected on his right and on his left by so attentive a premier, de Gaulle was free to devote himself to the most important matters — the perfection of his plans. Apart from Algeria, his main concern was France's relationship with the two superpowers.

He invariably began his day by reading press summaries at breakfast. Then he would have a look at British, German and Polish newspapers. A very lengthy series of interviews followed. At eight in the evening, the general knocked off and devoted himself to his family. Here there was no need to strike an attitude.

Renewing his acquaintance with Frenchmen, de Gaulle found them unchanged, as "habit-ridden and circumspect as ever." These people who in turn had followed Pétain, the Fourth Republic and the Americans now placed their destiny in the hands of de Gaulle. How long would they do so?

Between them and him the screen of the Elysée interposed itself, a glacial palace where men overly concerned about winning his favor came and went. On occasion the general thought nostalgically about those millions of individuals who busied themselves with commonplace concerns and ordinary pleasures. One day, upon hearing loud voices in an adjacent room where some aides-de-camp were milling about, he called in one of them, who explained: "That, my general, was a friend who has just told his latest joke. He has an inexhaustible supply of funny stories."

"Is that so?" the general answered morosely. "Then why doesn't he tell me any?"

The general was a captive of his own legend. This delighted him. After the war, on the advice of his ophthalmologist, he stopped smoking. His collaborators marveled at his ability to make so great a sacrifice so easily. "It's very simple," he replied. "You just tell your secretary about your decision."

Actually, it was not so easy. For months the people around him noticed that he was chewing gum nervously.

According to another legend of later vintage, the chief of state feigned unawareness of the preposterous emotions and humdrum satisfactions that are the lot of ordinary human beings. Once again de Gaulle was feeling melancholy. In Algiers, during the war, he had referred to his mood as "the box of troubles."

. .

Having departed via the corridor of honor, Pompidou immediately entered through the garden door. Discreetly as always, he resumed his easy chair at the Rothschild Bank, where, as expected,

Baron Guy entrusted him with additional responsibilities. Once again it was the Quai de Béthune, old friends, the good old life; he did not contemplate making any more changes.

Every four or five weeks he paid a visit to de Gaulle at the Elysée. His name was not always on the official list of visitors. Sometimes de Gaulle summoned him, at other times Pompidou himself telephoned the faithful aide-de-camp, who transmitted the request punctually.

"In those days," according to the aide-de-camp, "Pompidou had no intention whatsoever of returning to our 'affairs.' Often he said to me quite emphatically: 'Yes, I like politics well enough, but from a distance.' He would come to see the general out of affection and admiration. It gave him pleasure. Besides, he passed along to the general whatever information he had picked up in business circles."

Feeling somewhat cloistered at the Elysée, de Gaulle would give way to curiosity and seek Pompidou's company. "What are people saying about us?" he wondered. As a banker, his former chief of staff saw all kinds of people. He brought de Gaulle some aura of the outside world that was lacking in the lives of most statesmen. And Pompidou's judgment was sound. However, it would be a mistake to believe that he gave advice. He knew the general well enough never to depart from his role. Occasionally, it was de Gaulle who confided in him, revealing plans in order to study Pompidou's reaction. He sometimes exaggerated his own way of thinking, or even said the opposite of what he really believed, in order to see how far he could go. The general was an expert at this game. But Pompidou was never caught off guard.

Once one of the general's collaborators imprudently said to him: "Have you been chatting with Pompidou?"

The general let out a blast: "Let me tell you, sir, that no one 'chats' with General de Gaulle."

He would also be surprised if anyone were to say, "Your friend, Pompidou." It was a term the general might use publicly when alluding to a minister or collaborator. But it was not to be taken literally. General de Gaulle had no friends. He admired Malraux. He had affection for General Catroux. But friendship was quite another matter. To be the general's friend, one would have to share with him such things as age, social origin, milieu. One would also have to be capable of rising to his height.

"I don't know whether I've ever had a friend," the general said to one of his former ministers in 1969. "Perhaps I did have one, yes, about thirty or forty years ago."

Too many factors — age, tastes, social contacts, birth — separated de Gaulle from Pompidou for the latter ever to become the general's friend in the true sense of the word. Pompidou was merely someone who had rendered a service and who could be trusted, a man of quality whom de Gaulle had deigned to notice. In politics as in war, replacements are always needed.

.   .

February 1960, the barricades in Algiers. Citizens and paratroopers opposed to de Gaulle's liberal politics took up positions in the heart of the city. And once again, as in May 1958, fear of civil war mounted in France. And in Paris. It was the first bolt of lightning to strike the Fifth Republic. By the time the storm was over, de Gaulle had learned his lesson. He could now size up the men around him, their weaknesses, fears and misgivings. The conclusion he reached was a harsh one. What de Gaulle questioned was not the merits of a Debré or of any particular minister but rather something he called their "solidity." He decided that he himself would have to take charge of everything.

Nor was he alone in this belief. After the episode of the barricades, the government asked the Assembly for special powers. During the debate, the socialists, who formed part of the opposition, clearly indicated that they would grant such powers only to General de Gaulle, not to his cabinet or his premier.

At the Elysée, official advisers and confidential ones like Pompidou were now saying out loud that there was quite a distance between the general and his premier, between one segment of the cabinet and the majority of Gaullists. Actually, there was an abyss. De Gaulle himself arrived at this conclusion with some difficulty.

"Here are men who exist only through me," he said. "They have been elected because of my name or appointed by virtue of a decree signed in my name. What else can they do save follow de Gaulle?"

After the episode of the barricades, Geoffroy de Courcel, secretary general in the president's office, Pompidou and others underscored the dangers of excessive confidence. They felt that the constitution represented a concession to the political parties because it stipulated that the government was responsible to parliament. They saw an opportunity to press their point again. The constitution itself must put an end to the obvious differences between de Gaulle and his government.

The general listened, reflected for a moment, then answered: "This is not the United States. The Americans have a federal system in which the states can decide a good many things. The president does not hold all the power. In France there must be a premier."

Turning to Geoffroy de Courcel, he added: "Can you see me going to the parliament to do battle every time the price of milk has to be fixed?" He repeated: "The constitution is good. So is the text."

But he was willing to make procedural changes. Henceforth, most of the government's business would be handled at the Elysée.

"There was a sudden increase in meetings of a select group of council members over which de Gaulle himself presided," one minister of that period recalls. "Often the general summoned a member of the government and gave him instructions in the absence of the premier. Everything that remotely or directly affected the Algerian affair was decided by de Gaulle. At this point, you began to sense a certain irritation in Debré."

De Gaulle began to have certain misgivings about Debré, about his ministers and his majority. Whenever Pompidou came to see him, the general voiced his doubts to him. He said: "I'm going to get rid of X . . . If I don't, he'll betray me. But I haven't decided who will replace him. Think about it. Then come back and see me with a name to suggest."

Pompidou got busy. His work at the bank afforded him enough leisure to engage in political consultations. And the Rothschilds were not displeased — far from it — to see one of their directors serve the chief of state.

Not content to visit de Gaulle from time to time or to receive his confidences, Pompidou kept himself well informed about everything the government was doing. Far from being a mere observer any longer, he was actually at the very center of political activities. And he was constantly enlarging the scope of his contacts. De Gaulle knew this and was pleased, convinced as he was that for once he was not working with someone who was intent on "playing his own game."

Once a month, usually late in the day, the former chief of staff would go to the Hôtel de Matignon to see Debré. The atmosphere there was usually feverish, at times dramatic. Pompidou's visits tended to have a soothing effect on the premier. Debré was suffering. Pompidou administered balm to his wounds. He was the evening visitor, "friend Georges," as he was called at the Matignon. He would offer a little advice, but only on matters of secondary importance. Then he would button his light-colored flannel jacket and, a cigarette invariably dangling from his lips, he would leave to keep some other engagement.

He knew about everything. And he remembered the most innocuous details. But he did not limit his activities to gathering information. He also settled family squabbles among the Gaullists. All the important French leaders came under his scrutiny. A character out of Balzac? No one thought so as yet. He was, however, without doubt a spectator of this human comedy, which consisted in the exercise of power by people in high places and which — if we exclude de Gaulle — was certainly worthy of Balzac. If this human comedy was reminiscent of Balzac, the one enacted at the Elysée was worthy of a Goethe or a Châteaubriand. Pompidou had a certain contempt for mankind, for its weakness, stupidity and cowardice. The teacher who had inculcated this attitude was de Gaulle.

Pompidou was careful not to appear on stage. "He has a good life," de Gaulle murmured one day. And it was true, Pompidou enjoyed his life. He had a finger in almost every pie: business, politics, the arts, high society and café society. He lived a life of ease and enjoyed perfect health.

During the summer of 1960 he went to the United States. The trip was not exactly a diplomatic or secret one. But before leaving he went to see the general who asked him to gather information, to sound out the American public, especially businessmen.

Meanwhile, the general was trying to overcome his own impatience and weariness. The Algerian affair was as yet no closer to a solution. "In three months it will all be settled," the general would say one minute. But in the next he would toss in the towel: "There's nothing to hope for from the rebels or the *pieds-noirs*. At least I've done what I can. And I'm the only one who can see this war through to the end."

. .

On January 16, 1961, at five in the afternoon, after a very painful discussion, Debré once again offered to resign. Coldly, the general refused. "Besides, I have no one to replace you."

The premier himself uttered the name of Pompidou. No answer. Upon his return to the Matignon, Debré, upset and smarting, found a member of the government in the antechamber. He asked his colleague to step into his office and, his head in his hands, admitted: "It's all over. The general is losing patience. And I can't stand it any longer."

This crisis was to be followed by many others during the course of 1961. On several occasions, Debré offered to resign, suggesting each time that the general appoint Pompidou in his place. De Gaulle never answered. The Algerian affair seemed endless — it would soon be three years since de Gaulle's return to power and the knives had not yet been laid aside.

The general was not insensitive to his premier's dilemma. "I, too," he told one of his collaborators, "have had my calvary," adding, "but I don't boast about it."

Debré's suffering and remorse made de Gaulle angry. The general felt that he had been misunderstood, practically betrayed by his eminent collaborator. When one of de Gaulle's oldest companions came to him to complain about Debré's "somber prophecies," the general replied: "Does that surprise you? You know Debré. He's a regular Jeremiah."

If de Gaulle was determined to have a new premier he said nothing about it. But Pompidou did represent a striking contrast to Debré with all his nightmares. And his visits to the Elysée became increasingly frequent. Occasionally de Gaulle would express irritation at having to carry the entire government "in my own arms." But this situation came as no surprise to him. He felt that it was up to him and him alone to point the way out of the dilemma. In this charged atmosphere, darkened by the Algerian drama, Pompidou retained his calm. At times he even pleaded the premier's cause and alluded to his selfless loyalty. The general would nod silently.

When leaving the general's study, Pompidou never failed to go and greet Madame de Gaulle, who had not forgotten his help in administering the foundation. She would say: "You ought to come more often. Your visits are good for the general. He needs them at this moment."

One evening, the general and Madame de Gaulle dined unobtrusively with the Pompidous at their apartment on the Quai de Béthune. Looking back, observers sought to read some political significance into the incident. Actually, it was no more than an "excursion" to the home of a man who had no part in the government and who was good company. De Gaulle was rewarding Pompidou for his extreme discretion.

"In those days," Pompidou recalled, "a good many people complained to me about Debré. I told them: 'Be quiet. Because if ever the general should part with Debré, I'd have to take his place. And I really don't want to be premier.' "

. .

A short while after Debré's big scene, de Gaulle finally had a chance to move his pawn on the Algerian chessboard. This was in February.

All the contacts the French had made with the rebel leaders in 1958 were broken. All, that is, except one: a Swiss journalist had arranged clandestine meetings between the French premier and leaders of the Algerian insurrection. But all confidence, or whatever was left of it, had disappeared. Both sides demanded authorized instead of clandestine emissaries.

Toward the close of 1960, after the general had launched his explosive slogan, "An Algerian Republic," the Swiss, who served as a liaison, crossed the Mediterranean and informed the Algerian leaders, assembled at a congress in Tripoli, that a fruitful meeting was now possible.

The Algerians thought it over, put their heads together, weighing the chances; finally, they said they were interested. In Paris, the premier was immediately informed. He sent two highly regarded men to Switzerland: one, a counterespionage agent, the other, one of the government's technical advisers. These two ambassadors extraordinary returned to Paris and reported to the Minister for Algerian Affairs. The rebel chiefs, they said, were quite willing to meet with a Frenchman but stipulated that he must be de Gaulle's personal representative and not an agent of the government.

To insure the success of this secret meeting, which would be only preliminary in nature, the French emissary would have to be someone who was not in the service of the state, someone unobtrusive who would in no way commit the country. But he would also have to represent the general. Otherwise the mission, like so many others, was bound to fail. De Gaulle did not take long to decide. Pompidou fulfilled all the stipulated conditions.

"To be sure, Pompidou is the right man," was the rejoinder of one of the ministers to whom de Gaulle confided his decision. "But do you think he will accept? After all, he has his position with the Rothschilds to consider."

"Don't worry," the general answered. "In any case, I foresee his return to our 'affairs.' I have already spoken to him about it."

Through diplomatic channels the Swiss government confirmed that the chance of success was good. Pompidou made two trips to Switzerland. During the first, he merely listened and questioned the Algerians about how the renewed negotiations should take place. Thereupon three burning issues were raised.

Upon his return, Pompidou reported to the general. He was pessimistic: "It's going to be difficult to reach an agreement with these people." Nevertheless, de Gaulle sent Pompidou back to Switzerland and from then on, Debré ceased to have any role in the secret negotiations.

The second meeting assumed a more official aspect, in spite of all the odds. The general's envoy opened all the files, especially the file on oil in the Sahara, a subject that was his own special preserve at the bank.

The meeting took place in Neuchâtel. The discussion was more concrete and the bargaining sharper. As an expert, Pompidou studied the various proposals and examined the figures, dotting every *i*. This kind of shoptalk eventually produced results.

Pompidou, however, remained skeptical. He gave de Gaulle a detailed account of the second meeting. The newspapers mentioned it but revealed nothing specific. At the next meeting of the Council of Ministers the Algerian affair was not included in the agenda. The general said absolutely nothing about it. He did tell his premier something, but he was very vague. More tormented than ever, Debré confided to a colleague: "In short, if I'm not mistaken about Pompidou's reaction to his trip, the Algerian rebels are ready to sign an accord. On condition that we give up everything."

For once the general agreed with him. His mood was somber, the situation elusive. "We're not getting anywhere," he said. And so Pompidou returned to his office at the Rothschild Bank.

Then on March 30 a communiqué announced the imminent start of negotiations.

. .

Suddenly everything seemed to collapse — the army, the government, the state. The April putsch undid all the patient preparations.

Under the orders of the prestigious General Salan, an insurrectional force was established in Algiers during the night. One by one the French regiments stationed in Algeria seemed ready to join the insurgents. The government's representatives in Algeria were placed under house arrest by army rebels. This was the last spasm of French Algeria against an independence that was, by now, inevitable. But perhaps it would be a bloody spasm, a revolution.

Again, France, terrified, expected an invasion by paratroopers. But this time the coup was directed against de Gaulle. It was the end of all hope. The Matignon — where the barons were taking turns lending support to Debré — was in a state of panic. There was stupefaction at the Elysée where de Gaulle scarcely heeded the innumerable bits of advice that were being showered on him.

Saturday: endless waiting. Sunday: Pompidou went to the Elysée to find out what was happening. The general remained locked in his office with Courcel. He had made up his mind: he would take his "box of troubles" and republican legitimacy and leave Paris. "I won't allow myself to be trapped."

As in 1940, de Gaulle departed virtually alone, accompanied only by Madame de Gaulle and Courcel. But this time, thanks to the constitution, he was the sole custodian of honor, country and state.

Pompidou sweated out the terrible hours. Like everyone else, he hoped the general would speak out that night. But de Gaulle consistently refused to act under the pressure of events. The strategy he had learned at the Ecole de Guerre was guiding him now: let the enemy tip his hand first. All the same, he ordered television cameras for eight o'clock that night.

At the Matignon, the barons — Guichard and Foccart — reinforced by Chaban-Delmas were powerless to break through the general's awesome silence. Pushing Debré to the fore, they all had a part in drafting the famous appeal to be issued on television by the premier: "Go to the airport, on foot or by car . . ." By the end of the afternoon, the general had reluctantly given his consent: "Well, then, let Debré speak if he thinks it will be of any use."

Consultations between Courcel, Pompidou and the barons were resumed. Debré's appeal was postponed and rescheduled for the dinner hour to give him prime time.

In Paris night fell, a night filled with stars but with no sign of planes. In good-natured disorder, volunteers, night owls, romantic souls and veterans came to offer the government their bare, fragile arms. The general still waited. Time was on his side. Victory was in sight. Then suddenly, two hours before the agonizing homily of his premier, de Gaulle himself broke his silence by speaking directly to the French people.

Pompidou went home. He now realized that during historic moments, de Gaulle asked no one's help, no one's advice. But Pompidou had witnessed history in the making. That in itself was intoxicating.

It was a day he was to remember eight years later.

. .

After the putsch that failed, France recovered her habitual rhythm. Negotiations with the Algerians were resumed but proved unsuccessful. The country felt the shock. So did de Gaulle. The small group of retired generals who hoped for a coup d'état had been conquered; so much was true. But the state had vacillated, or at least the men who symbolized it had hesitated. De Gaulle realized how fragile the foundations of the regime still were. Without him the Fifth Republic, like the Fourth, would have collapsed.

At the Elysée the general's collaborators were hastily ferreting out those to be blamed — ministers, officials, deputies — the architects of disaster. Courcel insisted that Debré be replaced immediately.

At first de Gaulle seemed to acquiesce. Then, having thought about it, he said: "No. I will appoint a new premier when the war in Algeria is over. At that time we'll go on to the next chapter and there'll be many new faces. But it won't do to change horses in midstream."

At that moment — Courcel can vouch for this — the general had already decided who would be his next premier: it was Pompidou. Apprised at once, albeit in rather vague terms, the former chief of staff could proceed to make his preparations. To be sure, the general didn't say to him in so many words: "You're going to run the government." Instead, de Gaulle hinted his intentions, doing so ambiguously and a bit at a time. He resorted to aphorisms. Pompidou, for his part, voiced his lack of enthusiasm for a career in public life, his love of family, his preference for personal freedom, his want of experience. But as the weeks wore on, de Gaulle spoke ever more plainly. Criticizing Debré, he sketched his idea of a good premier, of the kind of man he yearned for: someone free from ties to a political party or clique or to parliament — someone without preconceived ideas and ideologies, who had neither enemies nor friends.

The general revealed his plans to Courcel, of course. He also disclosed them to Foccart and Frey (the latter had been promoted to Minister of the Interior during the April confusion). Thanks to the barons, Pompidou was kept informed about major developments. But he did not display an excessive interest. On the contrary, he never missed a chance to announce how much he enjoyed his position at the bank, how deeply attached he was to the Rothschilds.

No one from the outside could have guessed that this man was destined to have a great national career. With consummate skill, he concealed his secret. At the Rothschild Bank he redoubled his activities. He even edited an anthology of poetry, something that presupposed a certain amount of leisure time, even for a former professor. Almost every evening, he could be seen at a restaurant or club in the Saint-Germain-des-Prés district, in the company of VIPs — starlets in the public eye, a countess, a painter, a singer, a dancer, a few gentlemen of leisure. In the summer, he never failed to go to

Saint-Tropez — surely not the ideal beach for a future chief of state. The constant presence of people in the swim of things was one way of distracting attention from oneself. Perhaps, too, he wanted to prove that it was possible to lead a happy life far from the affairs of state, from political responsibilities and honors. It was perhaps his way of making himself all the more desirable.

For months, for years, he was to repeat: "Those who know me can testify that I never wanted to return to public affairs."

. .

While Pompidou affected a fine insouciance, Debré continued his descent into the inferno over the question of Algerian independence. Occasionally the general was seized with remorse in regard to his premier. But in the end the daily tragedies, endlessly repeated, wore him down. And Debré was decidedly misfortune incarnate. How could Frenchmen ever recover tranquillity, bonhomie or hope under a man like Michel Debré — regardless of his devotion to the state and his yearning for reform? De Gaulle no longer attempted to conceal his impatience. Debré now knew that he would be replaced. And he knew who his successor would be. Despite his penchant for self-sacrifice, he did feel a certain resentment. Little by little, Debré grew accustomed to the idea of having a rival. Acting in accordance with one of the most elementary rules of politics, he hoped to draw Pompidou into his camp. In August 1961, on the occasion of the resignation of the Minister of Finance, Debré had his chance. Pompidou was then vacationing on the Riviera. Debré immediately suggested that he be offered the finance portfolio.

De Gaulle, who had not consulted Pompidou, did not say no. After all, a few months at the Rue de Rivoli would be good experience for a future premier. Six years later the general was to assign this particular purgatory to Couve de Murville, prior to his appointment to the premiership. Pompidou was recalled to Paris. He arrived at the Elysée with a beautiful tan. Respectful of protocol in such matters, de Gaulle said to him: "The premier wants you to take over the ministry of finance."

It was a trap. Pompidou found all kinds of good excuses. Assuring the general of his devotion, he shrewdly observed: "That would be a poor choice. The director of the Rothschild Bank appointed Minister of Finance!"

The general did not insist. In no way convinced by the reason given, he concluded that Pompidou was deterred by the prospect of working with Debré. This was something he could understand. Pompidou took the train back to Saint-Tropez with his future, about which he was certain, intact.

· ·

Another summer, then the fall, and finally the winter. The Algerian affair was still not over. But despite rebellions and exhortations, de Gaulle was close to a solution. The outcome was certain — it was only a matter of time: months, perhaps only weeks. The general did not hesitate to make this clear.

Pompidou's handsome office at the Rothschild Bank became the antechamber of the government: the barons had gossiped. Everyone knew that the next premier was being pursued all the way to the Rothschild Bank. Pompidou merely shrugged his shoulders.

The general proceeded cautiously. During the early days of 1962 he ceased to talk about appointing a new premier. In small doses, Debré was swallowing the poison of the Algerian affair. Already dreaming of the future, the premier breathed new life into his associates. He had them draft a series of plans for reform which he hoped to implement as soon as the Algerian war was over.

Early in February contacts with the Algerian leaders were resumed at Evian. On the twenty-first an agreement was reached. Already considering what to do next, the premier talked about dissolving the Assembly and holding new legislative elections. De Gaulle did not contradict him.

In March came the peace negotiations, the cease-fire, the announcement of a referendum. Debré was called upon to plead for a "heart-rending" cause. Pompidou remained discreetly in the background. The general had repeatedly assured him that his time would soon come.

There were two premiers, and for a while de Gaulle was satisfied with this ambiguous situation. He had just asked a former companion, Christian Fouchet, to move from the embassy in Denmark to the post of High Commissioner for Algeria.

He gave Fouchet twenty-four hours to think it over. "And you needn't worry," the general explained, "you'll be taking orders from me alone. You have my permission to call me from Algeria at any time, night or day. All decisions will be made by me — and also by you. Besides, it so happens that the premier will soon be replaced."

Upon leaving the Elysée, Fouchet went to the Rue Laffitte to seek Pompidou's counsel. He found instead a de facto premier already ensconced in power. Pompidou said to him: "You haven't the right to refuse. I know of course that your mission will be a difficult one. Like the former minister, Pierre Mendès-France, you'll unleash a torrent of passionate feelings. And you'll probably be unwelcome in Algiers. But you have to accept."

The following day Pompidou went to see the reluctant Fouchet, to play upon his emotions. "There are just a few of us — you, me, and a small group of others upon whom the general must be able to rely, to lean on."

People were astonished by de Gaulle's plan to replace the premier. Some complained. Others were jubilant. Still others come to the Elysée to invoke custom, the established rules of the political game. De Gaulle let them all talk — "futile tempests," he later said. Of what use was all this agitation offstage in view of the government's best interests? For months the general had been weighing the advantages and drawbacks of appointing a new premier. In the back of his mind was the feeling that his philosophy of government was being challenged. The important thing was to emphasize the difference between the state, personified by the guarantor of republican legitimacy who was elected for a period of seven years, and a premier responsible to parliament, who was merely an intermediary of sort.

"Two premiers every seven years," he said. "That's a pretty good arrangement. And Debré has been in power for three years and three months."

The year before, the state had had a rough time. De Gaulle had not forgotten this. During periods of crisis it is the president who leads. He alone. To one of his companions, the general confided in all seriousness: "What is a premier? He is chief of staff for the President of the Republic."

Pompidou was the right man. Someone from the outside, someone who had not won his spurs within the confines of the political seraglio, who belonged to no clique, no school, unless it be that of the barons. His kind of temperament could work wonders. Placid, patient, a peasant type, he was also a "shopkeeper" who would keep a tight rein on the "store," who would know how to promote economic prosperity and reassure everyone. He would be a Pinay of sorts, but docile, altogether de Gaulle's creature. Would he gravitate toward the right or the left? Would he be in favor of progress or would he turn out to be a conservative? The general did not even ask himself any of these questions. At least not for the moment.

"All in all," said one of de Gaulle's collaborators, "the government is being transformed into a board of directors headed by a technician."

Someone who would look after everything, who knew all the secrets of Gaullism, would be able to compose and reassure the opposition which comprised many of his own acquaintances; someone capable of arranging, bargaining, compromising — Pompidou alone was the man who could do all this. And what a relief after Debré, with all his gloomy complaints!

. .

Michel Debré was waging his last battle. He planned to dissolve the Assembly following a referendum on Algeria, and to issue a call for new elections. Then the general, if he still wished to do so, could appoint a new premier.

De Gaulle vacillated for a few days. This parliament, this majority had created difficulties for him throughout the entire Algerian war. The thought of making a change was certainly tempting. In any case, it was time for Frenchmen to open their eyes. The nation's policies were no longer being decided in the corridors of the Palais-Bourbon. "Deputies, deputies," grumbled de Gaulle, "what did they do last April?"

The general suspected that his current premier was merely trying to gain time. He consulted all the members of the government cabinet. Many were on Debré's side.

Obviously, Pompidou as well as the barons — with Frey in the lead — advised against new elections. Finally, de Gaulle gave his verdict: "We'll keep this Assembly." It was one way of underscoring Debré's disgrace.

Very late in March 1962, while still at the Rothschild Bank, Pompidou had already begun to serve as premier. He invited advice from political leaders of every camp, listened to their suggestions and jotted down names on his memorandum pad. Olivier Guichard, poker faced, shuttled ceaselessly between the Elysée and the bank. Pompidou wished to form a ministry of conciliation, made up of men who had opposed Debré, including the socialists. De Gaulle approved.

At the Matignon, Debré was showing signs of exhaustion. He knew nothing about the deals being made by Pompidou and de Gaulle. Not until early in April did he learn the truth from some of his colleagues. He was livid. About the general's ingratitude he had nothing to say. But he spoke openly of betrayal when referring to "friend Georges." "I, who have always trusted him," he sighed.

On April 8, ninety per cent of the French voters approved the termination of the war in Algeria. The next day, the premier — "that poor Debré" — paid de Gaulle a lengthy visit. The interview was painful. De Gaulle called attention to the fact that Debré had often offered to resign. Then he enumerated all the ordeals that had accompanied the Algerian affair. The time had come, the general went on, to make a fresh start with a new government. Debré had conducted himself in exemplary fashion. He richly deserved repose and time for meditation. "Frenchmen must no longer associate your name with the drama we have just lived through," de Gaulle explained.

Seeing that Debré was furious, the general turned on all his charm. Debré should travel. He should separate himself, at least for a while, from the nation's affairs, from "the daily political grind." In due course, a day would come when the nation might need him. Able to recall only a few phrases of the conversation, Debré left the Elysée.

De Gaulle for his part believed that his parting advice would be heeded. He sincerely hoped to hold Debré in reserve. He wanted to give the outgoing premier time to become a popular figure again, a figure unsullied by the events of the recent past. Debré must be able to project a new image. But unfortunately Michel Debré was loath to quit the field.

·   ·

Pompidou was now free to act openly. To finalize matters, he installed himself at the ministry of foreign affairs, in an office lent him by Couve de Murville. Along with Guichard, of course. Here he repeated the ritual of May 1958, but this time as the principal officiant. Assuming a modest, cajoling manner, he often called on political personalities himself instead of summoning them. "With an inexperienced premier like me, the government needs men of your quality," he said.

After Debré, he merely turned the page. His presence heralded new methods, serenity. "I detest loud, angry voices," he declared.

To de Gaulle he promised a government of national union. But he was not able to achieve this. Despite his considerable charm, he managed to enlist only two new recruits.

On April 14, a Saturday, the general called a final meeting of the Debré ministry at the Elysée. Speaking gravely for ten minutes, he complimented a few people who were present and then adjourned the meeting. The following day Pompidou published a list of his ministers. And on Monday morning, accompanied by Guichard, he went to the Matignon.

Debré greeted him at the top of the stairs, on the first floor. Pompidou glanced at the office that had once been the general's. The building was empty. The drawers and wastepaper baskets were empty. This was in accordance with custom. Even the lists of telephone numbers usually placed on the telephone tables had been burned. There was literally nothing left save a rather heavy hand to shake.

Pompidou looked on as Debré departed. How many Gaullists had Pompidou seen who had been sacrificed in this way? Better not to think about it. The laws of politics were pitiless, like those of the state, to say nothing of the general's.

Pompidou was not to forget this picture of a solitary man, overcome by sorrow, with only the memory of his suffering to remind him of his unique honor. He resolved to do everything in his power to avoid a similar tragic end.

CHAPTER 6

The Initiation

HIS FIRST DAYS PASSED QUIETLY. The Hôtel de Matignon, scene of so many historic dramas, had until now played host only to professionals, to men fully prepared for the exercise of power. Pompidou didn't even venture to install himself in the premier's quarters. Three Frenchmen out of four, when asked their opinion of him, had none; ninety out of one hundred knew that from now on de Gaulle would rule with Pompidou as his intermediary. The new premier assumed the pose of a victim: "The general had me in a corner," he remarked apologetically. "Oh, well! It's just a matter of a few months."

Assembling the members of his cabinet for the first time, he told them: "I have no intention of exerting my influence in areas that are your responsibility. Nor will I deprive you of your freedom of action."

The promise was superfluous. Except for three or four ministers, the cabinet consisted of men who had already been deputies and were quite capable of eluding Pompidou's guiding hand. To some of these the general had said: "With Pompidou you'll be able to work peacefully."

The change was a total one. "Debré controlled everything," one minister recalled. "And with thirteen years of parliamentary life behind him, his experience was considerable. Pompidou was a neophyte. The authoritarianism of his predecessor was repugnant to him. He did not get up at seven in the morning to ascertain which files would require his attention."

Pompidou continued to play up his amateurism. For several months he was seen on certain evenings in small fashionable restaurants. Thus he seemed to be saying that power had not overwhelmed him because it was not he who exerted it. This was part of his contract.

Pompidou deliberately allowed some of his ministers to deal directly with de Gaulle. He himself would begin by attacking a problem that was exclusively his own: the battle in parliament. This of course was most difficult. His debut was not only unimpressive, but despicable or catastrophic, depending upon whom you talked to. However, even that is part of the legend. The deputies who were powerless against the general took their revenge upon this intruder.

Pompidou's first speech was the product of a collaborative effort. Several ministers had helped to compose it and de Gaulle had given his approval. To questions asked by the deputies, the premier responded after a lapse of twenty-four hours, the time required to submit them to the Elysée — at least such was the insinuation at the Palais-Bourbon. "I had never before delivered a public speech," Pompidou said.

When the general was told how meager had been the applause, how light the vote that Pompidou had been able to muster at the Assembly, he answered with magnificent indifference, "He'll work into it."

Frenchmen did not take seriously this Monsieur Pompidou from Montboudif in Cantal, who had parachuted down on the Hôtel de Matignon; they were still bleeding from their Algerian wounds. His presence seemed to them something of a huge joke, calculated to make the citizenry smile. Oh, the stares he received in restaurants where now his shaggy eyebrows, his nose and mouth were readily recognized! And the press was without pity — "vile," to use the general's epithet. Besides, there were politicians aplenty who rightly believed that they were worthier than Pompidou of honors and responsibilities.

Fortunately, he had de Gaulle.

.   .

As soon as Pompidou was appointed to the Matignon, his relations with the general changed. The general's esteem for Pompidou had not vanished — far from it. But the chief of state, like the head of an army, must keep his distance from his subordinates, and envelop his activities in a cloud of mystery. "Nothing increased authority so much as silence," de Gaulle wrote in *The Edge of the Sword.*

De Gaulle outlined the plans that were to be pursued. But he neglected to confide the threads of his thought to his premier, precisely because Pompidou was the premier. The general was more reserved with collaborators than with strangers. He was less likely to open his heart to the premier than to the director of a bank.

Georges Pompidou remained ever respectful of the general's need for secrecy. In fact, his discretion was so thorough that, although one might manage to guess de Gaulle's opinion of Pompidou, the nature of Pompidou's feelings about the general remained almost impossible to decipher. During the six years he spent at the Matignon, Pompidou never said to his colleagues: "The general wishes that . . ." Nor did he ever reveal any disagreement between himself and de Gaulle. Only by careful analysis is it possible to distinguish the respective accomplishments of de Gaulle and his premier during the seven years they worked together.

To guess the premier's reactions, one would have to decipher the expression in his gray eyes beneath the thick eyebrows. But no one indulged in this sport. Besides, Pompidou was no enigma. All he was supposed to do was to stay on the straight and narrow path.

In 1962 he had learned the lesson of Gaullism. A chapter in history, an entire generation, experience at the top — all these separated him from the general. Pompidou knew exactly what it was that the general expected of him: to coordinate the activities of the cabinet, to smooth over quarrels and nip rumors in the bud.

From his place of exile, Michel Debré observed with chagrin the tranquillity of his successor. His partisans were heard to murmur:

"Pompidou — he's nothing but Gaullism reduced to the habits of a provincial notary public."

The man from Auvergne let them talk . . .

.   .

During the past years the Gaullist family had grown. To be sure, the Algerian affair had precipitated the departure of a few leaders. But many of the 1940 companions remained. Pompidou knew them very well. Then there were such diverse groups as the Gaullists of 1958, the moderates who had rallied to the cause of an independent Algeria, some ambitious young men, and a handful of VIPs from the provinces. All in all, there were cliques, clubs, coteries, constituting a small but avid and disparate court to which the general deigned to be gracious from time to time.

Not being a member of the family, Pompidou could afford to ignore these people. The general described them as "a handful of busybodies, grumblers and imbeciles." But he also discerned a few faithful ones, "ready to go through fire."

The premier approached these men with infinite caution. Although included in the Gaullist aristocracy, he had no pedigree. Everyone knew that he had been hand-picked by de Gaulle — a fact that conferred supreme legitimacy upon him. Nevertheless, they regarded him as a usurper. They were still in mourning for Debré.

But Pompidou did have a few allies, notably the barons: Frey, Foccart, Guichard, and even Chaban-Delmas took pleasure in his promotion. Debré had not been wholly one of them. Pompidou was. In fact, he was their leader. With Georges at the Matignon, Roger at the ministry of the interior, Olivier working with Georges, and Jacques at the Elysée close to the general — to say nothing of Chaban at the Assembly — the barons had their hands on all the levers.

De Gaulle, of course, was well aware of this. He yielded a part of his power to them: finance, police, domestic policy, the U.N.R., parliament, the peasants, the trade unions, the shopkeepers and academicians. In short, all Frenchmen. For himself, he kept France. The customs established during Debré's tenure of the premiership were maintained. Algeria, Africa, the department of justice, the army, foreign policy — all matters pertaining to them were decided at the Elysée. The premier was kept informed in a general way only.

Anyone less accustomed to serving the general would have suffered from such an inequitable association. But the new premier easily accommodated himself to it. The prestige of the chief of state was then at its zenith. Frenchmen who were neither lawmakers nor politicians readily accepted this interpretation of the constitution.

Pompidou was being taught at the right school.

Later he told a member of the parliamentary opposition: "Everything I know I learned from the general."

. .

Pompidou was naturally mistrustful of dramas. He could tot up Debré's manifestations of anger or chagrin, the many times he had threatened to resign. When Pompidou came to the Matignon, he made it a rule never to clash with de Gaulle. He knew that the general's opponents always lost. De Gaulle frankly admitted that he did not like people who opposed him. "I listen to advice, but in the end I alone make the decisions," he said.

When Pompidou settled in at the Matignon, he realized how genuine Debré's anguish had been. At a time when France was separating herself from Algeria, the country experienced a moral crisis. Attempted assassinations multiplied. Each day in the south of France, ships arrived at ports, unloading hordes of *pieds-noirs* with their various belongings. Pompidou was called the first premier of the peace. But there was no peace in the hearts of men.

General Jouhaud, one of the authors of the April 1961 putsch, was condemned to death the day before Palm Sunday, twenty-four hours before Pompidou's appointment to the premiership. Jouhaud's file was absent from the dossiers in the office of the new head of the cabinet. The decision to allow Jouhaud to die or to grant him clemency was to be made by the chief of state, and by him alone.

A few days later, on Maundy Thursday, General Salan, the prime leader of the putsch and Jouhaud's boss, was arrested. Jouhaud had made his plea for mercy. De Gaulle hesitated.

"For several days," an aide-de-camp has related, "the Jouhaud dossier was plainly in evidence on top of the general's desk. Upon entering the room, I often noticed that the general was deeply engrossed in reading and rereading the documents. He refused to look at the letters sent to him by people requesting clemency for Jouhaud. 'I alone can decide,' he would say. 'I must heed my own conscience.' But Madame de Gaulle gave him a certain number of letters and managed to convince him that he ought to read them. I really believe that in this affair she was the only person he listened to. The general has always shown great respect for his wife's common sense."

De Gaulle kept postponing his decision. A few days after Salan's arrest, the Public Prosecutor's High Council met at the Elysée and examined the dossier. Jean Foyer, Minister of Justice and a friend of Debré's, said to the general: "In any event, Jouhaud's execution can't take place right now. The tribunal will want to summon the former general as a witness at the Salan trial."

This was a case of *force majeure*. The general allowed himself to be persuaded. What had he decided? No one knew. Even Madame de Gaulle and all of his closest associates, including of course Pompidou, were kept in the dark.

The Salan trial lasted several days. De Gaulle began to show impatience. In his opinion, everything was crystal clear: a crime had been committed against the state, against legitimacy, against France. And a crime had been committed against Charles de Gaulle, who for the moment constituted the epitome of all three. The verdict was announced on a Wednesday evening at a time when the Elysée was brilliantly illuminated because of a reception being given in honor of an African president: Salan's head was to be spared.

The next day the cabinet met at the Elysée. Pale and preoccupied, de Gaulle presided. The floor was turned over to Foyer, who gave a lengthy account of the Salan trial, never once uttering the name of Jouhaud. The general commented laconically: "The High Military Tribunal is encouraging subversion."

The cabinet went on to discuss current business. Then the meeting was adjourned.

"The general was very upset," a collaborator later recounted. "He was both distressed and furious. Someone had told him that one of the judges on the High Military Tribunal was a Freemason who, out of fraternal solidarity, had refused to condemn Salan to death. The explanation was perhaps somewhat simplistic. But the general did not reject it."

After the cabinet meeting, de Gaulle summoned two of his ministers, Jean Foyer and Pierre Messmer; the latter was in charge of the army. Pompidou had already returned to the Matignon.

The atmosphere in de Gaulle's office was electric. The general curtly told Foyer and Messmer: "I reject clemency for Jouhaud."

He gave Messmer his orders: the execution was to take place the day after the next, a Saturday, at dawn. He added that a precedent had to be set. The two ministers left the Elysée in a state of great anguish.

Foyer hastened to the Matignon and informed Pompidou of the general's decision. The premier was completely taken aback. Although he had said not a word, he too was crushed by the news.

"Jouhaud's execution would be an iniquity for which history will never forgive Charles de Gaulle," said Foyer. "I'm going back to the Elysée this afternoon and I'll tell the general exactly how I feel about it."

"Don't do anything of the kind," Pompidou answered. "Wait until tomorrow, I beg you. I'm asking this as a personal favor."

That afternoon Pompidou decided to go to the Elysée himself. He tried to plead the cause of Jouhaud and of civil peace with de

Gaulle, arguing that peace could not be maintained if capital punishment were meted out to this *pied-noir*. The general exploded. It was precisely the well-being of the state he was thinking of. Not Charles de Gaulle but France herself was being challenged. The cabinet must be made to understand this. Resorting to rough language, the general then accused Pompidou of failing to consider the higher interests of the state. The ministers, including Pompidou, must either obey or resign.

Weakly, Pompidou said all right, he was ready to hand in his resignation. But de Gaulle, not listening, reminded Pompidou of the realities of the situation. He had not named Pompidou premier to put up with his arguments. The interview ended on a cool note.

At the Matignon, Pompidou was reliving Debré's nightmare. When Christian Fouchet came to see him, he said: "The general treated me abominably. I cannot accept that. I have tendered my resignation."

Fouchet reassured him. He knew the general well and was accustomed to his rages. Differences were soon forgotten. All the ministers had had a taste of de Gaulle's temper at least once. He himself had been dressed down by the general on occasion. It was unpleasant, but no more than that.

Pompidou shook his head. He was not merely a minister but the head of the cabinet, and as such responsible to parliament.

"Believe me," said Fouchet, "wait until tomorrow."

The next day, a Friday, Jean Foyer went to see the general at nine-thirty in the morning. He was sharply reprimanded for his pains.

"Your job is not to defend criminals," de Gaulle told him. "I will be obeyed, whether you like it or not. Jouhaud will be executed." A few even less amiable remarks followed. Foyer had to take it. As he left, he ran into Pompidou in the antechamber.

"Well, how is he? What's his humor like?" Pompidou asked.

"Abominable."

The premier sighed, then entered the room assigned to the general's aides-de-camp. Ten minutes later de Gaulle summoned him.

He was even colder than the day before. No one, he said, would be forced to remain in the cabinet. Should anyone wish to leave, he would be replaced immediately.

What irritated the general the most — and Pompidou was quick to see this — was the blow aimed at his responsibilities as chief of state. In the Jouhaud affair, as in everything else, he alone would decide. The cabinet was not even to be consulted. To each his proper place. It wasn't a bad idea to remind people of this on occasion, and forcefully!

De Gaulle, however, was fully aware that since Salan's head had been spared, it would be difficult to execute Jouhaud. Later he was to say: "If Salan had been arrested before Jouhaud, then, yes, Jouhaud would have been executed."

.   .

It was Friday, twenty-four hours before the date fixed for the execution. The general allowed his hand to be forced. What followed was something of a tragicomedy.

Foyer, upon leaving the Elysée and the fireworks there, went to a meeting of magistrates at which he was to preside. In the midst of the kind of speeches usually delivered on such occasions, he was told that Jouhaud's defenders were waiting to see him in his office at the Place Vendôme. Foyer hurried there at once. The lawyers gave him an idea for a new clemency plea that would at least serve to delay the execution. Their position had been found to be valid by the higher magistrates. At last Foyer perceived a small silver lining in the darkening sky — "a good way out," as he later put it. Somewhat calmed, he went home for lunch.

At this point Foyer was summoned by the President of the Assembly, Chaban-Delmas, who upbraided him vehemently.

"If Jouhaud isn't executed, there will be a tremendous increase in terrorist activity. Ministers will be assassinated, and you, Foyer, will have their deaths on your conscience."

"On the contrary — quite the contrary," the minister replied. "It's Jouhaud's execution that would provoke fresh violence."

The dispute lasted for a while, each man holding to his position.

Shaken, Foyer returned to his office. But the High Judicial Council sent him word that the new plea for clemency, based on the Salan verdict, precluded the execution of Jouhaud scheduled for the following day. Without losing a minute, Foyer went straight to the Matignon, entered Pompidou's office and told him triumphantly: "Don't resign. You've been saved!"

The most difficult task of all still remained: to inform the general. Mustering their courage, Pompidou and Foyer went to the Elysée. De Gaulle listened to his Minister of Justice. Then, interrupting him acidly, he hurled the charge of betrayal at Foyer. Glacially, he added: "Well, gentlemen, our interview is over."

After dinner that evening, the premier went again to the president's office. Speaking deferentially and very solemnly, he offered to resign. De Gaulle listened paternally but pretended not to hear. He would not part with Pompidou until he believed it necessary. Certainly not yet. As he accompanied Pompidou to the door, he said wearily: "I know it's difficult. But the people who work with me, Pompidou, don't give in to their feelings."

The final scene was enacted at the Elysée the following day. The general was at his desk. Pompidou, Foyer and Messmer sat facing him. The die was cast. Once again de Gaulle accused the Keeper of the Seals of disloyalty. Foyer stood up: "Under the circumstances, my general, you will understand that I must submit my resignation."

Slowly Foyer walked to the door. Pompidou grasped his arm. The ensuing silence lasted only a few seconds. Suddenly de Gaulle, mollified, amiable, his fury spent, said: "Oh, come now, Foyer, sit down."

The crisis had only slight repercussions. Foyer, Pompidou, and the others were forgiven. The general forgot about his display of temper and about all the recriminations. Jouhaud himself was to be pardoned. He might have been pardoned in any case. Pompidou never again mentioned the unfortunate episode in the presence of de Gaulle. Later, when Bastien-Thiry, a colonel who had attempted to assassinate the general, was condemned to death, the premier carefully refrained from intervening.

Yet the incident remained a secret, nagging sore point. Pompidou had been subjected to the same treatment as a man like Foyer. He had thought of himself as a privileged being toward whom the general displayed a special indulgence. Now de Gaulle had demonstrated that his personal feelings, what ordinary men call friendship, would never affect the administration of the state.

Very quickly the Jouhaud affair became something of a legend. Public opinion learned of Pompidou's opposition to what in effect would have been a state crime. The general himself confided to visitors, somewhat complacently: "The premier was quite emotional. He offered to resign. He wasn't the only one to plead with me . . ."

De Gaulle gave credence to this version of the conflict. The effect was twofold: the Matignon benefited from having pleaded for clemency; the Elysée was credited with firmness. De Gaulle had gained on two fronts.

"There was no friction," Pierre Messmer confirmed. "Pompidou must be given credit for having braved the tempest; afterward, the general was grateful to him."

A few weeks later, de Gaulle, by then completely appeased, said to Pompidou: "I chose the lesser of two evils. I couldn't appoint a new premier after only six weeks."

CHAPTER 7

Baptism of Fire

THE DRAMA was not always orchestrated by de Gaulle himself. Often Providence had something to do with it.

On August 22, 1962, the car in which the general, Madame de Gaulle, and their son-in-law, Colonel de Boissieu, were traveling was attacked by a sizable group of terrorists between Paris and Villacoublay, in Petit-Clamart. One hundred and fifty shots were fired. One of them left a hole in the body of the car only a few inches from the place where the chief of state was seated.

Ever since 1940, the general had become adept at interpreting the signs of Providence. He also knew how to exploit them. Upon his return to the Elysée, while strong emotions were spreading throughout the country and even outside it, de Gaulle went to work. Paris was empty. Most of the ministers and administrative officials were still at the beaches. De Gaulle summoned a lawyer who was his adviser on constitutional matters. After listening benignly to the polite formulas usually invoked on such occasions, the general said: "All right. Now we must take steps to insure the future. We must go on to the second stage . . ."

De Gaulle intended to make sure that in the future, the President of the Republic would be elected by all the French people. Until now such a change had not appealed to him. But now that his life had been threatened, the moment had come to include in the constitution provisions inspired by this nearly tragic incident.

In reality, de Gaulle had been preparing for this second step during the past eighteen months, from the very moment in April 1961 when he had seen the state flinch in the face of a rebellion by a handful of retired generals. He had confided in one or another of his associates, but without much conviction.

The idea, he had come to see, was not yet ripe for implementation. He reflected, and questioned people, proceeding as he always did before he embarked on a major undertaking. He had not yet decided to act. To alter the constitution, which was only three years old, was to acknowledge its imperfections.

"The matter had already been studied," one of de Gaulle's ministers later pointed out, "in nineteen sixty and again in nineteen sixty-one. But in any case, the Algerian war and the presence of the African states within the French Community prevented us at that time from proceeding to hold a constitutional referendum."

As early as the month of April, the premier had soothed the deputies and certain ministers by firmly assuring them of his opposition to the use of a referendum for the purpose of electing the president by universal suffrage.

"The time is not right for upheavals and conflicts," Pompidou had said. "The country is still ailing and it would therefore be foolish to plunge it into fresh battles."

A few weeks before the attempted assassination of de Gaulle, Pompidou had stated confidentially to Pierre Sudreau, a member of the cabinet: "The general has again talked to me about a constitutional referendum. But I can assure you that it will not take place as long as I am premier."

Forty-eight hours after the gunfire at Petit-Clamart, Pompidou was summoned to Colombey. The general stated his intention of staging a constitutional referendum. But, as was his wont, he pretended to ask Pompidou's opinion. He of course wanted to sound him out.

"You understand that I am contemplating this change not for myself but for the individual who sooner or later will take my place," said de Gaulle. "Perhaps it will be you. Think about it. Then tell me your opinion three days from now."

In reply, Pompidou observed that he didn't need three days to think it over. Having already considered the matter, he could say that he was in favor of the proposed move. He didn't want a repetition of the Jouhaud affair. Nonetheless, de Gaulle was later to say: "My premier was not overly enthusiastic about the nineteen sixty-two referendum."

The faithful continued to shower the Elysée with advice. Several ministers, especially Roger Frey, suggested new and radical changes in the regime. Frey even advocated the installation of a vice president, since the question of de Gaulle's succession had suddenly become acute, as a consequence of the attempted assassination. The general did not say no, but he failed to see what sort of practical role a vice president might play.

De Gaulle had not waited for the opinions of his advisers. He immersed himself forthwith in law manuals. Once again he began to scribble. Twice a day he summoned his adviser, Boitreaud, and for more than an hour at a time he would discuss, line by line and in the manner of a professional, proposed changes in the constitution.

He had quite made up his mind to stage a referendum. "The people must declare their wishes." And he added: "This is urgent."

The difficulty was to find in the constitution the necessary authority to lay such a reform directly before the people without first going to parliament. "For goodness' sake!" he would say impatiently. "I'm the one who wrote this constitution. I know very well what I put in it."

People kept saying, "No, look at Article Eighty-nine." To which the general would reply, "Yes, but look at Article Eleven." Then he would close his manuals and say to his aides: "What I propose to do is entirely in keeping with the spirit of the constitution. You know that very well." Whereupon one of his aides would point out: "Yes, my general, with the spirit but not with the letter."

.   .

Time was pressing. De Gaulle no longer bothered to reassure and convince people or plead his cause. On September 12, 1962, three days after a triumphal trip to Germany, he informed the cabinet of his decision; Pompidou had been apprised of it the day before.

The general immediately made it clear to everyone, including his premier, that he would not lend himself to any accommodation. Since he was about to take the offensive, he would not mince words. Facing his ministers, he said:

"This reform, which I have every intention of pushing, may pose a problem for you. I will find it perfectly understandable if you should feel that you cannot assume the responsibility that will devolve upon you in accordance with the principle of ministerial solidarity. That is your affair. Within a week you must either cooperate or resign."

The question concerned only de Gaulle and France — or at any rate the French nation. Neither deputies, senators, ministers, nor Pompidou would be allowed to block the general.

· ·

The general fired the first salvo on September 20, 1962, in a speech to the people, and the second twelve days later in a message to parliament. Against the wishes of all the non-Gaullist politicians, he proposed a presidential regime in which the chief of state would be elected by universal suffrage. In France's history such dramatic changes have invariably produced coups d'état. The deputies immediately drafted a motion of censure against the Pompidou government. De Gaulle had foreseen the possibility, which in realistic terms was quite ridiculous. "Well, what is undemocratic about all of this?" he asked one of his aides.

The earlier referenda on Algeria had been mere formalities. This one heralded a new era for France. De Gaulle threw himself into the campaign with all the fervor of a young army officer. Gone was the shadow of death that had hovered over him a month before. Forgotten was the sinister word "succession." Would the referendum constitute a vote of confidence? Well, yes it would. Let those who wished — the breadwinners, the soreheads — be shocked if they must. If he achieved a large popular consensus, the general could get on with his job, forge ahead, raising France to fresh heights. He could take risks as well, since to hold power meant to innovate without cease. "A man who is out of the ordinary tries to change his times, not merely to follow prevailing trends meekly," said de Gaulle.

No sooner was the referendum announced than the battle began to rage. The various political parties raised the cry for a "sacred union" against de Gaulle. Many and varied were the rancors that came to light, some dating from the Liberation, others from the start of the war in Algeria. The "wise men" of the Council of State were themselves hostile to the idea of a constitutional referendum. But all this nonsense was dismissed by the general.

"Frenchmen are more intelligent than you think," he insisted. "They understand instinctively that something essential is at stake. If this were not so, would they have been on de Gaulle's side at every bleak moment of our history?"

Leaving the premier to deal with the parliamentary revolt, the general donned his uniform and went off to review the army's annual exercises. To renew his ties with the military, his own vocational group, was to break for a while with the "turbulent, intriguing" masses. Before leaving, he held one last council of war with Pompidou. The premier foresaw the worst — in other words, his own downfall — when the parliamentary debates ended.

Without a trace of bitterness, de Gaulle told him: "The Assembly will vent its wrath and realize its impotence. Our path has been clearly marked out. All you have to do is to stand firm."

Pompidou went to the Palais-Bourbon like a warrior leaving his trenches. Sure of defeat, he was indeed flouted, mocked and castigated. Without too much conviction, he counterattacked. The former councilor of state struggled as best he could amid the jungle of constitutional laws. This was a domain in which he was not at home. But he remained clear-sighted, not yet convinced that the referendum would be successful. His want of spirit was obvious to all. When de Gaulle later heard about Pompidou's lackluster performance, he shrugged his shoulders. "What good was it to bow to a sectarian Assembly?"

On October 5, at four o'clock in the morning, in the chill aftermath of a sleepless night, the Pompidou cabinet fell. The vote against it was 280 out of 480.

Defeated, the premier went directly to the Quai de Béthune, his familiar domicile, without even stopping at the Matignon. This setback was not his own doing. Everything had been prearranged, organized, controlled by de Gaulle. Pompidou could sleep peacefully. His conscience was clear.

For thirty hours he did not know what fate held in store for him. By long-distance telephone, he gave the general — still absent from Paris — an account of the parliamentary battle. De Gaulle would have to choose between dissolving the Assembly or getting rid of his premier. He was careful not to reveal his intentions. He merely said that he had foreseen the outcome. Henceforth this kind of thing was bound to prove a waste of time.

For thirty hours Pompidou could dream of his new-found peace of mind. All doors remained open to him, including politics — meaning perhaps the presidency of the republic, or the bank. He would put his faith in Providence, which had always been kind to him. Whether he left tomorrow at the general's bidding, or in six months when a presidential regime was installed, was of no great moment. He had always been able to adjust himself calmly to changing circumstances because of his unshakable confidence in his own capabilities. Politics was a vocation with many delights, not all of which had he as yet experienced. At fifty-one he still had quite a bit of time.

Meanwhile, the general had returned. In no great hurry, he saw Pompidou late the next morning. "Naturally, you will stay," he said. "We'll hold legislative elections after the referendum."

Pompidou concurred but without any genuine sense of satisfaction. To some of his associates he said: "All this is very good"; but to others he complained: "The French are weary and sorely tried. I wonder whether fresh ordeals are really necessary."

. .

For seven weeks France became the scene of electoral jock-eyings.

The opposition lost no time. The political parties — the "parties of long ago," as de Gaulle contemptuously described them — talked about the need for a massive uprising. The right and the left, radicals and clericals, Pétainists and former Resistants, advocates of a French Algeria and champions of the Evian accords — all combined to present a united front against the "monarch." A tidal wave was in the offing.

The general gave in to his black demons. "The jig is up," he said. "They called de Gaulle when they were in a funk; they dumped the Algerian affair on his back; now they're going to throw him over so they can go back to their knitting."

Roger Frey arrived with prognostications that were not as yet clear, but he stubbornly believed that de Gaulle would win. "It's going to be difficult, my general. The end of a certain kind of political philosophy is approaching. All in all, the groundwork looks good. The man in the street has received the message."

Maybe, de Gaulle conceded, the constitutional referendum would be accepted. But then the legislative elections would follow. There lay the danger. How could he remain in power with a vengeful Assembly, determined to sabotage his every move? Abroad the rumor was spread that de Gaulle would lose "his" elections. In London especially, where the general had not been forgiven for his refusal to approve Great Britain's entry into the Common Market, his adversaries were already claiming victory.

"The British Conservatives urged their followers to be patient," Couve de Murville recalled. "They said that de Gaulle would be beaten and that France's European policy would be altered."

.   .

The opposition parties were firing their big guns. Newspapers trumpeted the latest news. There were colloquia and banquets; new clubs were formed. But the general did not deign to take notice. He spoke only to the French nation. The stake was France herself.

"If the yes majority should prove weak, unimpressive, uncertain," said de Gaulle, "my job will plainly be over, and over for good. What could I expect to accomplish without the enthusiastic support of the nation?"

Disheartened, virtually paralyzed, the cabinet — which had been dealing only with current affairs since its defeat in the Assembly — let the general wage his fight alone. Pompidou confined himself to issuing various directives to the prefects and to supervising the everyday preparations for the campaign; he attended mainly to administrative and financial matters.

"I am obliged to exhibit a certain degree of discretion," he explained. "Inasmuch as I have been overthrown, the very sight of my person will only make polemical discussion more acrid. The result is bound to be harmful."

Like the majority of Frenchmen, he hated division. He had managed to remain neutral during the German occupation and silent during the Algerian tragedy. He was fearful of great moral crises that could split France in two; and he did not like to take sides.

Knowing his premier well, the general accepted Pompidou's detachment. Besides, only the man of destiny could alter the course of events.

During the two-week campaign that preceded the referendum, Michel Debré and Christian Fouchet were virtually the only members of the Gaullist clan to make themselves heard. Delighted to escape the tedium of retirement, Debré did his best to arouse the Gaullist troops, the U.N.R. deputies, and the militants. Fouchet, who had been appointed Minister of Information two weeks earlier, made abundant use of radio and television. He spoke with the same kind of passion that had marked his broadcasts from Algeria.

"Pompidou was afraid of television," Fouchet was later to remark. "His debut as premier had been rather awkward. He was not very sure of himself."

On October 24, however, four days before the balloting, Pompidou did appear on television. Had his silence lasted much longer, he would have been accused of treachery. Naturally, he preached common sense. He sought to reassure the country about the scope of the proposed reform and to minimize the issues that were at stake. "This will not entail any substantial political change," he insisted.

Once again Providence proved to be the general's most reliable ally. Five days before the referendum, the Cuban missile crisis arose on the other side of the ocean. There was at once great fear of another world war, the same fear that had pushed Frenchmen into the general's arms in 1958. De Gaulle did not believe that the Cuban crisis would develop into a global war. But the incident itself did at any rate illustrate a very ancient truth: when great danger arises, a groundswell of sorts pushes the strong man to the fore. Naturally, his is a difficult task; it is he who must make the principal effort, and it is his intervention that is bound to prove decisive.

De Gaulle had no need to exploit the situation. Fear accomplished its own obscure task. He finally permitted one of his ministers to state that "de Gaulle will enable France to make her full contribution to the defense of the free world." The opposition parties were obliged to mute their war cry.

. .

The referendum took place on October 28, 1962. Sixty-two point twenty-five per cent of the electorate voted yes. That evening, as the ballots were being counted, several ministers gathered around Pompidou at the Hôtel de Matignon. But the general, who was at Colombey, had not yet been heard from. The long wait augured nothing good.

Finally, Pompidou, loath to break the silence himself, asked one of his ministers to phone Colombey. At the other end of the line, de Gaulle expressed his disappointment. "I stated some time ago that if the results were not brilliant or decisive, I would go. Well, the figures are not impressive."

The minister replied: "Allow me to remark, my general, that such is not our feeling. From here it seems that in view of the size of the coalition of political parties arrayed against us, you have won an undeniable victory."

De Gaulle became more explicit. If the number of abstentions were taken into account it would be impossible to deny that fewer than one out of every two Frenchmen wanted to see him back in the saddle. "I will think it over," he promised. "I will see you on Wednesday."

Recollecting the general's abrupt departure in 1946, some members of the cabinet feared the worst. Throughout the following day Fouchet and even Pompidou lived through hours of anxiety. But the others were calm and undismayed.

"Believe us," they said, "when the general returned to power in nineteen fifty-eight, it was with the firm intention of remaining there until he died."

At long last the general summoned his premier to Colombey. He spent little time underscoring the results of the Sunday balloting rather, he drew up plans for a campaign battle in the legislative elections. This time the entire government would have to be mobilized. The stakes were high; the situation was difficult and fraught with danger.

But de Gaulle's enthusiasm had its limits. He told Pompidou quite coldly: "Whatever happens, I will give up power within six months. I have accomplished the essentials. I will leave, and you will take my place."

At the cabinet meeting at the Elysée on the following Wednesday, de Gaulle issued a call for a general mobilization: "The political parties will have to give up their stranglehold on the Assembly. They will have to be made to realize that the chief of state and the people are stronger than they are," he said. He went on to announce that in a few days he himself would address the French people. Then, with deliberate amiability he asked Pompidou: "Does that meet with your approval, Monsieur Premier?"

Pompidou was taken by surprise. But he soon perceived the significance of this remark. The general had every intention of putting

Pompidou into the battle; this time, he was to serve in the front lines.

The Gaullist party, the U.N.R., hurriedly threw itself into the campaign. Scarcely a month before, no one had expected that elections would be held. There had hardly been time enough to select the candidates. The condition of the party's exchequer was far from satisfactory. At that time Frenchmen were not yet ready to employ American-type electoral tactics, with their reliance on modern public relations techniques. (They were to be adopted by the Gaullists in 1968 and 1969.) The party leaders divided up the work as best they could. The barons — Roger, Jacques and Olivier — as well as the secretary general of the U.N.R., were to take care of the candidatures. Debré and Malraux were to be in charge of doctrine as well as speeches. From the Matignon, Pompidou was to supervise the overall strategy and handle all financial problems.

The general did not underestimate the importance of this campaign. Once again, it was his person that was the focal point. The referendum would have to be confirmed by giving the chief of state the wherewithal to act: a parliamentary majority — no more, but also no less.

"You who have voted for me in the past, vote now for those who are supporting me," he adjured the French people.

.   .

They did. The U.N.R. obtained 229 seats. The combined strength of those who had favored a yes vote exceeded by far an absolute majority (242) of the new Assembly. In the entire picture there was but one shadow: Debré suffered defeat at the polls.

Pompidou was confirmed in his functions as premier. He had been "reenlisted," to quote the general. Was he pleased? Yes, after all! Little by little he became accustomed to his fourth profession. His course had been marked out by de Gaulle. All he had to do was to follow it. Time was on his side.

"I am an Auvergnat, that is to say, a mountaineer," he said. "I husband my strength. I advance slowly."

On December 13, 1962, Pompidou was once again in the center of the political arena at the Palais-Bourbon. Nine months after his debut as premier, he was again to confront the deputies and lay his plans before them. With a sizable majority to support him, he now had nothing to fear. There were no radical changes or reforms to announce. He painted a future as untroubled as a lake's dormant waters. And he employed neutral phrases:

"The problem of agriculture is fundamental . . . In the social domain, it is better to prevent than to cure . . . Nothing is more fragile than prosperity . . . We are just as dedicated to the concept of a unified Europe as we are to the Atlantic alliance . . ."

Who cared if people sneered or mocked? The general ruled. And Pompidou was beginning his career as de Gaulle's major domo.

CHAPTER 8

The Daily Grind

GEORGES POMPIDOU was back in his office at the Matignon, blessed with those twin gifts from heaven that natives of the Cantal so greatly appreciate: tranquillity and stability. Save for some unforeseeable eventuality, he would remain premier until the termination of the presidential mandate — December 1965. Debré had held on for three years and three months; Pompidou could expect to hold on for the forty-five remaining months. Then the seven-year interval would be over with only two premiers, which was the way the general wanted it.

Pompidou proceeded to settle in. He transported some of his own furniture and had his favorite pictures hung on the walls — mostly abstract paintings by Soulages that would stupefy the general if ever he came to visit his premier at the Matignon. Pompidou was still not resigned to "living next door to his office." Every night he would return to his apartment on the Quai de Béthune, near Notre-Dame. Thus he violated a tradition — this one and others as well. In a variety of ways he indicated that he had no wish to resemble a Fourth Republic premier, or any type of political leader, for that matter.

There was no mistaking it: Pompidou was a financier in charge of the country's exchequer, its petty business, "the shop," as de Gaulle put it. Everything seemed to indicate that the country's economy would be his prime concern during the next three years. De Gaulle had called upon an expert to manage the ordinary affairs of the nation. During the war in Algeria, a politician had to be put at the

Matignon. But now the time had come for a technician who would concern himself with the treasury, with the problems of employers and trade unions — a man who would husband the pennies.

No one expected him to harbor any particular concept of France. At the Elysée, the general — with the help of Couve de Murville and a few lesser diplomats — was already outlining the nation's policies. Pompidou had no connection with foreign affairs save insofar as they affected the nation's economy.

Once a week the Minister of Foreign Affairs would come to the Matignon to go over things. According to Couve de Murville's colleagues, their boss submitted the names of future ambassadors to Pompidou for his signature. Nothing more.

Besides, what kind of dialogue could there be between the two men? One was the grandson of peasants, the son of teachers, a clever man elevated by luck and tenacity within a time span of fifteen years to the very apex of the social hierarchy; the other was an accomplished diplomat, a Protestant member of one of the great bourgeois families. Their relations were correct but frigid. Couve, even more than Pompidou, was a master of the art of silence. Occasionally recalling these interviews with the premier, Couve would admit with a slight smile: "I didn't help him any."

De Gaulle was not yet inclined to draw a comparison between the two men. Couve was an asset. But, as the general once remarked, "Diplomats are not men of action. Their job is to negotiate, not to decide." Couve de Murville was fortunate in that he belonged to a family which made a fetish of service to the state.

At the start of the year 1963, Europe was the general's major preoccupation. In fact, it was virtually his only one. Just as he had done during the war, de Gaulle was carrying on a lively dialogue with each of his Anglo-Saxon partners. This twenty-year-old dialogue had origins as yet still unknown to Pompidou.

Once again the general suspected the British of conniving with the Americans. "At a time when Great Britain plainly wanted to join the Common Market, the general wondered whether England would ever be able to shake off the American yoke," Couve later explained. "We had our doubts from the time of the Conservative party congress in October nineteen sixty-two. Prime Minister Macmillan's visit to Rambouillet in mid-December opened our eyes. By the end of the year no one believed that England would join the Common Market."

On January 14, 1963, in the Salle des Fêtes at the Elysée, the general uttered the words which the British press was to describe as the "death sentence." "It is quite possible that one day England will be metamorphosed sufficiently to join the European Community without restrictions or reservations . . . It is also possible that England will not change, and the feeling that this is what will happen seems to be the outcome of the very lengthy conversations in Brussels."

In a few sentences, de Gaulle had committed his country to a policy from which there could be no retreat. Pompidou was given the text of de Gaulle's statement that morning. This was quite understandable in view of the fact that the premier would have to defend the general's European policy before parliament.

"Several times the general availed himself of opportunities to explain his point of view to the cabinet or to a special group of ministers," Couve has noted. "His statement of January fourteenth could not have surprised any member of the government."

After the death sentence was pronounced, the execution itself took place on January 29 at Brussels, in the gloom and chill fog of a Belgian winter. For the time being, this settled the question of Britain's entry into the Common Market.

. .

That winter Pompidou was busy with domestic problems. The season began in melancholy fashion. The trade unions were not at all pleased with the premier, a man who had come straight from the citadels of capitalism. During the previous April, immediately after Pompidou's installation at the Matignon, a rash of strikes had broken out. They had gone on more or less continuously ever since, affecting one sector after another, subsiding only to start up all over again. They were becoming a part of the nation's daily life, much to Pompidou's chagrin.

On March 1, 1963, it was the miners' turn to stage a work stoppage. A difficult period began for the premier. He did not emerge from it unscathed.

At first Pompidou thought that this was a large-scale attempt to intimidate him. He had had no experience with social movements (the Popular Front of 1936 had been a matter of indifference to him). He knew only the business world, with its recourse to the kind of negotiations that amounted for the most part to bluffing.

And so he approached the miners' strike like a poker player. The workers scored from the very outset: 97 per cent of them went off the job. Pompidou decided to counter with equally strong measures.

March 2 was a Saturday and the general was at his country house. Pompidou went to Colombey and asked him to intervene. His arguments were impressive. This was a political matter. The authority of the state was at stake. The strike must be countered with a solemn gesture; power had to be brought into play.

The general was easily convinced. Never one to hesitate when told that the power of the state was threatened, he immediately responded to this kind of language. If Pompidou, who always liked to smooth things over, rejected any idea of accommodation, negotiations were clearly impossible. In the small study he had occupied during his long years of exile, de Gaulle signed the documents that the premier had drawn up. A statement condemning the miners appeared in the *Journal officiel* the next day.

This move was to have protracted consequences. The strike lasted almost five weeks. It aroused dismay and anger everywhere, even among Gaullists. The social crisis became a political and national one. Even the church intervened. Waves of recrimination submerged the Matignon and even swept on to the doors of the Elysée. Time, that precious ally, finally brought order. But at what a price!

Pompidou never forgot this cruel misadventure. His most serious mistake was to have involved the general in a matter that was entirely in his own jurisdiction. In short, he had driven a nail into his own coffin. "I just lacked experience," Pompidou was to explain afterward.

Despite this fiasco, the premier remained at his post. His authority and his burgeoning prestige suffered, but he continued to retain the general's confidence. He had lost a battle but not the war. A few incautious souls went to the Elysée and suggested Pompidou's recall. The idea had not even occurred to de Gaulle. "What a strange idea people must have of a state in which minor figures can oust a premier by voicing complaints," de Gaulle said.

Pompidou was the general's man. Only the general could replace him, and he would act if and when he thought it necessary. Never in the presence of Pompidou did de Gaulle allude to this deplorable episode.

.   .

Which kind of man, the general asked, would make the best possible premier? Pompidou, unruffled, intellectually agile, but indolent and inclined to allow events to carry him along? Or Debré, with his passion, his eagerness for reform, his enthusiasm and intransigence? In June de Gaulle invited one of his closest collaborators in the Free French movement to come see him. The two men exchanged anecdotes about those epic days. Suddenly, just as the visit was about to end, the general said to his visitor: "As someone who is not involved in politics, how do you feel about Debré and Pompidou? Which of them has the qualities of a true statesman?"

Debré, Pompidou, and others as well — the general looked them all over. Occasionally, in the presence of old associates, he would think out loud: "After me, the chief of state must be a man who is far-sighted and experienced in world affairs. He should be someone whose name is known abroad, who can make the voice of France heard. Couve is a statesman. What about Couve here and Pompidou at the Matignon?"

Many times the question of who would succeed the general was discussed. Presidential elections would take place thirty months hence and already the political parties were agog with impatience. The Gaullists themselves tried to pry the secret from the general. "You'll be here for a long time, my general, God willing. But after you, will France degenerate into impotence as before?"

De Gaulle would answer: "Have confidence in France. She will bury us all. If I was not convinced of this, I would have died of despair long ago."

.   .

Summer, filled with peaceful, lovely days, had come. The premier took himself off to Turkey, leaving his minister, Louis Joxe, to do battle in the Assembly over the right-to-strike laws. After all, Turkey was as important as the chamber . . .

But de Gaulle's mind was on other things. His work had not yet been completed. He still needed to transform, alter, reform.

Six months before, French institutions had been completely overhauled, yet already the general was thinking of making fresh changes. To pave the way for succession meant not only choosing a man, but also and primarily bequeathing a strong state, confident in itself and possessing the necessary tools for decisive action.

Senate, parliament, institutions — de Gaulle was forever thinking of how to renovate them, in keeping with his 1958 promise: "The state must be overhauled." He was preoccupied with the France of tomorrow.

Of himself, he said: "De Gaulle was not put on this earth to busy himself with the daily grind."

In midsummer, the realities of daily life suddenly interrupted the general's vision of the future. For weeks the country had been threatened by inflation and bankruptcy. Artfully contriving to take everyone by surprise, de Gaulle had been deep in the study of figures, balance sheets, budgets. A crisis impended. And drama was the general's element.

.   .

Although no expert in finance, de Gaulle viewed inflation as a political disaster, as material proof of impotence and of the country's tendency to yield to the easy life. For twelve years he had persistently accused the Fourth Republic of forever accepting the evils of inflation. Once back in power, he tersely observed: "The cash register is empty."

In November 1958, the general turned to his Minister of Finance and virtually ordered him to draft a plan for the country's recovery. "That's your department," de Gaulle had told the minister, and then confirmed it in writing.

But in 1962 inflation again raised its head. This was the period when a considerable increase in wages had been awarded to workers in the private sector, which in turn caused wages to rise in the public sector. Prices climbed. The infernal spiral was once again on its way.

The general was entirely preoccupied with constitutional affairs. Consequently, he did not at first perceive the economic perils. After the referendum and the legislative elections, the moment was hardly propitious for an announcement of new sacrifices. Besides, the new majority had said that it hoped 1963 would be a good year, a year of generosity, not of austerity.

Months went by. The black clouds of inflation loomed larger, but public opinion was lulled by false dreams. The U.N.R., imperturbable, predicted fresh generosities, and Pompidou allowed these pipe dreams to spread. He himself insisted that additional aid would have to be given to the unemployed and to all the poor and needy.

"In the government no one, not even the premier, was sufficiently worried about the economic situation," one of the barons subsequently asserted. "This was not our major concern at the time."

One man did alert the general: Couve de Murville. "I brought it up several times," Couve recalled. "I told the general that we would have to deal with the situation just as we had done in nineteen fifty-eight. I warned him."

The general listened silently to the technical explanations of his Minister of Foreign Affairs. Once again, de Gaulle had to make an important political decision. He did not go into the financial or monetary aspects of the situation. He understood little about such matters. But he saw the need to reverse directions. Economy was the foundations of politics, the pedestal upon which the work of art rested.

The general held many consultations, questioning a variety of people. Debré, likewise preaching firmness, wrote to him. De Gaulle knew that a certain number of remedies were available and that his decision would entail formidable political consequences. Before taking matters in hand himself, he took all kinds of precautions.

. .

Pompidou, the financier, declared himself against a program of austerity. And he had an abundance of arguments. Knowing the general's dislike for purely technical explanations, he underscored the political aspect. It would be unfortunate suddenly to give up the prospects of "a good year," and dangerous to put a freeze on the national economy right after France had taken in hundreds of thousands of repatriated Algerians. According to Pompidou, a policy of economic liberalism should be followed, expansion should be encouraged, and the country should be urged to produce more and improve quality in order to meet foreign competition, especially European competition.

Valéry Giscard d'Estaing, the Minister of Finance, was at first reluctant to recommend the purge. He was not eager to urge austerity upon a parliamentary majority that wanted just the opposite — to reap the rewards of victory.

When spring came, the recognized experts, the inspectors of finance on the Rue de Rivoli, all those who were respectfully alluded to as public servants, took turns in demanding a sudden halt to the catastrophic downhill swing of the economy. Thereupon Giscard too went to de Gaulle to advocate a policy of firmness, one worthy of a Poincaré. And of course the general was never deaf to any mention of historical precedents.

But Pompidou remained reticent. De Gaulle remembered the historic conflict of 1945 that pitted two ministers, René Pleven and Pierre Mendès-France, against one another over a similar question. At that time de Gaulle had backed Pleven, but for ten years he had been reproached for so doing. In the spring of 1963 he hesitated, not knowing whom to back, Pompidou or Giscard.

One of these men was, of course, the premier, who as such was responsible to parliament and attuned to the mood of the Gaullist majority. But the other was no ordinary man. Giscard was thirty-seven. The general liked to show kindness to brilliant young men like Giscard. He had a special liking for him. Was Giscard ambitious? Why should he not be? He came from a good family and displayed no unseemly greed for power. De Gaulle, long accused by sectarians of behaving like an old recluse, appreciated the young Minister of Finance and gave him a good deal of advice. "Never invoke special interests in public. Talk only about the country's interests and have only its interests at heart." Or else he would say: "There is only one force to which men submit: the truth. It doesn't matter whether the truth is obvious today or becomes plain later. Always rely on the truth."

By early summer, de Gaulle was still undecided. But he was growing impatient, irked by the slowness with which Pompidou moved. The government had as yet taken no action to correct the situation. At the Elysée there were some who predicted dire consequences. They spoke in this vein to the government. But the desire to take the easy way out persisted.

Then a fresh warning came from Couve: "You'll have to make up your mind now. At the end of this year, we plan to ask for an agricultural Common Market. But such a step will be impossible in a period of inflation. We simply couldn't hold out."

Early in August the decisive argument was presented to the general: it was the balance sheet for July. De Gaulle could see with his own eyes the extent of the catastrophe.

The ministers were all on vacation, enjoying the beaches in the west and south of the country. At Saint-Tropez, where vacationers were at their most garish, Pompidou was strolling gaily about, his smiling face the cynosure of eager photographers.

Fashionable places where well-known people congregate have always exerted a mysterious attraction on Pompidou. He still marveled at being admitted into the inner circle of actors and starlets, noted artists and unsuccessful painters, society women and demimondaines. This was his weakness. The general could never understand how a man capable of assuming the highest duties in the service of France managed to find pleasure in such mediocre company — indeed, that he could even bring himself to seek it. But what was once merely an excusable weakness had now become a crime, or even worse, a failing.

In Paris the financial reports were plainly disastrous. Yet on the beaches one witnessed the most blatant kind of indolence. De Gaulle flew into a rage. "They" were not attending to business, "they" were only thinking of themselves. Having fulminated against the entire cabinet without exception, the general summoned his ministers to an emergency meeting of the cabinet. It took place at the Elysée on August 13.

. .

Pompidou returned hastily to Paris. Told about the tempest that raged at the Elysée, he declined to get excited. During the past sixteen months he had learned to exhibit an ironclad philosophical calm in the face of a multitude of crises, both large and small. Before the cabinet meeting, he went to see de Gaulle.

Coldly but without rancor, de Gaulle warned Pompidou of his intention to put an end to the prevailing economic disorder. The premier agreed that the moment was well chosen: Frenchmen were at the beaches. But it would be dangerous, four months before the all-important erection of an agricultural Common Market, to interrupt economic activity, paralyze production, convulse the October meeting. He advised the adoption of stopgap measures, carefully chosen with an eye to the unhampered continuation of economic expansion.

The Minister of Finance, who was also consulted by the general, reminded him of his past warnings and once again suggested salutary economic action on a scale worthy of the general and history. This was a fine chance to correct the financial disequilibrium once and for all — something that had not been attempted since the days of Colbert. The franc, wages and prices, had to be brought into line with the current stability of French institutions. De Gaulle listened to the words he had been waiting for.

At the emergency cabinet meeting, which took place in a deserted Paris, most of the ministers were unaware of the conflict that pitted Pompidou against Giscard. The general entered the drawing room of the Elysée, whose windows opened onto a park bathed in sunlight. Contrary to his wont, he led off. Speaking with solemnity, he turned to the Minister of Finance. His admonitions, however, were not addressed solely to him but to the entire cabinet, "which is doing nothing to halt the inflation." "I shall expect you, gentlemen, to propose decisive measures within two weeks," the general commanded.

The stabilization plan was launched after having been worked out at the finance ministry, Rue de Rivoli, and nowhere else. "The general convinced me that we can rely only on ourselves," Giscard explained.

The finance minister jealously guarded his freedom of action. He had been in the government long before Pompidou. In addition, he enjoyed the special protection of the chief of state.

Upon leaving the now famous cabinet meeting of August 13, Valéry Giscard d'Estaing went straight to his office and summoned the various department heads. The citadel on the Rue de Rivoli had witnessed other upheavals. Now, it was there that every feature of the stabilization plan was readied for implementation amid great secrecy. Some of Pompidou's closest collaborators tried in vain to insinuate themselves into the proceedings. Pompidou remained ignorant of a few of the measures — the increase in the price of cigarettes, for example — until Giscard revealed them to the public.

The premier's authority was obviously being challenged. But he managed to obtain the general's consent to having the austerity program announced at a press conference at the Matignon, over which Pompidou would preside. De Gaulle granted him that consolation. The ceremony took place on September 12. In the presence of 200 journalists, Giscard and Pompidou enacted their comedy, deliberately giving the impression that they were cooperating harmoniously.

The austerity program, however, actually marked the effective end of their collaboration and the beginning of a cold war between them that held mistrust on the one side and jealousy on the other. Giscard played the role of a clandestine premier. By diminishing the influence of parliament, the new institutions of the Fifth Republic enabled the Minister of Finance to become the conscience of the government. Giscard was quick to realize this and to exploit it. Whenever the conflicts that pitted the two men against each other became extremely serious, Giscard would turn to the general and request his arbitration. Often de Gaulle sided with Giscard.

But de Gaulle was careful not to put an end to the real conflict caused by the question of who would succeed him. Giscard and Pompidou were both quite sure that the general himself would choose his heir. Their fate was in the hands of the chief of state. It therefore behooved both the premier and the Minister of Finance to prove themselves worthy of the presidency and of the supreme responsibilities it entailed.

Giscard made no secret of his ambition. Since early youth, his life had consisted in an imperceptible rise to power. From birth he had received his share of the future, having been raised as a thoroughbred and trained for the greatest of all races. Never once had he made a false move. For the past twenty years, his course had been marked out for him.

Pompidou's itinerary consisted of many detours. For him the future had been first the university, then government service, finally banking. And now at the age of fifty-two another prospect loomed. He might one day, if the general was willing, become the number-one man of France.

· ·

Pompidou had rivals. Each day the list grew longer. Before long, it could easily mount to ten, with Giscard in the lead.

Pompidou's sole strategy was to project to Frenchmen the image of himself as de Gaulle's chosen understudy. His legitimacy depended upon the confidence accorded him by de Gaulle.

People had seen him on television, an amiable man, his feet solidly on the ground, giving a "fireside talk," adapting his peasant background to modern political techniques. In contrast to the melancholy passion of Michel Debré, the glacial reserve of Couve de Murville, or the remote intelligence of Giscard, he offered the public a countenance on which his every trait or feeling could be easily deciphered: wryness, pleasure, perspicacity, caution, combativeness — and rancor. People told him and wrote to him that they liked what they saw in him. Why shouldn't he have believed them?

François Mauriac hailed the metamorphosis that was taking place in Pompidou "under our very noses." "Nothing in his hands, nothing in his pockets," wrote Mauriac, as if the premier were a magician.

The only difference was that Georges Pompidou already knew what the future held in store — or at any rate, his own future. But he tried very hard and successfully not to let this be seen.

As premier he was in a better position than anyone else to please the general, to be mindful of his moods, to fathom his reservations. His rule was to avoid the storm, and he was good at it.

"At cabinet meetings, Pompidou would watch from the corner of his eye to see what the reactions of the general, who was seated opposite him, would be," a minister recounted in 1963. "As soon as impatience or boredom was evidenced by a mere fluttering of the general's eyelids or a twitch of his mouth, the premier would intervene, interrupting the discussion to say: 'I believe, gentlemen, that we are wasting the general's time. We can, if you agree, study the problem ourselves. When our thinking has crystallized and we have had time to go over the matter, the cabinet can reconvene to review it once again.' Then we would go on to some other topic."

De Gaulle appreciated his premier's deftness in protecting him from petty annoyances. He praised Pompidou's "agility," his "savoir-faire." From then on, the cabinet sessions resembled meetings of a board of directors in charge of some family enterprise.

Never did the premier betray any personal aspirations, either in the presence of the general or even among friends. On the contrary, he pushed all controversial questions aside. "The general's mandate expires at the end of nineteen sixty-five. We have two years to think about it," he said.

De Gaulle, for his part, observed his premier. He realized what unavowed intentions were taking root and knew how the strategy of patience operated in his man. But none of this shocked him. Over the past twenty years or so, he had had ample opportunity to observe the growth of ambition in the men around him, including those he most trusted, his "friends." Pompidou therefore merely illustrated a fact that the general had always noted, although with a certain melancholy.

The chief of state pretended to be unaware of everything that was going on along the periphery of the government or in the political arena. During a visit to the south of France in September 1963, he calmly declared: "The main concern of General de Gaulle, President of the Republic, is to be useful to the French people. This has been my guideline for a quarter of a century. I am determined, so long as I have the strength, to continue."

Seven months later, illness, pain and hospitalization were to remind de Gaulle that no man is master of his own health nor of the fate reserved for him. By then, the assassination of President Kennedy had tragically underscored this truth.

Part III
GRAY DAYS

*Faster than spring-time showers comes thought on
    thought,
And not a thought but thinks on dignity.*

Henry VI, *Part II, act 3, scene 1*

CHAPTER 9

"Even his horse . . ."

STRENGTH, ENTHUSIASM, HOPE RETURNED. After the operation he underwent in 1964, the general forgot about the fatigues of aging. But he did not allow himself to become inebriated by this unexpected rebirth. He consulted several physicians. His strength still seemed fragile, questionable. At seventy-four, de Gaulle feared that he would be unable on his own to recognize the onset of the aging process. He listened to his own heartbeat, checked the sharpness of his mind, his memory, his reflexes. When delivering a speech or receiving a visitor, the slightest lapse of memory struck him as a warning from above. He forced himself to work on some thankless files for three hours at a time in order to test his intellectual capacities. He had the doctors explain to him all the symptoms of senility. The specialists reassured him. His lungs, his heart, his nerves were in good shape. But de Gaulle trusted only his own judgment. "I have lived through so much," he sighed. "Some day I will have to foot the bill."

People congratulated him on how well he looked. This only annoyed him. He alone was the best judge of his health. And if it were true that he was made of iron, as people kept saying obsequiously, he would be no less inclined, with full awareness of what he was doing, to abandon power with all its concomitant sorrows. He often expressed the hope that he would not "become diminished." Even the greatest of men always tended to stay on a quarter of an hour too long. "Napoleon accomplished great things," he used to say, "but unfortunately he came to a bad end."

Great epics are those which instill in successive generations a feeling of regret. De Gaulle had accomplished his mission: the war, Liberation, the economic recovery of the nation, decolonization, the recovery of France's independent position — all these would guarantee him a fine place in history. Would it all be lost through an old man's obstinacy?

He thought about his own death. The whole world also thought about it. Foreign countries were waiting for the moment when France would again become accommodating and subservient. And politicians of every persuasion were already burning with impatience to sit in his armchair. De Gaulle would sneer: "Frenchmen have nothing more to fear, neither paratroopers, nor scamps, nor a third world war, nor hunger. And so they want to enjoy life. De Gaulle stands in their way. They are tired of making an effort."

On August 15, 1964, the general went to Toulon. There the police discovered a bomb in a jar that had been placed at a point along his route. When he returned to the Elysée safe and sound, his associates begged him, in a long, detailed memorandum, to avert what they termed a "deadly blow." They advised him to alter the constitution once again and create the office of vice president, thereby insuring the continuation of Gaullism.

But de Gaulle wanted no part of such expedients. "A vice president?" he asked. "What would he have to do? Await my death?"

. .

Pompidou was the confidant of these dark thoughts. In his presence the general talked about the degrading miseries of aging. His sentences were cryptic. "When you are in my place . . ." Or: "That business . . . I'll leave it to my successor."

In his paternal way, de Gaulle kept giving more and more advice. He also pushed the premier more and more into the limelight. "You must be ready," he said.

Pompidou now used the first person when he spoke. The general's good will and the homage of public opinion combined to assure him of his destiny. His voice took on a different quality. For the first time he made an official trip to the Cantal. There, naturally enough, he discovered the delights of popularity. Toward the end of the summer, when the Gaullist family foregathered in a hotel for retired Britishers at Dinard, Pompidou hazarded addressing it as their leader. No one doubted the growing favor he enjoyed.

"That's his first mistake," the companions of the earliest years noted. "With de Gaulle, you mustn't be in a hurry to pocket the cash . . ."

At the Elysée, the men surrounding de Gaulle observed Pompidou without benevolence. Among them the word "successor" was taboo. People were already predicting with glee that at the last moment de Gaulle might nudge the premier off his precarious pedestal, just as he had done before to so many others.

The general permitted himself not a single confidential remark lest it be misconstrued. But he deliberately mentioned the other Gaullist princes — Chaban-Delmas, Couve de Murville, Fouchet.

Not a word about the Dauphin . . .

. .

In the autumn, fifteen months before the presidential elections, de Gaulle made the longest trip of his seventy-odd years. On a navy cruiser, the *Colbert,* he crossed the Atlantic to visit ten South American countries. At the close of a very trying year, de Gaulle showed himself to be once again in full possession of his strength. The voyage aboard a military vessel, far from the daily routine of his official existence in Paris, afforded him opportunity for solitary meditation.

In Paris, Pompidou tried to carry on with the utmost discretion. He was empowered to preside at cabinet meetings, and he exercised this authority on September 30. In the absence of de Gaulle, the government did not venture to address itself to international affairs. The meeting of the cabinet, although of no great moment, nonetheless gave rise to all kinds of speculation and hypotheses. The premier announced that he would call another cabinet meeting two days before the general's return. But from South America de Gaulle let it be known that a second meeting presided over by Pompidou would be pointless. The meeting was thereupon canceled. The transfer of power had not yet begun.

Upon his return, de Gaulle showed neither fatigue nor ill humor. He had spread the voice of France to the four corners of the gigantic Latin American continent. And he had been heard. He was satisfied. His trip had demonstrated how advantageous it was for France to have at her head a person of "historic and worldwide stature."

"Not forever will the world remain in the hands of the two giants," de Gaulle declared when he returned to the Elysée. "For one thing, there is China with all her vastness. Soon there will be a movement on the part of all governments hostile to the hegemony of the two superpowers. It will be France's task to influence the development of this movement."

For a France of the millennium, a country historically capable of leading other nations, General de Gaulle was a necessity. He realized this. For places like Cantal and Lozère, for ordinary Frenchmen, a Pompidou would suffice. But the President of the Republic must be far-sighted and visualize things on a grand scale. Solemnly the general declared: "France must be France."

. .

De Gaulle was meditating — "hesitating," some people said. The spring of 1965, destined to be decisive because it was nine months away from presidential elections, found the general totally preoccupied with "his" problem: to be or not to be a candidate.

He questioned all his visitors. Sometimes he answered his own questions in order to ascertain whether his remarks brought satisfaction or disapproval. He cited many names, those of adversaries as well as supporters. Or else he would sigh, putting an end to the discussion. "You see, what France really needs is a king."

As a military strategist, he examined all the possible alternatives and attempted to guess, though the campaign was still far off, the intentions of the enemy. For centuries, France had repeatedly been confronted with obstacles that stood in the way of her bid for supreme power. Sometimes she overcame them, but she also lost many a fine opportunity that would have altered the course of history. The will to act was a necessary quality in a statesman. On certain days, de Gaulle — "an old man worn out by troubles" — wondered if he still had enough life left in him.

He listened to what was being said and read newspaper and magazine articles on the subject which had already begun to divide Frenchmen. To diatribes against "personal government," he countered with statements on the dangers inherent in a system of impersonal government, in the kind of presidency whose titular confined himself to "opening flower shows."

It was up to him alone to decide, to search his soul and his conscience. For the moment he kept his own counsel, secrecy being his favorite tool.

. .

After twenty years of zealous and attentive attendance upon de Gaulle, Georges Pompidou, better than anyone else, should have known or guessed the general's intentions. In an effort to figure them out, he went over in his mind all the things he had heard the chief of state say. If anyone could flatter himself that he understood a man as enigmatic as the general, it was Pompidou. The premier never failed to remind himself that in this respect he enjoyed at least one advantage denied other Gaullists. But even Pompidou did not have all the keys to the mystery.

"The personality of Charles de Gaulle is a skillful blend," a friend of his said in June 1940. "The general had himself so described it in broad terms during the years nineteen twenty-five to nineteen thirty, without realizing that a fantastic role would one day devolve upon him. It was in nineteen forty when fate, or Providence, had invested him with a heroic mission, that his own metamorphosis had taken place. It was a total transformation. Within a few months, de Gaulle stripped himself of his entire past. But Pompidou did not know this. In nineteen sixty-five he saw a polished personality, accomplished, emptied of old memories, a man who had consolidated his own majestic place in history."

The premier relied on realities, but they were contradictory. In any case, the general, whose reactions depended on the day, the hour, the mood of the moment, the conjunction of events, the outcome of public opinion polls, was unpredictable. Pompidou was somewhat at a loss and definitely confused.

Because the general wished to preserve his freedom of choice until the verdict was pronounced, he felt that every avenue should remain open to him, including sponsorship of Pompidou's candidature. The general, however, gave his premier no assurances. Instead, he resorted to enticement and indirection. "The general used expressions in my presence that had not only double but triple meanings," Pompidou was to say.

In May de Gaulle invited his second in command to accompany him to the departments of western France. He presented Pompidou to the electorate and shared with Pompidou the applause which was obviously intended for him alone. A little later, during the summer, he urged Pompidou to take a trip to Brittany, a center of Gaullist strength. This time, Pompidou barnstormed alone.

"We must continue," the general declared. "That's what the people want now, just as they wanted it in the past."

Pompidou tried to project the image of a "continuer." He had a well-known newspaper publish his biography. The piece was to be used for electioneering purposes. Each deputy of the majority party received a copy of it. The article recounted a golden legend, the "secret destiny" of Georges Pompidou. At the Elysée, this was considered excessive. De Gaulle, the first reader of the piece, did not reprimand his premier. He merely smiled slyly. But Pompidou was guilty of neither bad taste nor ill-timed eagerness. He kept telling the barons: "It's a little too soon. I've been premier for only three years. I'm just completing my apprenticeship."

For two or at the most three months, Pompidou lent himself to the general's game. All sorts of homage and attentions came his way.

· ·

The temptation to give up the game was strong. Several times de Gaulle admitted: "Seven years — that's good measure. If I stay any longer, the French will get bored with me. They're always longing for change."

The general seemed already to be moving toward the relinquishment of power. He described the only kind of departure worthy of him. It called for giving up the "burden," returning to silence and solitude, exhibiting neither rancor nor regret. Like all the other episodes of his career, this finale would become a part of history.

He estimated the amount of time he still needed: six or seven years to write his memoirs and leave behind a complete work. Once again he recalled the horror of shipwreck; memories of Pétain, of his quavering voice, of the dead body of Churchill haunted him. But the careers of elderly statesmen were cited to give him encouragement: Adenauer, Clemenceau and de Valera, the Irish president.

"Duty?" the chief of state kept repeating. "Where does my duty lie?"

Madame de Gaulle expressed her opinion and the general respected the simple wisdom of his wife. She said to the faithful who came to the Elysée: "The general will question you. Tell him that he has served his time, that he has accomplished his mission. He'll listen to you."

But one of the chief's associates answered one day: "Can you imagine, Madame, the general, who is so vigorous and healthy today, retiring to Colombey and suddenly finding himself deprived of all activity? He'll make your life miserable."

A little sadly, Madame de Gaulle agreed.

. .

Bets were being made. Most of them were lost. Virtually all the leading Gaullists, from Foccart to Couve, from Debré to Malraux, expected the general to return to the sidelines.

The Gaullists' chances of winning the elections seemed better than ever. The opposition was split. The general's adherents were eager to destroy once and for all the traditional enemy, the "politicians of the past." With great glee, people kept saying: "The general can get anyone elected, even his horse. Even his horse . . ."

The regime had been consolidated and continuity seemed assured. Perhaps there would never be another chance. De Gaulle was not insensitive to this argument.

According to the testimony of one minister, this was no exaggeration: "At that time, there was such a wave of optimism, especially among officials of the government, that the election of any Gaullist approved by de Gaulle appeared to be a mere formality."

The general had only one Gaullist available: Pompidou. Michel Debré had just returned to parliament but had remained aloof from the affairs of state and government.

Several times de Gaulle, using the conditional tense, presented the problem to his premier. Somewhat later, three influential members of the cabinet stated that Pompidou had advised the general to quit. But in exchanges between the chief of state and his eminent subordinate, precise language was never used. De Gaulle, for his part, merely accepted the law of necessity. "This doesn't mean that Pompidou is the man I would want to see in the presidency of the republic," the general remarked to some of his confidants.

At the Matignon, as well as elsewhere, experts examined the possibility of the premier's candidature. "It's a little early. In any case, the contest doesn't have to be decided in advance, far from it." Everyone agreed that Georges Pompidou would be a presentable candidate.

. .

Resorting to his usual tactics, the general waited for his adversaries to tip their hand. His decision would depend primarily on the identity of the opposition candidates. But secrecy also reigned in the other camp. Days and weeks went by as this strange cold war continued. Each adversary waited for the other to show the tip of his ear before emerging from the trenches.

. .

On September 9, 1965, less than three months before the elections, the general opened his press conference with the following allusion to his candidature: "I will respond to your question by promising you that within two months you will have my answer."

His words made people smile. But the general was sincere. He decided not to reveal the secret until one month before the elections. He felt that thirty days of campaigning would be sufficient for himself as well as for Pompidou. And he did not change his battle plan.

But on the 9th of September something occurred that exerted a decisive influence on the general's decision: the announcement of François Mitterand's candidature. Mitterand was emerging as the principal if not the sole standard-bearer of the opposition. Perhaps de Gaulle might have been willing to see some leftist win, but not this particular one. In mid-December, between two campaign tours, he said: "If there were a worthier candidate to compete with, I wouldn't be running."

The general regarded the name of Mitterand as a personal challenge. Most Gaullists felt even more strongly. Michel Debré went to the Elysée and after an impassioned diatribe against Mitterand's candidature, he said to de Gaulle: "My general, it is now too late for you to abstain from running."

All the princes of Gaullism, including Debré, Couve de Murville and Malraux, felt that Pompidou could not defeat Mitterand. Pompidou himself was less pessimistic. After all, the premier had often opposed the leftist leader in the Assembly; and more often than not he had come out on top.

In any event, as soon as it was known that Mitterand would be the candidate, de Gaulle made up his mind. The people who saw him every day at the Elysée were struck by the fact that he now had the tranquil countenance of a man who no longer hesitated.

But he kept his own counsel.

Pompidou guessed what the general's decision would be. He called a halt to the distribution of his biography and said to his colleagues: "I'll stay at the Matignon another two or three years. I think it's better that way."

Nonetheless, no clear answer was offered. The general's silence provoked impatience among government officials. One of them said: "He'll run this time and again in nineteen seventy-two when he's eighty-two."

De Gaulle was determined to make his decision known at the appointed time and not before: one month prior to the elections on December 5. His disciples remained worried until the very last moment. On October 11, at a hunting party, Pompidou told one on his associates: "Both you and I have been placed in a ridiculous position."

And Christian Fouchet has testified: "We were all uncertain, even Pompidou, until, at the very last moment, the general finally spoke on television."

. .

On November 4, precisely the appointed date, de Gaulle announced his candidature to the French people in a short, seven-minute speech. He struck a self-sacrificing note: "I feel that I must hold myself in readiness to continue my task in full awareness of the effort this will cost me."

As usual, the premier was informed on the very morning the speech was delivered. The barons made a date to meet for dinner at the home of the Assembly's president. But Pompidou begged off at the last minute, saying other friends were expecting him to dine with them. "Honestly, that day the premier seemed relieved, as if a great weight had been lifted," a colleague stated later.

For the general, however, the prospect of this new mandate did not seem a happy one. When it came time to wage the electoral battle, the general seemed far from delighted. He uttered bitter words — "burden," "responsibility," "duty," especially "duty." But at any rate France would be spared having to put up with the activities of "a Mitterand or someone like him."

To his visitors, he reiterated: "There is still work to be done.

We've had Algeria, reform of the state's institutions, money problems. All these have been settled and well settled. But we still have social problems. We intend to propose to the country a vast reform of its social structure."

This last undertaking, visualized as the crowning achievement of his career, was something he had dreamt about ever since his youth. He had read, studied and thought about it.

Once the lines had been drawn and the reform accomplished, de Gaulle would be ready to quit, but not before.

CHAPTER 10

The Coup of December 5

A PRESIDENTIAL ELECTION was something that directly concerned de Gaulle and the French people. It was a new phase of the curious dialogue that for a quarter of a century had absorbed the general and this ancient incorrigible people. In the past there had been misunderstandings, quarrels, outbursts. But there had also been collusion and a deep bond. The Mitterands and all the other candidates were spoilsports. Besides, they were playing at the wrong game.

The members of the cabinet, and above all Pompidou, were to remain on the sidelines. On the fifth day of December 1965, the general planned to stage a ceremony that would thereafter be perpetuated, a republican sacrament of sorts. With this in mind, he declared: "Today one cannot govern a country — with all the dramatic options that this involves — without the force of immense popular support. There are some who talk about plebiscites. That's nonsense. I am not eager to remain in office until I die, but I am working for the men who will come after me. One day people will appreciate what I've done — perhaps the very individuals who today criticize everything I do."

The phrase "electoral campaign" was no longer appropriate, he went on. This was not merely a matter of choosing an official or of voting for a political label. Frenchmen must realize that this presidential election was different from others. The legitimacy of the republic was at stake. "I am the one who reestablished the republic in August nineteen forty-four," the general reminded his listeners.

"Moreover," he added, "Frenchmen know and understand me. I have confided everything to them during the past twenty-five years."

An order was issued to Foccart and to Pompidou: "No campaign." The general would not demean himself to answer the other candidates. He had no desire to appear as the head of a party competing with rivals. Frenchmen had no need to be taught how great was the distance that separated a Mitterand from a Charles de Gaulle.

De Gaulle condemned his faithful to a stoical silence. Pompidou, Debré and the barons took turns at the Elysée begging for permission to answer the opposition's attacks. They too fell victim to the blows of the opposition. But the general remained undaunted and exacted a like attitude from his men.

From the very start of the campaign, Roger Frey warned the general: "The appearance of the other candidates on television gives them an advantage. It will be a hot campaign."

But de Gaulle refused to believe that there would be a real battle. Every day the Minister of the Interior laid before the Elysée the results of the most recent public opinion poll and the prognostications based upon them. Frey tried to estimate the distribution of votes in the first round of the balloting and was alarmed by his own figures. He passed this information along to Pompidou and even to the general himself. But de Gaulle's orders remained unchanged: the Gaullists were to do absolutely nothing.

The members of the cabinet were in a state of panic over the general's attitude and Debré was telling everyone that the whole thing was a scandal. He accused Pompidou of dereliction of duty because of his failure to exert sufficient pressure on de Gaulle.

But the general remained deaf to all appeals. "De Gaulle," he said, "is not a politician. From someone like me, polemics and shouting would be most inappropriate."

On November 30 the general's bitterness became obvious on the television screen. That evening he reluctantly broadcast a speech — "to please his faithful," he said. He had planned to deliver only one speech at the very end of the campaign, on December 3, 1965. He regretted this change in his plans. The screen disclosed an old man whose weariness was self-evident. The following day de Gaulle said to his collaborators: "You see! I was wrong to listen to your advice."

Three days later, making a second televised speech, he created a better impression. But the game was already over. Before his last decisive speech was taped, Foccart gave the general the latest information. "You don't have to beat around the bush," de Gaulle said.

That Friday, thirty-six hours before election day, the general went off to Colombey, resigned to whatever the verdict might be. He had envisaged all the possibilities, including defeat. If he failed to obtain 40 per cent of the popular vote, he would remain in Colombey on his own land, abandoning his countrymen, after the issuance of a brief message whose content he had already pondered. To Burin de Roziers and Foccart, who tried to look cheerful, he said: "I will give you my instructions on Sunday evening."

. .

That Sunday night, while a storm rattled the windowpanes of his country house at Colombey, de Gaulle kept his own counsel. At the Matignon, leaving ministers, officials and curious onlookers to drink their tepid champagne, Pompidou retired to his office with Guichard. The results of the balloting — a bare 44 per cent for de Gaulle — had been broadcast throughout the world. The premier was filled with anxiety. This new silence and uncertainty about his own fate taxed his nerves. In an adjacent room, other Gaullists were already making plans for the second balloting. They said: "The general has no choice. The constitution obliges him to continue. He has to go through the ordeal of a second balloting."

But Pompidou remembered the 1962 referendum. De Gaulle would refuse to remain in power without the massive backing of his countrymen.

With the help of Guichard, always imperturbable in moments of crisis, Pompidou drafted a communiqué which would be submitted to the general. At least it would serve as a valid excuse for calling Colombey.

At eleven-thirty that night, Pompidou finally picked up the phone. The general's voice seemed to be coming from another world. As he was to confess thirty months later, de Gaulle was submerged by "great waves of sadness." The general listened to the text which Pompidou read to him. "Go ahead if you wish," he said.

The general did, however, make one change; in the sentence, "Divisive and diversive candidatures have prevented the national will from expressing itself," he deleted the word "prevented" and substituted for it a phrase stating that the expression of the national will had been merely "delayed."

But this was not much to go on as an indication of the general's true state of mind. More significant was his tone of voice, which was lugubrious. He seemed to have accepted the voters' decision with a muffled fury. He had no intention of governing Frenchmen despite themselves. Let them have their way, let Mitterand, the communists, defeat, chaos, civil war come, and let them leave de Gaulle alone to finish out his last days in peace.

In conclusion, the general coldly announced that he would remain in Colombey in order to meditate in solitude, and that he would make his decision known before Wednesday. Then, with a certain solemnity, he expressed his gratitude to Pompidou.

The premier was horrified. "That night and even the next day," he recalled, "I really believed that the general would quit power. I lived through some terrible hours."

In 1968 he was to say the same thing after experiencing tense hours of a different kind.

· ·

Fear pervaded the entire headquarters of Gaullism. Pompidou made no secret of his apprehension. The old-timers sadly reminded him of the general's departure in 1946. Then, the blow had been delivered by the Assembly and the political parties, not the people. De Gaulle had even greater reason to retire now.

Feverishly, they tried to imagine what would happen if the general did decide to quit. The President of the Senate, a sworn enemy of the Gaullists, would proceed to the Elysée amid great pomp, and he would occupy it. The second round of balloting ordinarily took place two weeks after the first, but in this instance the two remaining candidates would be equally hostile to Gaullism. The Gaullists discovered a little late that the constitution had not made provision for every eventuality. There was nothing to indicate clearly what could or should be done in case one or two presidential candidates were removed by sickness, death or withdrawal.

Early in the morning of the following day, Monday, the general's brother-in-law, Jacques Vendroux, was despatched to Colombey. He returned that very evening with bad news. "He wants to quit. He's sorry he ran. He says that his mission is over and that in any case, such a meager indication of confidence would make it impossible for him to undertake large-scale reforms. So, what would be the point of staying on?"

But on Tuesday calm returned. That morning the general called the Elysée to say that he would be coming back to Paris that very day. By way of explanation, he said: "We're going to have lots of work to do." At one o'clock, all the chieftains of the Gaullist family — cabinet members, barons, Pompidou — lunched together. The discussion centered on the new-style campaign to be waged, on the best way of mobilizing public opinion. A plan of battle was worked out, as if de Gaulle were no longer the strategist, or at any rate not the only strategist.

But Pompidou threw cold water on these burgeoning enthusiasms. "Gentlemen, let's wait for the general's orders," he said.

.   .

Walking over to the Elysée, the premier felt anxious. He had no idea whether the general would be willing to participate personally in the battle. De Gaulle might very well decide to adhere to the line of conduct he himself had laid down several weeks before. As matters now stood, he would have to confront Mitterand in a bilateral contest. There was every reason to believe that the general would not be enchanted by such a prospect.

But from the very outset, the general acknowledged both his mistake and his responsibilities. They must fight! Whether pleased to do so or not, the chief of state would perform his duty. But he added that he had no intention of remaining in office seven years. The vote of December 5 was a warning that he would remember. He did not fix a date but he firmly declared: "I won't be here for long."

In emphatic terms he repeated this to several ministers and to some of his intimates: "De Gaulle suits Frenchmen when things are going badly. But today people are no longer afraid. They want to go back to their old idle habits. I've had enough. Enough of everything. Of the French, of politics, quarrels and complaints, and of Mitterand. All of this is pure waste of time."

Pompidou, like all the faithful, knew that the general was often subject to fits of depression; in earlier days such moods had proved short-lived, lasting only two or three days at the most. Now they lasted several weeks. De Gaulle was aging. Troubles, obstacles, sorrows weighed heavily on him. Yes, he had become increasingly sensitive.

The premier heard him out and then changed the subject. Bringing the general back to the realities of the immediate future, he suggested a battle campaign. It involved the mobilization of all men of good will — ministers, deputies, militants — and the use of television, because, he explained, "we must employ every weapon at our disposal and that's one we've completely neglected." In short, it was to be an all-out offensive.

De Gaulle gave him a free hand: "We'll do the best we can."

These words were quite enough. Relieved, Pompidou returned to the Matignon. He assembled everyone there and proceeded to outline the scope of his sweeping plan: the press, billboards, television, meetings, the disbursement of funds — he knew all the devices of the electoral game. He had learned a great deal since the early days of the R.P.F.

That very evening there was a dinner for the barons at the Matignon, with Debré as a guest. During the meal it was decided that the general should consent to a fireside interview by a journalist. This sort of thing had worked very well for both Mitterand and Pompidou.

At a cabinet meeting the next day, Wednesday, de Gaulle tried very hard to conceal his disappointment over the outcome of the election. Right off, he said: "I alone am responsible for the result of this first round."

Then the general proceeded to cite the political explanations which a professor of political science, who was serving as secretary general of the Senate, had given him. "I made a mistake," de Gaulle admitted. "I thought of this election as a referendum of sorts. Experience demonstrates that it was no such thing. A referendum offers a simple choice between alternatives. Presidential elections are much more like legislative elections."

De Gaulle realized that the forthcoming contest was a political battle with all that this implied in the way of demagoguery, promises, and attacks on the adversary. He appealed to the ministers to join him in this dubious struggle.

The officials around him wanted nothing better. When the cabinet meeting ended, all the participants repaired to the home of one of the ministers. There, speaking like one of the king's musketeers, Roger Frey said: "Gentlemen, hang on to your hats! We're about to charge!"

But Pompidou was not given to romanticism. He totted up the number of troops and the supplies of ammunition. He looked after all the details. Neglecting nothing, he saw to the proper size of the billboards and distributed the necessary funds to all the Gaullist associations. He kept an eye on everything. Later, he was to say complacently: "Now I know how a presidential election is organized."

That Thursday he summoned all the Gaullist deputies for a meeting in the Salle Colbert at the Palais-Bourbon. Here he issued directives. They included: (1) the use of television; (2) the distribution of several million copies of a newspaper, *France-Avenir*; (3) the use of billboards and handbills "with a very short text printed in very large letters"; (4) the convocation of meetings "carefully prepared from every possible point of view, including announcements and agendas"; (5) the work to be done locally by the deputies, which included going "from door to door, from voter to voter."

The premier concluded his long pep talk by saying: "I am asking all of you to do your utmost." Then, in order not to sound too imperious, he added: "I ask this in the name of the general."

He had spoken as a leader, as he was entitled to do. De Gaulle had not hesitated to evade this thankless and unworthy task.

The general did, however, resign himself to appearing on television, to being interviewed by a journalist, as Pompidou and virtually all the other Gaullist leaders had urged. Three programs were planned. At first de Gaulle thought of entrusting one to Pompidou, one to Couve, Messmer and Bourges — "three ministers, that is enough to make a good sauce," he said — and to reserve the final appearance on television for himself. But he was finally persuaded to appear on all three.

These televised interviews made an extraordinary impression. They showed a different de Gaulle, a man unfamiliar to the French people — their leader in bedroom slippers, or, as de Gaulle put it, "in pajamas." But when he saw that the most recent opinion poll gave him only 55 per cent of the vote, he grumbled: "You see, none of this does any good."

The bond that linked him to the French people was wearing thin. History was being forgotten, the "personal equation" had been damaged and nothing could completely obliterate the scars of December 5. In vain did his disciples advance skillful arguments, assuring the general that the Fifth Republic would be "all the stronger for having been subjected to this ordeal by fire." The general did not believe them. That "certain image" that he held of Charles de Gaulle had been irreparably tarnished.

In the course of one televised tape the general declared: "In any

event, I will not remain in office for long." Only at the urgent insist-
ence of one of his advisers did de Gaulle finally agree to delete the
phrase that already heralded his farewell.

.   .

On December 19, 1965, de Gaulle emerged from the second
round victorious but displeased nonetheless. The sky was somber.
Elected for seven years! Already the general was counting the days
and awaiting a chance to make an impressive exit. The memory of
the balloting remained constantly in his mind. He would not overlook the lesson: France was no longer quite her old self.

To his collaborators who asked if there would be any ceremony at
the Elysée on January 8, 1966, to mark the beginning of the new
seven-year term, the general said: "Oh, we'll do a little something."

The immediate business to be taken care of was the formation of
a new cabinet. Obviously the recent happenings would have to be
taken into account. Prior to the presidential elections, the general
had considered the possibility of appointing a new premier. Not
that Pompidou deserved such treatment. But it was important to
underscore the point that there must be two changes of cabinet
every seven years. The replacement of a premier who had served
for three and a half years would be a clear affirmation of the separa-
tion of powers, a concept dear to the general's heart. In such a regime, the President of the Republic, chosen by the French people,
served for seven years; the cabinet designated by the chief of state
held office for three or four years; the Assembly was elected for five
years. In replacing Pompidou, de Gaulle intended to emphasize solemnly the point that the government was no longer an emanation of
parliament, a majority, or a political party.

However, by the 20th of December, he no longer had any choice.
Urgent considerations compelled him to retain Pompidou. The
presidential election had shown that political parties were still important. It had also demonstrated that Pompidou was a good majority leader. Moreover, the forthcoming legislative elections of March
1967 loomed as a danger. The present majority leader must there-

fore be kept. Finally, the general did not wish to give the impression that he was penalizing any of his ministers because of his own disappointment with the outcome of the voting.

"If I dismiss Pompidou, people will think that I hold him responsible for the results of December fifth," de Gaulle remarked. "No, I'll keep the premier." Then he added: ". . . until the legislative elections."

. .

Pompidou was told of the general's intentions. He was not surprised. His role between the first and second rounds of the balloting had earned him this fresh mark of confidence, he thought. Also, the events of December had afforded him priceless experience. He now believed himself capable of successfully waging a presidential electoral campaign — "I would have been elected had I run against Mitterand," he kept telling his friends. He had become the undisputed majority leader. And finally he knew that the general did not want to remain in the presidency until the end of his seven-year term.

Pompidou would therefore have to hold himself in readiness, to remain in the limelight. A disgrace like the one suffered by Debré in 1962 would be a catastrophic blow to his ambitions. "If I had to leave the Matignon, what would I do?" he wondered. "Of course I could travel, write, deliver speeches in Aurillac and Toulouse. But Frenchmen would soon forget me. It's too early to quit."

Pompidou now felt strong enough to impose one condition on the general, but he did it tactfully: the dismissal of Giscard d'Estaing, the finance minister. "By prolonging the austerity plan unduly, the Minister of Finance was largely responsible for the failure of December fifth," he explained. "If we keep him on at the Rue de Rivoli, we shall run the risk, for the same reasons, of suffering an even more serious setback in the nineteen sixty-seven elections."

But the premier could hardly conceal the rivalry that pitted him against his junior. So he went on to say: "The presence of Giscard threatens the cohesiveness of the cabinet. In a modern government, whoever is responsible for the country's economy plays an essential role. It is impossible for me to fulfill the functions of a premier if I cannot have a minimum of contact and rapport with, or confidence in, the finance minister. And I have not had this kind of relationship with Giscard during these last months."

At first de Gaulle refused to face the problem. His good will toward Giscard had not vanished. "He's a young man with a genuine feeling for the state," he said.

This was the supreme compliment. Nevertheless, Pompidou returned to the charge several times, discreetly letting it be known that he would decline to assume the responsibilities of premier if Giscard were kept.

"Economic affairs tend to produce incalculable political repercussions," he repeated. "The title of premier will be meaningless if I cannot have my say there."

Finally, the general allowed himself to be persuaded. "Whom would you suggest as his successor?" he asked.

Pompidou immediately named Debré. The former premier had long ceased to be a rival. In addition, he had proved his fervor during the recent presidential campaign. On December 9, Pompidou and Debré put the seal on the resumption of their friendship as all the Gaullist deputies in the Assembly looked on approvingly.

Besides, during the past few days, several of the general's collaborators had suggested that Debré should be reinstalled in the cabinet. But de Gaulle, his face puckered by unpleasant memories, had answered: "Debré will pester me with his tantrums."

The general ultimately agreed, but he demanded a compensation: "Giscard must stay. Ask him to take over an important ministry. Supplies, that's it, with a hand in Transportation, Construction and Tourism. He won't be bored with that."

Pompidou transmitted the offer. Giscard coldly turned it down. He never overlooked a chance to charge that his eviction from the ministry of finance was due solely to Pompidou's presidential aspirations. The general sent his young finance minister a warm letter and invited him to the Elysée for dinner six weeks later.

When the after-dinner coffee had been served, de Gaulle took Giscard on a tour of the presidential palace. Treating him as an intimate, the general dropped a hint in the course of their conversation: "Some day, when you'll be here . . ."

. .

On January 8, 1966, the general inaugurated his second reign at the Elysée by staging "the little something" he had promised. Both Debré and Pompidou were invited. There had been two premiers, and there would be others. But at twelve-thirty it was nonetheless the incumbent who was again appointed to the post. That evening, the announcement of the composition of the new cabinet publicized Pompidou's victory. Giscard at once departed. Debré took his place as Minister of Finance.

The general had assembled all the ministers at the Elysée and there were, thank heavens, few new faces. Pompidou, seated opposite the general, was a little more self-assured than he used to be. His eye was somewhat sharper, his plumpness a little more apparent. The general uttered a few banal words of welcome. The winter and a new year was about to begin.

De Gaulle looked at his ministers, who in turn observed him. How much passion, ambition and hope in all these faces! And how much treachery, perhaps. More than ever the general sensed his own solitude. His brothers, his friends, were dead. Before him were men who were still young and impatient. Pride, power, strength? All these were myths and illusions. What remained was fatigue, and the inexorable awareness that time was galloping on.

CHAPTER 11

Captain of the Musketeers

ONCE AGAIN Pompidou received a fresh lease at the Hôtel de Matignon with its delicately worked façade and its park to which memories of courtly gallantries still clung. The failure of the December 5 election was certainly not his doing, but the victory of the 19th could to some extent be attributed to him. People knew this. The premier was about to embark upon a stage of his career that would inevitably lead to the topmost position in the government. In the eyes of the Gaullists, of public opinion, and probably of the general, too, he was the Dauphin. However, he was in no hurry: "In a month, in a year . . ."

But no sooner had the new reign begun than a drama occurred. The general's fury brought home to Pompidou, if he had forgotten, that according to de Gaulle, a premier had no other function than to serve. No one had life tenure. At every echelon of government and state, each individual, whether big or little, must earn each day the legitimacy that only the confidence of the President of the Republic conferred upon him.

Without attracting great notice, the affair had begun during the election campaign with the abduction in the Latin Quarter of Mehdi Ben Barka, spokesman for the Moroccan opposition. Since then, each day had brought one or more bits of scandal: counter-espionage, the involvement of the French police, the names of officials in high places, of a Gaullist deputy. All this was fodder for the shocked public to feed on. The most honorable names in France demanded "the truth about the Ben Barka affair." Appeals, petitions, manifestoes and articles were all addressed to de Gaulle and to him alone. From the members of his entourage the general encountered either confused explanations or embarrassed silence. The scandal was naturally welcome to de Gaulle's enemies. "There are too many ties between the protagonists, between the accomplices in the Ben Barka affair and the men in power," a leading socialist charged.

De Gaulle flew into a rage. His fury was directed at the Moroccans, whose young king, the son of one of his "companions and friends," had recompensed him so poorly for his many acts of kindness. But his ministers, and primarily the premier, were the principal targets of his rage. In the presence of officials, the general gave full vent to his temper, alluding to "negligence," or incapacity — in short he placed the blame on the cabinet. It was no concern of his that Roger Frey, as Minister of the Interior, had failed to perform his duties. The chief of state had a team and the team had a leader. At such moments de Gaulle used the plural, "they," with the utmost contempt.

Pompidou waited out the end of the storm. To be sure, he had little liking for police matters or cloak and dagger antics. He was therefore not sorry when de Gaulle used the Ben Barka affair as a pretext for depriving him of all intelligence services; they were transferred to the army.

Much more serious was the criticism directed at him by the general on three different occasions in the presence of the cabinet. A young minister still serving his apprenticeship was astounded to hear de Gaulle reprimand his right-hand man. "You don't keep track of your services," the general shouted. "If the Moroccans want to cut each other's throats, that's their own business. But it is intolerable that they should do so with the complicity of our police!"

And to one of the ministers the general spoke even more plainly: "I am told that my premier chose not to soil his hands in this affair. The result is that France herself has been defiled. Such negligence cannot be tolerated. Today it's the Ben Barka affair, tomorrow it can be something else. For two years I have noticed many mistakes, many errors. I said nothing. But if the state should degenerate — and what is happening now is a bad omen — needless to say, you will see me act with dispatch."

The general's anger took long months to subside. The Ben Barka affair was the first mishap. At the moment, Pompidou saw it as a minor incident, part of the ups and downs of his job. But the general was looking beyond the episode itself. The premier's negligence led the general to ask questions. After all, the period of apprenticeship was over. The 1963 inflation could be attributed to Pompidou's inexperience. De Gaulle had intervened in time. But three years and nine months had gone by with the same premier still in office . . .

The general had other reasons for being annoyed. People were talking about the Dauphin and praising Pompidou for the role he had played in the presidential election. That was all very well. But de Gaulle had not chosen a party leader, nor had he designated a candidate for the succession to the presidency. He had appointed a premier. Nothing more and nothing less. Totting up the profits and losses under the stewardship of the Pompidou cabinet, the general noted that the loss column was getting longer. This was so despite the fact that some obvious good points — Pompidou's successes — had to be entered on the profit side.

Very gradually, de Gaulle began to think about someone to replace Pompidou. This became evident from questions he put to some of his closest associates: "How can we find someone who has the will to act, who is a statesman?" Sometimes the general murmured his own answer: "Couve, perhaps."

. .

The wound inflicted on December 5 was still bleeding. The general was no longer sure that he knew the aspirations of his fellow countrymen. "What on earth do they want?" he asked one of his ministers. "Is it my face they can't stand any longer?"

Nineteen sixty-six began — a long vigil before the start of legislative elections. The outcome of this fresh battle seemed uncertain. Frenchmen were no longer frightened. They might revert to their old tricks.

The general was impatient to move ahead, to transform society. Bored by the daily grind, he found that marking time sorely tried his patience. Yet it would be impossible to launch any sweeping reforms until the electorate had once again spoken. Throughout the year 1966 the Elysée occupied itself with small-scale social planning.

De Gaulle husbanded his strength. He occasionally spent entire days reading, meditating, trying to guess the shape of the future. And he spent long hours with his family. At dinner he entertained men who did not belong to his political seraglio. In the twilight of his life he indulged himself by savoring old memories, by reviewing various stages of his epic history. He had seen his contemporaries, the soldiers of World War II, disappear one after the other. Every death grieved him although he was careful not to show it.

Little by little, he left matters of state to Pompidou, keeping for himself practically nothing save the one area on which he continued to meditate: the foreign policy of France. He even began to lose interest in military problems, except for the list of promotions to the High Command. When the Minister of the Army, Pierre Messmer, came to the Elysée, there was often nothing for him to do but listen to the general talk about the past and the future, about war and peace.

. .

All the problems of the majority party, of the relations of Gaullists with affiliated groups, the selection of personnel, the designation of candidates for the legislative elections of March 1967 — all these were handled at the Matignon. In this work the premier was aided by his closest colleagues and friends, Guichard and Juillet. The barons — Frey, Foccart and Chaban-Delmas — were always consulted. Pompidou continued to attend their meetings and to preside over their luncheons. More than ever, the musketeers remained united. Debré, preoccupied with his voluminous financial files, tended to stay on the political sidelines.

Because the opposition was slowly uniting and increasing its contacts with the communists, the forthcoming battle promised to be a fierce one. In October, de Gaulle himself urged the candidates of the majority party to unite "openly." But he declined to become involved in the rivalries and squabbles that prevailed among Gaullists of every stripe.

Pompidou was given the green light to speak as the leader. Once so conciliatory, he now used the general's permissiveness to affirm his authority over Valéry Giscard d'Estaing. After the general's famous voyage to Canada and his cry of "Long live a free Quebec," Giscard had quietly joined the opposition. He still belonged to the majority, but he no longer approved of General de Gaulle's methods. And his attitude, expressed in the two words "Yes, but . . ." provoked the wrath of the chief of state. After this Giscard no longer belonged to the small circle of the faithful.

Again, it was the premier who obtained the general's authorization to throw members of the cabinet into the electoral fray. De Gaulle gave his permission, but he was not pleased. He had always hoped that his ministers would remain aloof from parliamentary contingencies and steer clear of the inevitable demagoguery of election campaigns.

But Pompidou advanced powerful arguments: "The nineteen sixty-five balloting should have taught us something. The opposition, which is already talking about a third balloting in presidential elections, will do everything this time to achieve victory. We can't overlook a single trump. The ministers will prove to be good vote getters."

Convinced, de Gaulle himself mobilized those ministers who still hesitated. He encouraged Couve de Murville to run in the seventh district of Paris where fifteen years earlier his brother, Pierre de Gaulle, had won. "The general personally asked me to be a candidate in the elections," Christian Fouchet stated. "He told me that we were involved in a difficult contest and that he was counting on all his old companions."

All the preparations for the campaign were perfected at the Matignon. Pompidou, himself a candidate in his native Auvergne, improved on the tactics first used in December 1965: newspapers, political rallies and handbills were utilized effectively. The Gaullist exchequer was not very flush, but funds were raised by tapping bankers and industrialists, although here Pompidou had to compete with that great champion of popular rights, Mitterand. The premier knew that in France oratory was indispensable for a successful political career. Forgetting his modest beginnings, he now spoke out loud and strong.

The general was not overly pleased with this performance. He did not like the way Pompidou "touted his wares." When the general learned that Pompidou had enlisted the help of a big public relations firm, he even showed some disapproval. In his view, propaganda as such smacked of something rotten. However, he also realized that to win it was necessary to seduce, and that no modern weapon could be overlooked.

Moreover, de Gaulle himself intervened twice: on February 9, 1967, at the very start of the campaign, and again on March 4, at its close. "A great deal has been accomplished . . . A great, great deal remains to be done," he declared. "We will have earned the right to entertain every hope if our Fifth Republic wins. For then it will be launched on a fresh march toward progress."

Despite all this, the election results were rather unimpressive, despite a first round of balloting that seemed to augur well. When he was informed of the outcome that night at Colombey, the general betrayed little disappointment. To be sure, the majority, led by the "arrogant" Giscard, was precarious, but the opposition was so weak! Two days after the election, de Gaulle said to one of his ministers: "Fortunately there are the others. Who are they, the others? Mitterand? No. The communists. And you'll see, all the rest will disappear."

. .

All the same, the election hurdle had been surmounted. A new government would now have to be appointed. Not a soul in France imagined that the cabinet would not be headed by Pompidou, no one, that is, save de Gaulle.

For several weeks de Gaulle had been seriously thinking about appointing a new premier. It would soon be five years that Pompidou had held the post. If he were reappointed, he would probably remain in office until the next elections, scheduled to take place five years hence. In all, he would have spent ten years at the Matignon. More than a seven-year presidential term! That was unthinkable!

The general explained his position as follows: "A premier must put up with the daily grind and undertake a multiplicity of tasks. Anyone saddled with such responsibilities wears out faster than a chief of state. After three or four years, certain habits are acquired. Insidiously, routine takes over. A man's enthusiasm if not his imagination tends to wither away."

Even Pompidou was unable to elude this fate. The fine agility he had displayed in 1958 had evaporated; or else de Gaulle had become accustomed to the intellectual precision that had formerly characterized the premier. The wear and tear on Pompidou became somehow confused with the general's weariness. There had been no dearth of opportunities to point out that a premier was the second in command and that he could be replaced after every battle. Another opportunity was now at hand.

Most of the visitors who came to the office of the chief of state heard a good deal of praise for Couve de Murville. De Gaulle was toying with an idea. He called Couve "the best foreign minister we have had since the century of Louis Quatorze." Or the general would say: "He reflects. He is foresighted. He is not self-seeking." Or again: "A statesman of the same quality as Clemenceau."

The interested party was not informed directly of the fate in store for him. But he had friends close to the general. "Couve knows that something is in the air," his associates admitted.

His hour perhaps had struck.

· ·

As usual, Pompidou knew what was afoot. For several weeks, in the most tactful terms, one of the general's advisers had given him to understand that de Gaulle was getting ready to appoint a new premier.

He received the news without any excessive display of emotion. To his friends, to Guichard and the barons, Pompidou confided his plans: "There's no majority leader. And I have always considered this to be bad for the smooth functioning of any government. Neither the general nor his premier can play this role. An active deputy is needed. Once I have been elected deputy by the people of Cantal, I will fill this void. And should Couve be my successor at the Matignon — and during the past few weeks I have had the feeling that he will be — my fate will in no way be affected."

For a few weeks Pompidou made pleasant plans for the future. After all, to leave the Matignon before the wear and tear had had its effect, to spare oneself the unpopularity that sooner or later was the lot of all statesmen — well, all that had many advantages. If he were a deputy, his name would not be forgotten — and this was one experience he had not yet had.

Besides, to be free again was not a little thing! To write, read, travel a bit, to have leisure and time to think and to live a little more for his family — his wife had been complaining that she was married to a man who expended all his energy on politics — to have time for his son who was also his dearest friend — all this counted.

But the outcome of the legislative elections, and in particular Couve's defeat in his own Paris district by an old parliamentarian named Dupont, changed both the general's plans and those of Pompidou.

De Gaulle immediately announced that he would retain his premier. "Couve's defeat and the unimpressive election results have forced me to change my mind," the general explained to one of his ministers.

With the majority party barely holding its own, and with internal clashes and squabbles galore, it would be difficult to parry the inevitable attacks. New plans would have to be formulated. De Gaulle of course realized that a balance as precarious as the one that would thus be achieved could not possibly last. It would end in a crisis, in the dissolution of the Assembly, or in a referendum. And so the king would have to keep his captain of the musketeers.

At least for a while . . .

CHAPTER 12

Whitecaps

POMPIDOU IMMEDIATELY WENT TO WORK. In the Assembly he bore up under the crossfire of the opposition: interminable debates, Mitterand's criticisms and sarcastic sallies, motions of censure. The majority, whose every vote counted, vented its ill humor. Little by little there was a return of sorts to the old games of the Fourth Republic, which de Gaulle had regarded as irreparably discredited.

As the leader of his forces, the premier tightened his fist and his voice. Bolstered by the reaffirmed confidence of de Gaulle, he assumed the stance of a political boss. Without loss of time, he settled disputes, defined strategy and tactics. He showed that he was responsible not only to de Gaulle but also to a half hostile parliament. It was he who decided to ask the Assembly for a delegation of powers to settle economic and social questions by decree laws. De Gaulle did not interfere. After all, it was Pompidou who was bearing the brunt of the battle.

At cabinet meetings, Pompidou intervened more frequently, making decisions after listening to the arguments — in short, in many areas it was he who dictated the methods to be employed. Again, de Gaulle refrained from interfering.

Pompidou used similar tactics with de Gaulle. Patient, insinuating, he often succeeded in converting the general to his own point of view. "He's baring his teeth," said one minister.

Upon returning from the Elysée, Pompidou rarely said: "The general wishes . . ." Or if he did, he would quickly add: "That seems fine to me."

Under the great shadow of Charles de Gaulle, Pompidou's shadow began to distinguish itself.

. .

With Pompidou, Gaullism took on a different air. The family was growing. A new generation was emerging. Suddenly it became plain that Pompidou's "young wolves" were taking the place of the general's "grumblers." Everywhere, the premier had friends and protégés: in the government — Guichard, a minister now, after his long period of penance, François-Xavier Ortoli, Chirac — three men who had been his collaborators at the Matignon the preceding year; in the Gaullist party; in the Assembly; in various key positions throughout the state. He had, so to speak, established his own dynasty. It owed its legitimacy neither to the Resistance, nor to May 13, 1958, nor to the general. The dynasty comprised many experienced men. And of course there was the club, the coterie of barons.

The changes took place gradually, unobtrusively. A species of "Pompidouism" sprang up within the Gaullist group, the offspring of five years of patience.

"Pompidou had no ulterior motives," said one young wolf. "He simply had a very natural desire to work with men whom he knew well and believed worthy of his trust."

But all his ardor, his friends and his power did not suffice: the premier's self-confidence was not as deeply rooted as it appeared to be. "Oh, Christian, they'll end up by skinning me," Pompidou said one day to Fouchet.

But he did not identify these threatening ghosts. Mitterand, Giscard, Couve, the Gaullists, the ministers? Or the general?

Between de Gaulle and Pompidou everything was not entirely serene. Five years had elapsed, five years of work, of clashes, of secret wounds and smoldering anger. Five years of living together. Things were no longer quite the way they had been in the old days. The general was watching Pompidou with a critical eye. And in his presence the premier spoke less deferentially. Their conversations had become briefer — there were moments of silence, of secrets jealously guarded. De Gaulle avoided clashes with Pompidou. He was careful not to raise his voice. Some unpleasant memories remained, unavowed resentments had piled up. A sense of impatience could scarcely be controlled. Time had done its work.

"In those days there were a few ups and downs," one minister has recalled. "Occasionally, one could read rejection of Pompidou in the general's closed countenance. But the following week he would again be quite amiable although somewhat formal toward his premier."

Admiration and filial feeling persisted in Pompidou. But could he continue to serve de Gaulle, to suffer the general's daily reproaches or silences, without feeling deep down a sense of rebellion?

Time . . . Time . . . It slyly erodes the best of sentiments. One day Pompidou, yielding to a burst of spontaneity, said to a minister: "There was a time when the general liked me, liked me very much. But today I feel that he likes me a good deal less. And that really hurts."

.   .   .

Pompidou was busying himself with the French, the general with France. Leaving the premier to attend to the small daily miseries of handling fifty million malcontents, de Gaulle was busily putting together the mysterious loose ends of the past and the future. Relentlessly, he mapped out a universe in which France would enjoy a privileged place. The hegemony of the superpowers that dated from Yalta, the division of our planet into two separate blocs, were for de Gaulle the subject of incessant meditation.

When he spoke of "all that remains to be done," he was thinking first and foremost of this problem. France could no longer invoke economic or military power. Her proper role henceforward was to point up the road to peace. And the mission of Charles de Gaulle as the representative of France was to be the bearer of this message to those nations whose eyes had not yet been opened.

In 1967 the general was the last witness of the Second World

War, the last statesman to have seen soldiers of all nations rushing to the holocaust. That gave him the right, he thought, to speak with authority about peace.

In May 1967 it was in the Middle East that the peace of the world seemed threatened. De Gaulle issued warnings at a time when the conflict was still exclusively a diplomatic one. On May 24 the cabinet met at the Elysée. It examined current problems, which were not negligible, especially the general strike that had paralyzed France one week earlier.

Suddenly the general took the floor. "Gentlemen, I am going to ask you to end this meeting. I must leave you in order to receive Mr. Eban, the foreign minister of Israel. He is visiting Paris for a few days. I want you to know what I am going to tell him. It is quite obvious, I will say, that Israel is on the verge of a resumption of hostilities. If hostilities are resumed, Israel will undoubtedly win very quickly. But this will produce three grave consequences. First, the installation of Russia in the Middle East and therefore in Africa as well — an eventuality that would be of some importance to France. The worldwide balance of power would be endangered. Second consequence: in the Arab world, moderate regimes will lose heart and fall, to be replaced by extremists. The result will be a threat to oil supplies to the West, especially to Europe. Finally, the Palestinian problem, which until now has been merely a problem of refugees, will become a great national cause. And in conclusion I will say to Mr. Eban: 'We wish only the best for the Israelis. The warnings we are giving you should be looked upon as a proof of our friendship and interest. Do not resent them.' "

The general was well aware in advance, however, that his warnings would not be heeded. The very next day he forecast the outbreak of war, which he declared to be imminent. He was even more explicit when he discussed the matter with Pompidou: "It won't last more than ten days."

For several weeks, de Gaulle continued to predict grave dangers. To visitors he recalled the Suez affair which in 1956 had almost plunged France into a terrible disaster.

"Once ignited," the general kept saying, "the conflagration may spread far and fast. I have always cautioned that we should not be the captives of military alliances. Look where France would be today if she had been Israel's reluctant ally. Our decolonization policy, the continuation of a French presence in Africa, our reconciliation with the Maghreb and the Arab countries — all that would have been wrecked."

In 1967, Pompidou, the future President of the Republic, realized that he lacked one important trump: experience in the area of foreign policy. He therefore tried more and more to inject himself into decisions reached by de Gaulle after consultation with Couve de Murville. But in this domain, more than in any other, de Gaulle continued to be secretive. And Couve was not inclined to share his privileges with Pompidou. Often the premier was apprised no earlier than other cabinet members — or at the most only a few hours earlier.

In July de Gaulle went off to Quebec where he issued his famous appeal to the French Canadians. Pompidou, who had remained in Paris to work on economic and social measures, was taken by surprise. He attempted to attenuate the painful impression which the general's outburst made on the French people. He deleted parts of the television broadcast on the incident.

For eighteen months, de Gaulle had been preparing for this glorious tour of Quebec. In 1966 he had told a young Secretary of State in Charge of Cooperation: "They're not all blacks out there. There are also many French Canadians. And, in a general way, it would be a great thing to emphasize their love of France. Ours is not a minor undertaking."

The general would not go to Montreal merely to inaugurate "flower shows." In any case, he discovered there such intense and vocal hostility against the Anglo-Saxons that he came away deeply affected. Cries of "Vive la France!" uttered by residents of America seemed to him a God-given sign.

The premier carefully refrained from expressing even the slightest reservations about the general's conduct. The world was a stage upon which de Gaulle trod as heroic protagonist. "As for me," said Pompidou, "I wouldn't know how to dramatize things. That's not my style."

.   .

For a long time, in fact ever since the start of the century, when the young Charles de Gaulle attended Jesuit schools, he had harbored a revolutionary dream. It was the era of the first strikes, which were repressed by the drawn swords of the military, and when the church was on the side of the army. But a few generous-minded Christians attempted to envision a better world in which workers and employers could live together in peace — a world in which it would no longer be necessary to wage the class struggle.

Then, weary perhaps of forever battling the workers, army officers likewise began to visualize a new form of social justice. De Gaulle was not the heir of capitalism. He belonged to a class which, although it had ceased to enjoy special privileges, nonetheless opposed socialism, Marxism, the Reds. In his native region of northern France, he had seen employees and employers pitted against one another.

When Liberation came, de Gaulle clamored for social reform. He could demand it all the more readily because the bourgeoisie, the haves, had not been the most ardent in resisting the occupiers. Often, until 1969, he reminded people of the muffled hostility against reform he had always encountered among the French bourgeoisie, who, to boot, "had been in favor of Pétain."

In 1948, after the war and during the period of the R.P.F., when the communists seemed to have reached the eve of their "great night," the general continued to pursue his dream. But he came up against obdurate realities.

"He often talked about this during the fifties," Léon Delbecque related on one occasion. "He wanted to give our generation an ideal, some formula midway between communism and capitalism. He was searching for a solution."

Once back in power, the general was too preoccupied with Algeria, constitutional changes and economic recovery to reopen his file on social reform. But in 1961 his intentions reemerged. Regularly, de Gaulle confided his thoughts to one of his collaborators, Geoffroy de Courcel: "A worker-capitalist association is a great idea," he said. "Sooner or later we must come back to it."

"Yes, my general, provided the trade unions are included in your plans. Otherwise they will suspect you of paternalism."

After the election of November 1962, the question of social reform entered the domain of practical politics. Thirty deputies met with René Capitant, father of the worker-capitalist project, to form a study group. Looking back, Capitant has recounted some of these early experiences: "At the Elysée our work was carefully followed by the general's technical adviser and by the secretary general of the presidency. Both men counseled haste. But the Matignon did not take us seriously. The premier made this clear to me."

Indeed, Pompidou made no effort to conceal his skepticism in regard to social reform. For de Gaulle it was a philosophy, even a religion; for the premier it was at best merely a technical modality. "The social terrain is too dangerous, according to the premier," one of his collaborators later testified. "Foreign policy or constitutional reform can be dramatized, but not questions of social policy."

Better than anyone else, de Gaulle was aware of the premier's reservations. This did not bother him. It tallied perfectly with his own image of Pompidou. "Social reform," the general said to an old-time Gaullist, "involves so much upheaval that a government geared to meet daily problems and avoid risks is bound to oppose it. It is a problem that will have to be worked out with the French people themselves."

De Gaulle expected his intermediaries, ministers as well as deputies, to obstruct his grand design. In 1958 he alone had reestablished the authority of the state. He had then gone on to impose peace in Algeria, combating winds and storms as he did so. Now he alone would take the lead in proposing a social revolution to the people of France.

Meanwhile, in 1963, 1964 and 1965, no progress whatsoever had been registered, despite the pleas of Capitant. Eventually Pompidou persuaded himself that the general had abandoned his idea of a great social reform. What a mistake he made! In no hurry, de Gaulle was still meditating. "Things are not yet ripe," he said.

The social domain was not a familiar one to the general. The transformation of the army had been an easy undertaking for someone like him. This, after all, was his world, his milieu, his profession. He knew military men; he knew which officers to promote, which to displace, which to remove from the ranks. Diplomats, prefects or high officials did not disconcert him. But the workers' world was totally alien to him. In his view, trade unionists were worthy men because they were waging a battle, but they were also dangerous. "Working class centers constitute a state within a state. When I say that I've said everything," he confided to one of his ministers.

The general was groping, hesitant to move ahead on his own. He consulted many people, and this course acted as a brake on his impatience to arrive at a decision.

But de Gaulle was convinced of one thing: he would not be able to "do something really new" through ordinary parliamentary channels. At various times in 1967 Pompidou told the general that a vast social reform was not possible, at least at a time when the opposition was proving so aggressive and the trade unions so active. De Gaulle seemed to resign himself to these dismal realities.

But in the spring, the cabinet requested and obtained full economic and social powers. De Gaulle thought the moment propitious for launching an initial experiment. One of the changes he requested that summer was a regulation dealing with "the sharing by wage earners in the profits of industrial expansion."

Capitant's group went to work with renewed enthusiasm. Pompidou watched anxiously as the project was being elaborated. Several times he warned the men around de Gaulle: "Business must not be made to bear the brunt of all this. Let's be careful not to put a brake on expansion."

The premier knew that industrialists were hostile to the plan: "I already have enough trouble with the trade unions," he said. "Don't add to my difficulties by making me quarrel with the employers."

In the presence of de Gaulle, Prompidou maintained a discreet silence, as if he were quite detached from the matter. But he commissioned his chief of staff, Michel Jobert, and one of his technical advisers to prepare an acceptable draft of such a project.

In August, after the general's return from Canada, a hot battle took place between the Capitant team and the team from the Matignon. De Gaulle let both sides fight it out in an adjacent chamber. Having studied both plans, he decided in favor of Pompidou's. "However, the statement of objectives, which gave explicit expression to the whole philosophy of participation, was our work," Capitant later observed. "The result was a curious disparity between the preamble and what followed."

The premier had won the battle. But the general had not given up his great design, which henceforth was called "participation." From de Gaulle's point of view the main thing was to lay the first stone, even if it were merely a symbolic one.

.   .

The succession . . . The question of who would succeed the general occupied everyone's thoughts. Rightists and leftists, city dwellers and provincials were obsessed with it. Even the faithful talked about Gaullism after de Gaulle. The phrase grated on the general's ears. "What's this?" he said accusingly to the members of his entourage. "I'm not dead yet."

Pompidou avoided the burning issue. On television, he declared quite bluntly: "Let me say this: if there is one person who does not talk about the succession and who does not think about it, it is I. This I say even though you may not believe me."

How could anyone really believe him? Pompidou stood in the very center of the stage. He was doing daily battle in the Assembly. He appeared regularly on television. And he had improved considerably in the use of this medium. The general himself congratulated him for it. National television had become the premier's special preserve. Politicians, including members of the majority party, could not appear on television without authorization from the Matignon.

The privileges of a second in command were obvious. Pompidou could even go to the provinces on political tours and be acclaimed by the people. The general would smile. He had once advised his premier to "show himself." It was plain that the advice had been heeded.

Very few men had remained at the Matignon as long as Pompidou. Very few had had the opportunity of following the Matignon files year after year, of getting to know individual politicians and learning about their ambitions, their activities. Although the premier was not as much of a slave to his work as Michel Debré had been, he nonetheless handled all the country's large and small problems, with the exception of diplomatic affairs. He controlled many people. Some owed their rise to him; others hoped he would forget their failures or machinations. Pompidou's path was strewn with both disappointed hopes and achieved ambitions. In politics, time is an absolute weapon. No one reproached the premier for having made good use of it, especially not de Gaulle.

But when the general talked about his successor — and this occurred more and more frequently — he was careful not to pronounce a name. He questioned visitors adroitly, as if the matter haunted him. But the conclusion he had come to remained a mystery. "Have confidence in France. She will find an answer."

De Gaulle was not preoccupied with what might happen after he had gone. A chief of state, especially if he is Charles de Gaulle, does not create a dauphin. And the word "succession" itself never ceased to irritate him. There would not be another de Gaulle, not for several generations. History invariably witnessed rapid transitions between epics. Louis XIV had a weak heir, Napoleon's place was taken by a king without glory. And after Clemenceau, Frenchmen chose mediocrity. The question of who would follow de Gaulle, therefore, scarcely mattered.

Only one thing did matter, and de Gaulle worried about it: after him France must not return to impotence and disgrace; no Fourth Republic must be allowed to follow the Fifth; the post-Gaullist era must not represent "a step backward," as the general put it.

. .

Yet alarming signs were evident. The Chamber of Deputies had once again become the scene of pointless quarrels. Little by little, the cabinet was forced to yield to ukases issued by the deputies. To one of his advisors, the general sadly remarked: "The scales are beginning to tip the other way. The balance of power is threatened."

The general also noted that the Gaullist party was behaving like any other political party. Deals, divisions, the grumblings of the majority — all these constituted a "pitiful soup," a sorry mess.

Unfortunately, events and situations always had a way of intervening to upset one's dearest principles. At a time when de Gaulle was becoming impatient with the growing role played by political parties, he was obliged to favor the development of a tightly disciplined Gaullist party. Consequently, he had to rely on the one man whom everyone was calling the Dauphin! In giving Pompidou this new weapon, the general knew that he was reinforcing the myth of Pompidou as his successor.

De Gaulle was not unaware that Pompidou showed a certain relish for politicking. Conversing with a few deputies who had come to call on him, the general discreetly expressed some amusement: "Pompidou is the man we need to take the majority party in hand. And this 'soup' doesn't seem to be displeasing to him."

In November 1967, Pompidou organized a Gaullist congress in Lille to which the local party members were invited for the first time. He demanded the assistance of all the big men in the majority party and placed government planes and helicopters at the disposal of the ministers. In short, he carried out a full-scale mobilization. But he showed no disapproval of anyone who chose not to go to Lille, including Capitant and a few of Pompidou's most fervent enemies.

At Lille only the flags and songs were Gaullist. Despite the innumerable references to the general, to his ideas, speeches and example, a sordid battle took place in the wings. For Pompidou uncovered a plot that aimed at depriving him of the party leadership. The revelation was bitter. This dark conspiracy was apparently headed by two of the most influential barons, Frey and Chaban-Delmas — the good Roger, the dear Jacques. In any event, this was the story recounted to the general by several witnesses, including Jacques Foccart.

The old camaraderie of the barons was now merely a legend. Roger Frey had been removed from the ministry of the interior where for six years he had guarded all the secrets of state. Jacques Chaban-Delmas had been confined to the presidency of the Assembly where he enjoyed full honors but no power.

Pompidou could now overlook the hidden resentments of these two old companions. He was no longer a mere baron, like the others. Also, he knew that friendship, in a profession like his own, could prove deceptive, that words and feelings were not to be taken at face value. The political world would enjoy the spectacle of his discomfiture. The premier no longer ignored the sorry realities concealed beneath fine phrases.

This was a lesson he had learned from the general — one more lesson. Men in power are alone, free of all the bonds that hinder ordinary individuals. People like Chaban-Delmas and Roger Frey might very well again become enthusiastic servants of Pompidou, when the right time came.

To the general, the goings-on in Lille seemed but a sorry to-do — "whitecaps," as he put it to Pompidou.

· ·

After Lille, de Gaulle was less ready than ever to rely on others. It was up to him to take in hand the social changes that would constitute the culmination of his great adventure. Elections seemed to him an idle business.

Once again the general considered the idea of a general referendum that would disclose, in an irreversible way, the desire for change. There would be a fresh battle to fight, a battle against the "others," against the deputies who by nature were loath to take risks; also a battle against Pompidou, whose tendency was to preserve the status quo.

"My premier does not favor a referendum," de Gaulle confided to some of the people around him. "He's not the only one. But every important accomplishment since nineteen fifty-eight has been achieved by a referendum, that is, by the French people themselves. And Frenchmen understand; they're not so stupid."

On occasion, the general was more explosive: "Everyone would like things to continue on their haphazard course; everyone is ready and willing to get along like this. But, I repeat, that just shows that people don't understand me. General de Gaulle is not the kind of man who will accept this sort of thing."

His great idea was slowly taking shape. It was a matter of urging French society to take a decisive step forward, to move completely into the century of tomorrow. It was a difficult step to take for an ancient people whose old wounds had not yet healed, whose defeats still rankled and whose most natural response was to cling to old habits and traditions.

At the age of seventy-seven, would de Gaulle have the strength to accomplish his task? Time was passing; now, more than ever, each month counted.

Pompidou was merely an auxiliary, the collaborator of the moment. His reservations, his want of enthusiasm, in short his entire person, were not very serious obstacles.

"At that time I warned the general about Pompidou's excessive ambition," Capitant said. "De Gaulle did not like to hear that kind of talk. But in the end he agreed to hear me out. And he listened."

Soon it would be six years since the general had rescued from obscurity an assistant whom he then needed. De Gaulle was not deterred by all the talk about a dauphin, a successor, which was strengthening the premier's position. The legacy, the succession — that was something he would decide. Pompidou was merely one man among many who were available.

What about afterward? After de Gaulle? "There's always an end to everything," the general would answer. "Every man comes to an end. For the moment, however, such is not the case."

Life went on, simply and peacefully; but May 1968 was approaching.

Part IV

THE RUPTURE

And lean-look'd prophets whisper fearful change;
Rich men look sad and ruffians dance and leap,
The one in fear to lose what they enjoy,
The other to enjoy by rage and war:
These signs forerun the death or fall of kings.

Richard II, *act 2, scene 4*

CHAPTER 13

A Most Unwelcome Storm

DE GAULLE SHUT THE DOORS of the Elysée behind him. Ten hours a
day the general reigned alone in his office. He sat motionless in the
dusk, facing windows that opened onto the deserted park. Visitors
were rare, travels even rarer. Any time off was spent mostly with
his family: the tea hour, lunch, dinner — or evenings watching television. The presidential palace had become a temple of silence.
People spoke here in hushed tones; even the footmen and the Republican Guards looked like wax figures.

Life outside filtered in only after it had been purified. Bernard
Tricot, the new adviser, and the faithful Foccart barred anyone or
anything that might anger or sadden the general. The chief of state
was the object of solicitude, of tender precautions that are the lot of
stricken monarchs. Interviews were granted only to trusted friends.
And those who did manage to see the general were important people.

"Geoffroy de Courcel used to insist that the general should see all
kinds of people — especially young people," a former aide-de-camp
said. "Someone had the idea of inviting the best students from the
best schools for 'private' interviews. After Courcel, others attempted to do something about the isolation into which the general
was gradually sinking. I must say that these attempts proved futile.
Then Bernard Tricot arrived. He was a high official who had had no
contact with the general prior to nineteen fifty-eight. The walls of
the ivory tower had grown thicker. And Tricot himself, involved as
he was in his files, saw very few people."

Pompidou respected the general's desire for solitude. Most of the state's business was conducted at the Matignon where the pace was fast. When the premier came to the Elysée his hands were empty, he carried no papers or dossiers. Putting his cares aside, he brought the general a bit of his own serenity. The dialogue between the general and his eminent collaborator consisted of amiable generalities; or else they exchanged philosophical comments on the state of the nation and the morale of its citizens. Tricot had to insist on being kept informed about the handling of certain problems.

With ill grace the general acquiesced to all this mollycoddling. He remarked that ever since December 1965, legitimacy had been steadily frittered away. Public opinion polls interested him more and more. In February 1968, one of them indicated that his popularity was lower than it had been in ten years, whereas Pompidou's had reached a record high. The chief of state kept saying to visitors: "Under various circumstances I have had more backing from the French people than any other statesman. But look at what's happening! Things are different now."

Nevertheless, de Gaulle was convinced that the time had come to pave the way for a basic social revolution. He said this when he made his New Year's resolution. 1968, he promised, "will witness an important step toward a new social order." The tepid response of the cabinet, of virtually all the Gaullists and of the majority of Frenchmen did not shake him in his determination.

On April 25, 1968, David Rousset, a former Resistant, philosopher, writer, leftist and non-Gaullist, was summoned to the Elysée. As was his wont, the general stressed the very thing that would appeal to the person with whom he was conversing. He talked about "his" revolution. "Capitalism stands condemned," he declared with vigor. "It must be deliberately condemned. And totalitarian communism must likewise be condemned. A new way must be sought: participation."

There was no one in his entourage who could draw Frenchmen into this new venture. The cabinet? No, that was not its role. The Gaullist deputies? They were too conservative and too tied to their

own interests, like all parliamentarians. "I'm cut off from my countrymen," the general acknowledged. "I'm searching for men of
good will who understand the significance of this battle. And I can't
find any. I'm alone, Rousset, alone."

Timidly, the visitor said: "What about the left?"

The general laughed somberly. What left? The left of Mitterand? Of the socialists? It was blinded by sectarianism. It united
only to oppose de Gaulle. "The left, Rousset, will claim to be my
heir only after I'm dead, not before."

De Gaulle repeated that the moment was ripe, the terrain favorable; he knew it, he felt it.

.   .

On the other side of the Seine, Georges Pompidou was convinced
that he was on the right track. He merely had to take care to avoid
accidents. On March 17, to the Gaullists assembled at Ajaccio, the
premier declared: "I have the feeling that no government measur-
ing up to the effectiveness of ours has ever governed France so long
a time."

A motion of censure put before the Assembly had been rejected
on April 24. Another was to be presented on May 13. This
amounted to guerrilla warfare. But Pompidou marched on from
victory to victory — against the opposition, against the strikers,
against the malcontents, against all those who foundered in doubt,
as de Gaulle, citing *Faust*, put it. "We are living in a period of rising expectations," the premier reiterated to the Gaullist deputies
during the closing days of April.

He saw nothing miraculous about his popularity, his growing authority. Nor was he inclined to give daily thanks to the good Lord
for all these blessings. Certain that he was the only true statesman
begotten by Gaullism, he did not dwell on the question of succession.

Pompidou regarded the general's dream of social reform as insig-
nificant, even dangerous. He felt it precisely his job to ward off
such perils. He was sure that his own amiable, insinuating way of

handling the general would result in the abandonment of these dangerous dreams. And he felt strong enough to oppose them openly if necessary.

At the last cabinet meeting in April, the ministers had witnessed a surprising scene. The general had reopened his dossier on his cherished project of social reforms. He was still trying to put some order into the mass of texts at his disposal.

Then Pompidou took the floor. Instead of displaying his usual tact, he bluntly opposed such grandiose dreams. He spoke as a man responsible for the well-being of Frenchmen, for the maintenance of domestic tranquillity. He also alluded to the state of the exchequer. This was the first time that he had ventured to disagree sharply with the general and to do so in the presence of others. For a number of political and tactical reasons, the premier no longer feared to speak out now and then on the issues that separated him from the general. He had boasted of this to his intimates, but in rather moderate language.

.   .

No one saw the approaching storm of May 1968 — neither the ministers, the police, the trade unions, nor the students; neither de Gaulle nor Pompidou. At the outset, recriminations against the chief of state and his government, long piling up but overlooked, provoked the explosion.

With the general's consent, the premier had gone off to "get acquainted" with the people of Iran and Afghanistan, traveling as a tourist for reasons of protocol. Accompanied by Couve de Murville, Pompidou was visiting the land of a thousand and one nights when he first heard echoes of the student demonstrations in the Latin Quarter. "From that distance," Couve later explained, "it was impossible to assess the seriousness of the situation."

Leaving Pompidou to continue his trip, the foreign minister returned to Paris, as had originally been planned. There he witnessed a stupefying spectacle. But the premier did not curtail his visit. "What can you expect?" he said. "I'm only the second in command. There's a President of the Republic by the name of Charles de Gaulle. He holds all the power. There's even an interim premier."

Pompidou had all sorts of reasons for not interrupting his travels; he called them diplomatic and technical differences of opinion. And so he continued, from deserts to mountains, from one wonder of the world to another. Each evening, at the close of his daily sightseeing, he was informed about the violence that day after day pitted the students in the Paris area against the police. But he couldn't hear the news clearly — voices tended to fade out over the long-distance telephone, and the radio was almost inaudible. He was tempted to give thanks to Providence for being where he was at such a terrible time.

"When I go back to Paris," he said to a man in his suite, "my name will be unsullied."

· ·

At the Elysée the general's meditations were interrupted by the noise of grenades, the fervor of the young, and the anxiety of their parents. But it was not the obligation of the President of the Republic to intervene personally to put an end to such "childishness," as he called it. There were ministers and the police for that. He demanded firmness, indicating that the only possible tactics were clubbings and the resulting tears. Then, reverting to the ways of a soldier, he became angry. Using barracks language, he excoriated his officers for their hesitation. Acts of rank stupidity multiplied.

But this was merely the beginning. Disorders, feverish outbursts, rebellion followed. On May 10, barricades were erected in the Latin Quarter. The distressed ministers, shocked and upset, were at a loss how to deal with the riots that occurred night after night. Neither Foccart nor Tricot dared to alert the chief of state to the dangers of the situation. De Gaulle fell victim to the devotion he inspired in these men. Finally, at dawn, Louis Joxe, the interim premier and an old companion, warned the general. Meanwhile, the battles had subsided, leaving the entire Sorbonne area strewn with ashes and debris. Joxe described Paris as being "on the verge of civil war."

Then came a rapid succession of developments. All the trade union organizations announced a general strike that was to begin on May 13; it was to be accompanied, needless to say, by a series of demonstrations. Everyone begged the general to intervene. He was reminded of the April 1961 putsch and of his silence, which had mystified the faithful. Once again de Gaulle considered the situation, examining each of the possible counteroffensives that he might set in motion.

"I can't sit still and fold my arms. I will speak over the radio tonight. And early next week I'll bring the trade unions right here, to the Elysée. Anyway, I've been wanting to talk to those people for a long time and to lay the groundwork for the program of participation."

But by the middle of the afternoon the general's mood began to change. Assisted by Fouchet, the Minister of the Interior, and also by the prefect of police, de Gaulle studied possible plans of action for that terrible day of May 13. He totted up the number of police officers, placing one squad here, another there. The causes of the students' rage were not even discussed. The sole question considered was how to parry their blows as quickly as possible, to close the breaches which each day were becoming more apparent.

No longer did de Gaulle think of intervening in person. "The chief of state should not be in the front line," he kept repeating. "He does not act under the compulsion of circumstances, when things are at their hottest."

The general's strategy can be summed up as a refusal to take any action until after he had meditated at length. Since the premier was returning to Paris that very evening, it would be up to him to appear before the public. To Fouchet de Gaulle said only: "We will not retreat; we will not capitulate."

At seven that evening there was another change. The general allowed himself to be persuaded to accept the idea of a truce based on conditions that might prove acceptable to the students. A little clemency, a little toughness — just the right dose of each. Before going in to dinner, de Gaulle instructed Tricot to prepare the draft of an armistice to be announced the next day, Sunday.

"In any case," he said, "during the next forty-eight hours, from now until the strike scheduled for Monday, May thirteenth, nothing much will happen."

. .

A few moments later, Georges Pompidou finally returned to Paris.

Although he possessed only the most fragmentary information, having been unable to consult with a single minister or with anyone else in a position of responsibility, he had decided on his plan of action while he was in Kabul. During the plane flight homeward, he had written the speech that he planned to deliver to the French nation that very evening, although he had seen and heard nothing.

Driving from Orly to the Hôtel de Matignon in his black Citroën, he listened to the account that his chief of staff, Michel Jobert, gave him of the recent happenings. But he changed neither his plans nor a single punctuation mark in the speech he intended to give. When he walked into his office, he appeared to have all the self-assurance of a man who had made up his mind one way or the other. He did not even bother to question the assembled ministers — Joxe, Fouchet, and the invaluable Guichard — who had immediately been summoned. He merely said to them: "This is what I'm going to do . . ."

His plan amounted to a formal repudiation of the policy that had been followed in his absence. He would keep the Sorbonne open and release the arrested students. Clemency without conditions, without bargaining or haggling, he said. Joxe, who deep down had been hoping for precisely such measures, reluctantly warned him: "I myself tried all day to convince the general. You'll never get him to agree."

"Yes, I will," Pompidou retorted, "because I intend to make this my own personal affair." And with his usual calm, off he went to the Elysée. He guessed that his resignation would be unnecessary and that right now de Gaulle would refuse to accept it. "Anyway, there was no need for me to suggest it to the general," he later asserted most explicitly.

The general saw before him a premier whose suntanned face looked somewhat worn from his travels, but who epitomized self-assurance. For de Gaulle this was a change from the "weaklings," as he called them, of the day before.

He listened attentively as Pompidou explained his plan. The premier's approach pleased him. The general wished to see his ministers assume their responsibilities without asking him for instructions. His role was to cover for them. If they failed, he would replace them.

The general readily accepted the premier's plan. De Gaulle allowed himself to be persuaded not to act himself at a time when things continued to be hot and the barricades were still smoking. According to Malraux, he told Pompidou: "It's your turn to play. If you win, so much the better. France wins with you. If you lose, too bad for you."

The premier nonetheless wanted to justify his tactics. On Monday, May 13, the tenth anniversary of the general's return to power, an immense crowd would march across Paris in response to an appeal from all the trade union organizations. If the Sorbonne were closed, it might be invaded by "a bunch of madmen." Pompidou's strategy would deprive the demonstration of its true objective — de Gaulle would call it a "strategic retreat." The general did not as yet ask himself whether such tactics might produce dire results. If they failed, there would still be time to take other measures and to replace the commanding officer. Pompidou was gambling his own fate. The general, who had so often challenged both Providence and the French people, respected Pompidou for his course of action.

But the battle of May 13 was not fought along predictable lines. This time the police did not lose their heads. The Parisian population joined the parade. That evening the Sorbonne's doors were open to the first revolutionary wave. The celebration began — and so did the folly.

When night fell in Paris, the premier had every reason to believe that he had won. Or at least that he had not lost. From that decisive day onward, one thing stuck in his mind forever: the cry, "Ten years, that's enough!" which was uttered by millions of voices.

These four words were addressed to de Gaulle. But they also represented a threat to Pompidou — or, perhaps, a promise.

. .

The next day, the general was to leave at dawn for Bucharest. Of all the countries in the communist camp, Rumania was the only one that showed some signs of independence. The trip might serve to illustrate the effectiveness of Charles de Gaulle's grand design. It would also give the chief of state an opportunity to exhort one East European country to emulate France by freeing itself from the tutelage of one of the two great blocs. He also planned to protest "the permanent presence of foreign forces on the soil of certain countries." At that moment, Czechoslovakia was experiencing a springtime rich with promise.

At the Elysée and the Quai d'Orsay, diplomats had been at work for weeks preparing memoranda for these Franco-Rumanian talks. On April 25, in the course of a conversation with David Rousset, de Gaulle dwelt at length on the message he planned to deliver in Bucharest. Compared to such prospective accomplishments, so important for the future of de Gaulle's "Europe from the Atlantic to the Urals," the voyage to Quebec was mere window-dressing.

But six hours before his departure, during the evening of this feverish May 13, the general hesitated, wondering whether he should leave after all. In the middle of the night he summoned, one after the other, all his closest collaborators. Fouchet begged him not to leave Paris. "The French people would not understand, my general."

Ten minutes later, Pompidou arrived, followed by Couve. The premier offered precisely the opposite advice. "The tempest is really over. If you don't leave, the people will think that the whole affair has not yet ended."

Pompidou had already convinced himself that his plan was succeeding. He counseled serenity and optimism. In Paris it was up to him alone to act, to see things through to the end, to victory.

De Gaulle gave in. Besides, Rumania was only four hours away by plane. He would go, but with "a bad conscience," as Fouchet observed. In accordance with established tradition, he authorized Pompidou to make use of the constitutional powers vested in the premier during a temporary absence of the chief of state.

In Rumania, despite the warm welcome, the flowers, the picturesque customs, the satisfaction of having been seen, heard and understood, the general remained taciturn. The news arriving from the Elysée was too vague to satisfy him. He left a student revolt only to find that a social crisis might now be in the making. The strike was progressively paralyzing all the essential mechanisms of the country's economy. De Gaulle had handed France, the state, over to Pompidou, and he was already regretting the confidence he had placed in his premier.

By May 18 he was ready to return. That evening he telephoned the Hôtel de Matignon. Accompanied by Foccart, Pompidou closeted himself in his office to talk to the general. Guichard remained in an adjacent room.

The premier dissuaded de Gaulle from interrupting his Rumanian trip. "You couldn't intervene, my general, even if you were here. It would be too late. I must close the breach until the horizon clears." Respectfully, Pompidou insisted. Then he hung up and told Guichard that he had convinced de Gaulle to stay on in Rumania. "The general will return exactly as originally planned, and that's a good thing. A hasty return will only aggravate the situation."

And so de Gaulle traveled from factory to factory and from city to city, from Bucharest to Kraków. Since he himself was not paying attention to affairs of state, he suspected his premier of being negligent, of making mistakes, or of playing his own political game. Ab-

sence inflamed his instinctive distrust. A great drama was being enacted while he, the man who loved storms, was far away. He
foresaw even worse: the likelihood of being faced with an accomplished fact that would not be to his liking.

Finally only a few hours ahead of the original schedule, he returned to Paris. "The holiday is over," he said to his ministers.
Then he added firmly: "We are going to take charge of the situation."

He encountered looks of annoyance. He sent immediately for
Pompidou. It was almost midnight. The general was soon told the
news: authority had been flouted, anarchy and destruction were
rampant, the general strike was in full swing. The state had been
made to look ridiculous. France had been struck down.

Vehemently, de Gaulle upbraided his premier for having given
him an inaccurate account of the disaster. His words were wounding. Pompidou tried to explain. "I felt, my general, that it was not
up to you to act. And I still think so. It takes eight or ten days for a
strike to get fully under way."

"The strike! As if that's all that matters! There's nothing but
whoring around here!"

The premier offered his resignation. That would give the general
a free hand. But de Gaulle shrugged his shoulders, rejecting the
suggestion. "This is hardly the moment. Come here tomorrow,
bring along those responsible for maintaining order, and we'll make
the necessary decisions. Tomorrow is Sunday and things should be
at a standstill."

·   ·

The following day, Sunday, Pompidou went to the Elysée, accompanied by Christian Fouchet, Messmer, the Minister of Information
and the prefect of police. As he climbed the staircase of the presidential palace, Pompidou continued to exude self-confidence.

"The general is furious," he admitted to Fouchet. "But I am
ready to answer him as follows: we are giving back to you a country

far calmer than it was upon my return from Afghanistan." Then, turning to the Minister of the Interior, he said: "I'm warning you, Christian, he's going to ask you to clear the Sorbonne."

As soon as his five visitors were seated opposite him, the general vented his wrath. "Well, so de Gaulle goes off and when he returns he finds that everything is topsy-turvy."

Without going into such questions as who was responsible for what, but obviously looking at Pompidou, the general drew a bleak picture of the sequence of events that had occurred during his absence. Everything had been sacrificed — order, the state; everyone had closed his eyes. What had been done to France? Resorting to strong language, de Gaulle described the defeat, which was none of his doing.

Pompidou settled back in his armchair but said not a word. Then the general issued his orders: "Clear out the Sorbonne and the Odéon Theater immediately!"

Fouchet looked at Pompidou, who was still silent. "And so I had to face the music alone," Fouchet later related. "I explained the risks involved in such an operation. It would be impossible to take over the Sorbonne without firing into the crowds. There would be casualties, deaths. De Gaulle turned to Pompidou and the prefect of police. Both of them agreed with me. Then he quieted down a little, but he still insisted that we clear the Odéon. And within twenty-four hours. The premier made no comment. We then returned to our ministries. I drew up a plan for an offensive against the Odéon. It was a delicate operation but not an impossible one."

Upon his return to the Matignon, Pompidou tried to get de Gaulle to change his mind. He talked to Tricot and Foccart. "It's madness," he told them. "The general has no conception of the chain reaction he'll provoke. And for what? For a theater and a few trunkfuls of costumes seized by a bunch of kids. This is a bad time to play with fire. Try to convince the chief of state."

Then he waited. Three hours later, de Gaulle again allowed himself to yield. After all, more imperious problems had to be dealt with, in particular the conduct of negotiations with the trade unions.

From that moment the premier was doomed. So far as de Gaulle was concerned, Pompidou had lost his wager of May 11. The general decided to replace him. In two days, in two weeks or two months — the time didn't matter.

CHAPTER 14

Descent into Hell

DE GAULLE DID NOT LACK REASONS for getting rid of Pompidou. He enumerated them: the premier had not foreseen the coming storm, although the first signs had already been visible in Italy, Germany, and Spain, to say nothing of Nanterre. When you're piloting the ship of state, even if you're only the second officer, you have to be able to sight trouble. In Bucharest, de Gaulle mumbled to someone in his entourage: "Yes, of course, it's fine to display your savoir-faire for three days. But it would have been better had he displayed it over the past six years."

Having made up his mind, the general was without mercy. And even had he been inclined to treat Pompidou with a certain amount of indulgence, considerations of public policy and concern for the interests of the state would speedily have brought him back to his senses. It was impossible to retain a premier who had allowed "such things" to happen.

He had already found a replacement: none other than Couve de Murville — an unyielding man. De Gaulle had watched him at work. A few days later, on Sunday, May 26, the foreign minister was summoned to the Elysée. The storm was then at its height. Without further ado, he was asked to prepare himself for his future responsibilities. This struck Couve as catastrophic.

"Couve was really reluctant to go to the Matignon under the circumstances. The future was too uncertain. Of course, he couldn't refuse the general's invitation. But I swear to you, he did nothing to encourage him. Besides, what could he have done at that moment but continue to implement the government's policy and retain all the members of Pompidou's team?" one of Couve's closest associates recalled.

Meanwhile, the general, making quite a show of his benevolence toward the premier, kept his own counsel and was careful not to let on to Pompidou. For the moment, at any rate, he had no choice but to allow the incumbent premier to wage his own battle in the Assembly where a new motion of censure against him had been presented. The general felt that he must give Pompidou a chance to surmount such a preposterous parliamentary obstacle. He also wanted Pompidou to begin negotiations with the trade unions.

Above all, however, the general was impatient to go into action himself. Before leaving for Rumania he had announced that he would address the French people on May 24. He had given himself plenty of time to perfect his strategy so that it would be foolproof. During the ordinary ups and downs of public affairs de Gaulle always allowed himself to be guided by events — "like a cork bobbing on the waves," as a former assistant put it. But this rule of conduct could not be observed when major issues were at stake.

On May 24 the general intended to suggest a referendum, something he had been pondering for several months. As soon as he returned from Rumania, he confided his plan to the ministers who had come to meet him at the airport. "As always during difficult moments, we will appeal to the people."

Subsequently, he discussed the matter in great detail with his visitors, as well as with all the ministers, who, one after the other, were summoned to the Elysée. No one objected. Three days later, in solemn tones, de Gaulle said to his entire cabinet: "Gentlemen, I will have extremely important things to tell you after tomorrow. We will hold a special meeting here."

In the crisis that was currently rocking French society, the general sensed a strong public desire for participation. Everyone agreed, even those who were loath to use the general's word for the project. From this de Gaulle inferred that he had not been wrong when he had said to Rousset and others: "The long-term results are coming to a head."

Realizing that Frenchmen were blinded by their own daily demands, he had planned to forge the revolution himself. And now he found himself confronted with a revolution that he had not authored, a street revolution! This was an excellent opportunity to take control of the flood and to use it for his own purposes. "The state rests on a foundation solid enough to prevent any backlash."

De Gaulle could not visualize the recurrence of a storm similar to those France had experienced in May 1958, in 1960 and in 1961, during the Algerian war. The Fifth Republic was strong enough to cope with misadventure. What was happening now represented an attack against a "mechanized, inhuman" society. All the prosperous countries, in the East as well as in the West, were being threatened by the same kind of reaction.

The first priority was to reestablish order — in factories, offices, universities, ministries, as well as in the streets. On Thursday, May 23, at an "extremely important" meeting of the cabinet, the general hurled reproaches at his ministers and especially at his premier: "You could have done a number of things a long time ago but you did not do them . . . Similarly, from the start of these disorders, you could have acted with greater dispatch. Instead, you decided to allow this to happen, to allow these things to go on . . ."

But it was too late for idle regrets or recapitulation. In any case, the state, which had triumphed over other upheavals, seemed no longer to be vacillating. Pompidou's diagnosis was moderate: "Today," the premier said to the members of the cabinet, "France has no special or profound anxieties. Paris is bored . . ."

But the disorders would have to be put down. All the Gaullists, Pompidou included, were assured that de Gaulle would manage to reestablish order.

But in this spring of 1968, the general was no longer quite the de Gaulle of history. His advancing age, ten years of power, the events of December 1965 — all these had affected him. The popularity he had once enjoyed had given him the will to act, to take the lead; this will was now greatly diminished. In earlier days, the chief of state had needed only a few days to make up his mind. But this time he had let three weeks pass without intervening. Silently, he had stood by. He was still capable of activating mechanisms that were familiar to him, but his stamina, his daring — to put it in a nutshell, his genius — were no longer what they once had been.

In his Elysée palace, that fortress of silence in a city gone mad, de Gaulle himself realized this. In vain he sought the inspiration that enabled him only yesterday to hold Frenchmen enthralled by a mere word or gesture. He no longer possessed that flair for clear thinking that had permitted him to assess with accuracy the limits of the tragedy. He had lost his faith. Yesterday, it was revolt; today it was revolution.

And the general admitted, even confessed, to his intimates that he no longer "understood." He had discovered in himself another Charles de Gaulle — a man who was wounded, impoverished, despairing. His greatest ambition henceforth would be to preserve appearances, and to do nothing that might destroy the image of his great epic.

Pompidou and his ministers were not yet aware of this. In their eyes de Gaulle, whether aging or not, could only be de Gaulle. The long silence they had just witnessed had been taken as something of a nightwatch. De Gaulle had always known how to tip the balance at the last moment. On May 23, the members of the cabinet left the Elysée comforted. No one opposed the general's plan for a referendum, which he intended to submit to the people the next day. Even the least optimistic ministers, including Guichard, were sure that at the height of any storm, the general invariably triumphed.

They were soon to lose their illusions.

.   .

As usual, the general prepared his speech for the 24th with jealous care, heeding no one's advice. What he came up with proved to be merely a speech, whereas the Gaullists had expected a clap of thunder. De Gaulle employed on this occasion phrases he had used successfully before, under very different circumstances. The very quality of his voice betrayed nostalgia for the past.

He acquitted himself of the formality with a certain sadness, as if he knew, even before he spoke, that his words had lost their magical power. The recording on the first floor of the Elysée lasted only seven minutes. The general's associates, as well as the television technicians clearly showed by their embarrassment how deeply disappointed they were. The general sat down in front of the tape recorder and judged the results for himself. But to everyone's surprise, he did not ask for a second recording. He nodded briefly, then, after absent-mindedly waving good-bye to members of the audience, he returned to his first-floor office without a word and closed the door.

That evening the French people were on time for the rendezvous the general had made with them. Everything, including even street demonstrations, came to a halt. Television viewers saw a pitiful old man, a pallid copy of yesterday's hero.

The night was a long one, with barricades, fires, and violence. Words of insolence, of rage, were hurled by the crowds.

De Gaulle was the first to measure the extent of his failure. "I laid an egg," he said honestly. "I put my chips on the wrong number."

De Gaulle was beaten. There was nothing but emptiness, a total void within and around him. His old, faithful associates, who had so often witnessed his crises of despair, suddenly found themselves contemplating the downfall of a man and his work. Anyone can forgive a mistake or a lapse. But no one who accepts defeat can expect a chance to avenge himself. The adventure begun on June 18, 1940, in proud solitude was over. Completely crushed, the general was resigned to this. He kept repeating: "There's only the good Lord . . . God is all that's left . . . The future is in the hands of the Almighty . . ."

If he still entertained the slightest hope, or a desire not to jeopardize the future, he would have packed his bags. But he remained to become a spectator of the chaos he himself had created, a morbid witness of his own downfall.

To leave or to remain physically present for a while — it all came to the same thing. De Gaulle had turned the page. His epic had terminated at eight in the evening on May 24, 1968; that was the date history would record.

The general was thinking of the future, which for him was but a march toward death.

.   .

He still attempted to pay his respects to custom. As if in a dream he continued to perform the duties associated with power. He donned his dinner jacket to receive the new American ambassador, Sargent Shriver. He asked Couve to hold himself in readiness to take over the position of premier. Nothing would change his plans.

He left it to Pompidou to wage the final battle — the negotiations with the trade unions — knowing that the battle was lost even before it got under way. Gaullists, barons, ministers, old companions — all were discovering a profound crack in de Gaulle's very substance — something Pompidou termed a "fissure." And they interpreted his condition as tangible proof of defeat. The premier alone continued to hope. He took up the torch with its flickering flame.

Pompidou viewed the general strike as a real social crisis. He intended to put an end to it by any means possible. Salvation would follow. The meeting with the trade union leaders was to take place on Saturday, May 25, in the lovely ministry for social affairs on the Rue de Grenelle. Before going there, Pompidou told a few deputies: "I promise you that tomorrow evening, at the very latest, the matter will be settled. We'll stay up all day and all night if we have to, but we'll arrive at some agreement."

He was ready to fire all his big guns, to leave no stone unturned. He believed he would succeed where de Gaulle had failed. "In two days, three at the most," he declared, "France will go back to work. And we'll have peace once again."

For two weeks Pompidou underwent his baptism of fire. This

was the first catastrophe he had ever experienced. Until now, his life, including even the span at the Matignon, had appeared to him in retrospect as an unbroken series of sunny days with only a few clouds that were soon dissipated. Now it was up to him to show his mettle as a statesman, working in the very eye of the tornado. For two weeks he never abandoned the ship. All his nights were spent at the Matignon. For the first time in six years he slept in the apartment reserved for the premier, next to his office. Until now he had managed to get the best of his weariness, knowing that fatigue was a bad counselor. He had been sprightly and alert, deliberately giving the impression of serenity.

What about the crisis? Well, there was nothing for it but to pay the price. Pompidou had faith in his talents as a negotiator, an arranger.

"The day before the meeting on the Rue de Grenelle," the Minister of Social Affairs, Jean-Marcel Jeanneney, has recounted, "I asked the head of the employers' association to stop by to see me. I told him that in my opinion the economy could not stand a general wage increase of more than five per cent, that such a rise would entail grave monetary risks. I thought I had convinced him. Yet no sooner had the conference begun than Huvelin suggested a twenty-five per cent increase."

When he heard that figure, Pompidou grumbled. "The man's crazy," he said. But he was beyond worrying about the exchequer. It was the country itself he had to save from extinction.

"As the person responsible for the nation's budget," Pompidou declared at the Rue de Grenelle, "I was shoved under the table from the start." He was submerged by the avalanche. The trade unions were dividing up the state's cash. The negotiations amounted to no more than a mad rush for the spoils.

Michel Debré, the Minister of Finance and an incurable Cassandra, hurried off to the Elysée to alert the general. He claimed that the premier was about to destroy the results of ten years' labor.

De Gaulle bowed to the inevitable. The Fifth Republic? It was dead. "People" were despoiling it and dividing up its remains.

Pompidou? He still thought he could play his own game. "Does that surprise you?" the general thundered to Debré.

There would be the unavoidable sequel: chaos, civil war, a contagion that had already begun to spread throughout all Europe. In the end it would sweep France into the hands of the "totalitarians." Pompidou would be able to pocket the profits of all his "maneuvers." De Gaulle proceeded then to describe the "France of Auvergne" that eventually would replace the "France of de Gaulle."

"But," the general added, "this won't last. A few months, a few weeks, even The abyss is there, waiting. France will fall into it, carrying Pompidou and Mitterand with her. And you, too, Debré, and me, if I'm still alive."

Michel Debré left the Elysée in a state of shock. There had been times during the war in Algeria when he had seen the general yield to despair, when he seemed ready to give up everything. But today the situation was far more serious. De Gaulle appeared to be far away, immersed in a deep depression; he was a shadow that was vanishing.

The general kept describing to his collaborators and a few intimates all the stages of the cataclysm he envisioned. And he spoke with hallucinatory precision: "You can't stop a worldwide revolution by sitting around a green baize table discussing things. Pompidou is making a mistake if he thinks that the French will go back to work. This is a tidal wave. It will bury us all, even the pope."

He observed in passing: "They can give in on every issue on the Rue de Grenelle, they can surrender down to our last penny. You'll see. It won't change a thing. No one will return to work."

De Gaulle was not wrong about this. Despite the pact concluded with the trade unions, the strike continued. France was indeed a madhouse.

· ·

During the next few days, the general, immovable, continued his descent into his own inferno. At a time when his country was facing shipwreck, he had suddenly become an old man who was himself sinking — a condition he had often dreaded. He still kept informed, received his associates and collaborators, responded to them, and presided over cabinet meetings; but his power was no more than a dismal comedy.

The only effort he did put forth was to conceal, when others were present, the sobs that were suffocating him. At the cabinet meeting on Monday, May 27, he again alluded to the idea of a referendum, since the topic had been placed on the day's agenda. He was, however, aware of the realities of the situation: it would be materially impossible to consult the French people.

"The text of the plan would have to be printed in Belgium," one minister pointed out, not without a certain cruelty. "And even then, it wouldn't work out. Postal workers are also on strike, so how could the text reach the voters?"

Christian Fouchet was consulted. He answered by declaring bluntly that a referendum was unthinkable under present circumstances; and he did not believe that things would improve in the immediate future.

"I would have liked, however, for the French people to say no. Then I wouldn't appear to be capitulating," said the general.

De Gaulle was condemned to the most humiliating kind of retirement; there was simply no other way out. To a few of his faithful who tried to talk to him about the recent past and to apportion blame, he said with indifference: "Let's not talk about what has just happened. There's no use. To be sure, it was a mistake to leave the Sorbonne open. We should have held out. The disaster began on May thirteenth. But what's the use of going over the past?"

And then he added: "I'm the one who is causing all this unrest. The French people want me to quit. Well, I won't cling to power against their wishes. I'm no Franco. Then everyone will be happy. I'll leave, I'll leave."

.   .

Tuesday, May 30, was a long day for the general as he bade his farewells. The communists were mobilizing. De Gaulle granted interviews until late in the afternoon. His old companions, trade

union leaders and military men all came to see him. In great secrecy he also received visits from a few intimates who entered the
Elysée through the service entrance.

He kept repeating, "Everything has gone down the drain. An inundation, an inundation. I no longer recognize my own country."

In the presence of stupefied callers, he painted a picture of the
apocalypse, a future of fire and blood. Soon, he said, the communists would be in power all over Europe. After France it would be
Italy's turn, then West Germany's. A long civil war would begin.
The Americans would come to France to support the resistance. In
Germany the Nazis would reappear. Finally, there would be an end
to the chaos "because the Russians would abandon the idea of making Europe the theater of a third world war."

Then de Gaulle came back to a more immediate future: his own
death. He could see signs of fear on the faces of his visitors. Thereupon, he stood up, walked to the door and shook hands with his departing guests. His final word was a prayer to God.

That Tuesday evening, at eight-thirty, the general summoned
Pompidou. In the antechamber, the premier noticed men standing
around looking like death. Tricot and Foccart placed their last feeble hopes in Pompidou. "Tell the general he can't leave this way.
It would be unworthy of him."

Pompidou was exhausted. Ever since 1962 he had often heard de
Gaulle say that he would quit the very next day. But this time Pompidou sensed that there would be no miracle. It had never occurred
to him, however, that the general would abandon the field so
quickly, thus hastening the onset of disaster. Pompidou felt
crushed. De Gaulle represented the last rampart; he was a symbol
that was desperately needed.

Before entering the chief of state's office the premier composed
his features in an attempt to appear serene and reassuring. "The
game has been won," he told the general. "Public opinion is beginning to tip toward us. The communists are staging a parade tomorrow in order to demonstrate their power. Then, everything will return to normal . . ."

"Ever since the crisis began you have been optimistic," retorted de Gaulle. "Alas, events have given you the lie. And I'm afraid the same thing will happen tomorrow."

The general reminded Pompidou that the communists were about to call for a general mobilization. This would mean revolution, and it would not be limited to France. It was the beginning of a world-wide upheaval. As for himself, he refused to run the supreme risk: to be encircled at the Elysée and delivered to the masses, like Louis XIV. Once again he expressed his regrets about the referendum because it would have given him the chance to make an honorable exit.

Pompidou suggested legislative elections. De Gaulle gestured, disconsolately. "Referendum, elections — it's all the same. All that is quite impossible. Besides, things have gotten beyond that. There's only one solution, I'm afraid."

Pompidou protested. De Gaulle's departure would serve as the signal for an explosion. It would mean the end of the Fifth Republic. With barricades in the streets, no Gaullist would have a chance to succeed the general in the presidency. And he, Pompidou, would no longer be in a position to control the situation.

The general would not budge. Yes, it would be the beginning of chaos. But you had to act with your eyes open. There were no longer any means, any instruments, with which to fight back. One couldn't hang on to power, it wouldn't do any good.

The interview lasted a long time. But de Gaulle steadfastly refused to change his somber plans.

After Pompidou, Christian Fouchet was summoned. The Minister of the Interior had also received advice from Tricot: "Tell the general he has no right to quit."

But powerless, Fouchet had to listen to a lengthy monologue: "Everything is collapsing, Fouchet. I had gotten to the point where I hoped Frenchmen would vote no at the referendum so I could leave with dignity. But we can't even go that far. Look at the picture: the country doesn't have a government anymore, or a bureaucracy, or even a police force. For ten years we have been trying to build up the state. But the French people don't want any part of it. Mitterand will last for a while because there's still gold and currency in the cashbox. Then there will be disaster. And thank God I'll no longer be here to witness it."

. .

That evening the general suddenly made up his mind. Within the next twenty-four hours he would escape from this "box of sorrows." All his faithful companions, who remained at his side and kept watching over him, ended up by exasperating him. He no longer could stand anyone, not even those members of his entourage who were closest to him.

Behind these masks of commiseration and devotion he detected the hunger for power always at the ready, betrayals always in the making. He was told that some Gaullists were already in contact with the enemy. This did not surprise him. He had witnessed a similar stampede in June 1940. But at that time he was twenty-eight years younger, and he had had the strength to rebel.

Yes, everything indicated that he must leave the Elysée, leave all the good and bad apostles who badgered him with their advice. He would carry off with him the republican legitimacy which he still embodied — but for how long? He would flee Paris and avoid becoming a prisoner in the Elysée, constrained by the hordes to sign his own abdication. He would remain unsullied, free to do as he pleased, if only for the last time.

De Gaulle was convinced that his retirement was inevitable. He ended up by deciding, however, that the least he could do was to stay on a few days, perhaps a few weeks, and at the same time spare himself a shameful end.

When the general left Paris on Wednesday, May 29, he held on to one last privilege — that of choice. He met one of his aides-de-camp on the stairway and calmly said to him: "I'll see you tomorrow."

Before leaving he wanted to reassure the premier and to erase the terrible impression he had made on him the preceding evening.

The general rejected the idea that his departure would be interpreted to mean that he was fleeing in the face of the enemy. On the phone he told Pompidou: "The cabinet meeting has been postponed for twenty-four hours. Don't worry, I'll be there tomorrow. I'm going to Colombey to meditate in peace."

Pompidou remained on the battlefield. As a token of encouragement and an expression of farewell, de Gaulle added: "I embrace you."

Two hours later the general had completely vanished. His helicopter at that moment was spotted emerging from the clouds above German soil.

. .

He did not intend to return. Pompidou had guessed it. The general had left, taking with him his nightmares and his tantrums. The appeasing words he had uttered on the telephone meant nothing. De Gaulle would not come back to Paris. In a few hours, perhaps a few days, the capital would be in the hands of the communists. Of this Pompidou was sure. In flying off as he had done, de Gaulle dropped a curtain of mystery behind him. This was his final gesture. Long after this dreadful month of May, the general stubbornly refused to explain his absence.

"Well, you know," he later remarked to Louis Joxe, "I always expected to dump everything: at Dakar, in Algiers, in Paris in nineteen forty-five, and even during the Algerian affair. You yourself heard me say so more than once."

Joxe did not venture to ask any more questions. "It would have been unseemly to revive such tragic memories," he explained. "The general will always feel the pain of that trip, when he rushed off to Germany with his family and all his luggage. But he'll keep the whole thing to himself."

On that Wednesday, May 29, as de Gaulle was flying somewhere between France and Baden, Pompidou realized the true reason for the general's departure: despair.

Left alone in Paris, the premier was at a loss. The general's ab-

sence deprived him of all legitimacy and made it impossible for him
to prepare for the future. His fate was linked with that of the chief
of state. He telephoned Tricot, who was also in a state of collapse.
"I absolutely have to know where the general is. Our last chance is
to hold elections. And he alone has the power to order the dissolution of the Assembly."

But at the Elysée there was total silence.

At the Matignon, surrounded by a small cohort of panicky Gaullists and barons who were urging him to assume the power that had
been abandoned, Pompidou was reduced to impotence. Frey, Guichard and Chaban wanted him to go before the French people immediately and affirm his right to succeed de Gaulle. They urged
him to begin his campaign for the presidency. But Pompidou felt
he had to wait.

"The President of the Republic goes off and his premier isn't even
told about it!" he exclaimed. "What could I tell the French people?
That I don't know where to find the president? What can I do?"

Pompidou was shocked by the clandestine flight. De Gaulle had
created a void, thereby preventing the premier from saving whatever could be saved. Although responsible to the electorate, the
premier had been relegated to the rank of a trivial assistant; he cut
the sorry figure of a man who had been left to God's good grace
without having been given a single key to power. He was no more
than the weaponless standard-bearer of an army at bay, facing enemies who had gone mad.

At six-thirty that night, the general put an end to the agony by
telephoning the Matignon from Colombey, where he had just arrived. His voice was strong again. He would be at the Elysée "at
the appointed time."

CHAPTER 15

The Flaw

DE GAULLE RETURNED, TRANSFORMED.

His extreme torpor had given way to a sudden spurt of energy — "the energy of a young man," according to a member of the cabinet. One could expatiate at length on the causes of the change. His conversation with General Massu, the commander in chief of the French troops in Germany? A night of rest at his home in Colombey? Or was it that de Gaulle, his eyes suddenly opened, realized that he had been guilty of a gross miscalculation? The communists had not seized power. After marching down the big boulevards, they had gone home, forsaking their allies, their dreams, and Mitterand.

De Gaulle had always been extremely sensitive to the general atmosphere. In Algeria, he had been carried away by the crowd. In spite of himself he had found himself shouting, "Long live French Algeria!" although he had always refused to do so before. In Quebec the same sort of thing had occurred. Again, he had been carried away by the "sea of human faces" crowding around him. Thus, his behavior was often determined by what he saw or heard.

In Baden, the spectacle he beheld affected him like an electric shock. He had left a country seething with anarchy. In Baden he found a bit of France, but an orderly France, with the tricolor floating at the top of the flagpole and officers proudly sporting their decorations. In General Massu's "eagle nest," he detected not the slightest sign of disquiet. He had walked past peaceful, unarmed soldiers and encountered officers eager to obey and to serve their state.

Turning his back on the unfamiliar and hostile world of politicians, trade unionists and university professors, he had returned to a universe that was his own; he was among men who were brothers in arms — "simple people," he said, "patriots." This was a pilgrimage to the very font of his destiny. What Massu or the other officers may have said to him was of no importance. The army does not question, a quality that made it "the finest of all things." Behind Massu's desk, photographs of Algeria reminded de Gaulle of how much mute suffering was to be found in military service, in obeying the injunctions of the army, of honor. The Black Forest spread out before him as far as the eye could see. Covering the seven hills of Baden, a thousand times more beautiful than the forests at Colombey, it inspired peace and wisdom.

De Gaulle tended to be swayed by sudden changes of mood. As he grew older, this tendency became more pronounced. How many times had Pompidou and others been obliged to buck him up! And how often had they found his joys excessive!

After his protracted depression, de Gaulle took advantage of the opportunity still open to him. Now that he had miraculously recovered his strength, he was determined to wage this final battle. He would hold out until the referendum, which would furnish a definitive answer. He had not changed his mind about the basic cause of the crisis: the spell between himself and the French people had been broken. But to quit power in the wake of a vote was quite different from capitulation in the very midst of a battle.

Upon returning to the Elysée on Thursday, the general worked out his strategy. He even wrote the text of the message that he intended to deliver to the French people. First, he would reestablish order by mobilizing the army of frightened men, just as he had done in 1948 at the time of the R.P.F. and when he had faced the colonels of Algiers. Then, as soon as calm had been restored, he would hold the referendum. But after that? Whether victorious or defeated, de Gaulle did not plan to remain much longer in public life. He knew that the crisis he had just undergone signified that his strength was declining. The great emptiness within him, which he had miraculously managed to overcome, was obvious proof that he had aged. Yes, to be sure, his memory was still good and his physical condition sound. It was deep within himself that de Gaulle had discovered a flaw, invisible but profound.

The referendum would be his last challenge. If he won it, he would at least have laid the groundwork for a new society. His successors would need only to follow in his footsteps. "Little by little, France will adapt herself to the change," de Gaulle said. "She will enjoy an advantage as she moves into the century of technology."

And what if Frenchmen answered no? Well, then he would return to Colombey and to silence. Later, much later, history would decide. De Gaulle may have suffered a terrible blow, but he was still on his feet; the institutions of his regime would be saved; and a precious legacy would be transmitted to France.

. .

Early in the afternoon, Pompidou visited the chief of state. The premier came to the Elysée firmly resolved to submit his resignation. The mysterious trip to Baden had been too much for him, at least so he told his friends. He still believed it was a blunder committed at the expense of his countrymen, a misguided action directed against the state, and against history, against the government as well, and against himself, Pompidou, the man de Gaulle trusted, the first of the general's collaborators.

He said to de Gaulle: "The French people want you to stay. That should be enough. There's no need for a referendum."

And again he offered to resign as premier.

De Gaulle refused to accept his resignation, at least for the moment. Frenchmen would not understand. The all-important thing now was to show that the state had not been adversely affected. With marked deference, Pompidou then stated his conditions: "The main thing is to dissolve the Assembly and to hold new elections. I

have been convinced of this ever since yesterday. And yet I am the
last person to have rallied to this idea."

De Gaulle reacted vehemently. To postpone the referendum in
order to hold legislative elections was pure nonsense. The state did
not reside within the Palais-Bourbon nor did it depend on a search
for a new majority party. The acquisition of a few more Gaullist
deputies was of no importance. What did matter was to get an answer to the following question: would the French people be willing
to allow de Gaulle to undertake this new task, the most important
and the final one? The general repeated: "I myself represent the
issue to be decided, Pompidou. I alone. It was against me that the
agitation was unleashed. This is a matter between the French people and de Gaulle."

Stubbornly, the premier urged that his plan be implemented.
From the very outset, the crisis had been fueled by divisions within
parliament, he argued. The cabinet was bound to fail if it were
forced to retain the present Assembly. Sooner or later a motion of
censure would be voted against him as premier. It would therefore
be wiser to replace the cabinet and its head immediately. Pompidou repeated: "Your hands are free, my general."

De Gaulle did not see the matter in this light. He was not opposed to legislative elections. He had remarked to Couve on several
occasions during the past few weeks that such elections must be
held. "You can't govern or initiate a great social reform with the
present Assembly," he had said.

But although agreeing about the elections, de Gaulle insisted that
they must take place later, after the referendum.

"It's the only way to restore calm," Pompidou nevertheless repeated. "I'm convinced of it. To be logical, if you keep the chamber as it is, you will have to appoint a new cabinet with a different
man to lead it."

This possibility did not disturb de Gaulle in the least, since he had
not given up the idea of parting with Pompidou. But all this would
be done after the referendum, not before. That was his refrain.
"I'm keeping you," de Gaulle said. "I don't want to make any deci-

sion that might appear to have been forced upon me by events. First, order, then the referendum — that's all I see for the moment."

Pompidou reversed the dictum: no referendum without a prior return to normal conditions. This meant elections, first of all. Once again he offered to resign. "If you lose the referendum, my general, your regime will be doomed. If I lose the elections, I alone will be the loser."

The general tried to control his mounting anger. Where was the Pompidou of yesterday? Confronting him now was a man with whom he, de Gaulle, had to reckon, to bargain and to reach a compromise; a man who sought to impose his own views, who raised his voice, who exhibited self-confidence and scarcely tried to conceal his own political ambitions.

Now, more than ever, the general was determined to dismiss the premier. Pompidou was getting in his way. But he could do nothing about it for the moment. He therefore yielded on the question of the elections, but vowed to get rid of Pompidou as soon as they had been held and after the call for a referendum had been issued. Having thus made a few concessions without, however, yielding on the major issue, the general kept his resentment to himself.

The rupture dated from that moment. De Gaulle had lifted an unknown administrator from obscurity; but Pompidou had apparently forgotten this.

· ·

When the general appeared for the cabinet meeting, he took pains to conceal his anger. He even began by complimenting Pompidou on his "ability," his "strength of character," his "skill" and "courage." The ministers had forgotten what such praise from de Gaulle usually heralded. They no longer remembered the fate of Salan, Debré and Giscard. Pompidou himself scarcely noticed what the general said next: "After the elections, the cabinet will resign. It might then be opportune to appoint a new premier."

This was hardly the moment to speculate about the future the general had in mind for Pompidou. The premier still held his post and his views had been adopted. Surely, he was indispensable.

De Gaulle agreed to alter the text of the speech that he was to broadcast by radio that afternoon. The first version was placed in a safe at the Elysée; it was destined to be added to the historical archives that had been accumulating for the past ten years.

Parisians took to the streets, this time shouting "Long live de Gaulle!" The demonstration on the Champs-Elysées had been organized by the barons, Frey and Foccart, and by former members of the Free French movement. Every type of group or association had been appealed to. Old-time Gaullists as well as last-minute ones were invited to demonstrate. Pompidou, who did not believe that this mobilization would be successful, remained at the Matignon. "My place is not in the streets," he said.

But when he learned that hundreds of thousands had participated in the demonstration, he was amazed. Later, he was to say: "Parisians marched on May thirteenth. And they marched again on May thirtieth, but for the very opposite reason. And these were the same people. Paris is a whore."

Standing at his window in the Elysée, the general watched the billowing waves of humanity flooding the Champs-Elysées, as they had done on the day of Liberation. But he guessed that this Gaullist victory, born of fear, would have no morrow. "There are a lot of people," he said to his aide-de-camp.

"Yes, my general, I'm happy for your sake."

"Oh, if it were only for me . . ."

Now, two days before the end of May, bruised by the experiences of the last three weeks, the general approached the final chapter, the epilogue of his adventure. Hoping to act quickly, he planned to leave behind him an image that would not be unworthy of the de Gaulle legend. But nothing could ever erase deep within him this springtime of sorrow and disorder, nor the shouts of ingratitude hurled on May 13 by the French people: "Ten years, that's enough!"

·   ·

Once the May crisis was over, the general again found himself face to face with Georges Pompidou, the number-one witness of his calvary. It was going to be difficult from now on to conceal his annoyance. He said to the members of his entourage: "The premier has been at his post for six years. He is worn out."

But the legislative elections had to be organized, since unfortunately they had already been announced. This was to be Pompidou's last task.

The France that the general was discovering corresponded neither to his ideas nor to his memories. "I no longer recognize our nation," he remarked to a minister.

Endlessly, he mulled over the question of how things had reached such a pass. A month earlier, everything had been in order. The state was "basically solid," the exchequer "well filled." Advance orders in business heralded a year of full employment and considerable expansion. Then suddenly the dams had burst and the flood had swept everything away. De Gaulle kept harking back to this defeat. As early as June 1, he drew a harsh conclusion from the crisis: "The state allowed itself to be overcome by events that no one could foresee or control. The government allowed itself to be intimidated. It dreaded bloody confrontations that would never have occurred."

The general reproached himself bitterly. He was the chief of state, the one person who had full responsibility. But deep down he raged against the cabinet and the premier. In June he told Joxe: "I'm not going to dwell on what happened during the month of May. But I cannot condone it."

De Gaulle had granted freedom of action to his trusted agents. This was the one thing he could not forgive himself for. But it was impossible to distinguish publicly between acts that could be laid at the door of the premier and those for which the President of the Republic was responsible. During the election campaign, the two were inextricably interwoven.

Only to the members of his intimate circle did the general talk about his dissatisfaction with Pompidou. He blamed the premier for having allowed the Sorbonne to remain open. He alluded repeatedly to this unwise decision.

"Yes, it certainly deserves to be criticized," he said to Couve de Murville, "because it did not produce the expected result. Thereafter the contagion was bound to spread. The factories were occupied and the state was disgraced."

Throughout the ensuing ten months the general constantly plagued Pompidou with it, sometimes in very cavalier fashion. In February 1969, gesticulating angrily, he said to Christian Fouchet: "The Sorbonne should never have been left open — never!"

"But then, my general, the police would have had to open fire and there would have been casualties."

"Well, what of it! Maybe fifty people would have been killed. I would have replaced the premier immediately."

Pompidou was told about the general's criticism. He too was to suffer a long time because of his decision, but he always refused to admit that he had made a mistake.

There was no debate on the subject within the cabinet. Only once did de Gaulle allude to the "weakness" of the government. Nor were questions raised about the negotiations with the trade unions, although the general deplored the fact that the cabinet "had given in to the very limit of the country's economic capacity."

"But no one has forgotten that when the negotiations began on the Rue de Grenelle, the government literally had a knife at its throat," Couve de Murville observed.

Now an enthusiasm no one honestly felt had to be whipped up. De Gaulle and Pompidou were involved in an election campaign. Better by far to give the impression of unity. In a televised interview on June 7, the general carefully avoided saying anything that might prove embarrassing. "I personally observed that throughout the crisis, the government remained entirely united around the President of the Republic. I don't know any other regime that has set such a fine example."

. .

Having accepted the idea of elections, de Gaulle now saw that he could use them to reestablish the state's authority, upon which grave inroads had been made. This became his primary objective. The premier, for his part, considered the elections his personal affair. He knew that he was gambling his future.

The preparations for the elections were quite different from prior ones. This time, the general did not neglect what he called the political "soup."

After the first round of balloting, which presaged a Gaullist tidal wave, the general said to an old companion with a coldness that the events did not warrant: "I won't stay long."

Eight days later, in the wake of his party's victory on June 30, he evinced even greater disillusionment. It seemed that the time had come to take stock. All the Gaullists, the barons, even public opinion attributed the miraculous reversal to Pompidou. Rumors of this reached the Elysée, where de Gaulle stoically bore up under this fresh manifestation of ingratitude. To some of his closest advisers, he nonetheless said: "These elections were bound to come out as they did. The situation was desperate, and the French heeded my appeal."

On the other side of the Seine, Pompidou looked upon the elections as a nod from Providence. The voters had confirmed his destiny as a statesman. He spoke as top dog. "Whatever happens," he said to a newly elected deputy, "I will never again allow the police to enter university property."

It was to him that the Gaullists swore their oath of allegiance.

. .

Between the two rounds of balloting, when the Gaullist victory was not yet certain, Pompidou once again offered to resign. He spoke of his "extreme fatigue." Good-humoredly, the general answered: "We'll talk about it some other time."

A week later, on the Monday following the second round, the premier was again summoned to the Elysée. In Pompidou's pres-

ence, the general congratulated himself on the outcome of the elections. The vote, he said, was a landslide greater than any that had
occurred in France in the last fifty years. This was no time for complaints: the massive majority, whether it consisted of progressives or
conservatives, would be loyal to de Gaulle. It would enable him to
govern. This was a great day.

Pompidou was about to leave; de Gaulle, before accompanying
him to the door, inquired solicitously: "And what about you? Have
you decided?"

The premier mentioned his weariness, as he had already done, his
longing to rest a little after the fever of the spring. He added that it
might be politically useful to appoint a new cabinet. The general
replied that such was not his opinion. "If you and I separate, it will
look like a defeat. We have won the election together. We must
continue . . ."

Pompidou repeated that he wished to resign. De Gaulle advised
him to take two days to think it over. He saw Pompidou to the
door, then shook his hand warmly. "I thank you. I still need you."

Pompidou returned to the Matignon. In the fever of the election
campaign, he had scarcely had time to think about the future. But
now he was incontestably the standard-bearer of the majority that
was flooding the Palais-Bourbon. Events had proved that he deserved the title of Dauphin.

Since de Gaulle indulged in the luxury of mystery, Pompidou, as a
good disciple as well as a talented actor, allowed uncertainty to
spread about his own decision. Choice was no longer the general's
exclusive prerogative. Henceforth, power politics was a game that
two could play. That Monday afternoon, the incumbent premier assembled all his deputies, paid them compliments and granted certain favors to a few.

On Tuesday and Wednesday, following the general's advice,
Pompidou thought things over. He questioned his friends, his collaborators at the Matignon and a few ministers. All of them predicted that the immediate future would be difficult. It could even

be stormy. The economy, the university, finances, the October rendezvous — all these were bound to preoccupy the cabinet.

What about the general? Some predicted that he would retire in six months, or at the most, in a year. Others insisted that he would remain in the presidency until his term had expired in 1972. Pompidou collected all these conjectures and predictions.

"According to one hypothesis, the general will quit next spring," the premier's advisers told him. "If this is correct, then it would be good strategy for you to withdraw. Your prestige would not be impaired. On the contrary, you would safeguard your future and avoid the troubles of this autumn. According to a second hypothesis, the general will remain in power for four years. If so, you should remain at the Matignon in order to make sure that you will not be forgotten after such a long time span."

Opinions differed widely. Pompidou was inclined to accept the first hypothesis. After the terrible May riots, the general would probably want to make sure that he could beat an honorable retreat. Besides, he had indicated such an intention quite recently. If de Gaulle stayed on for at least a year, his departure would necessitate a new presidential election and force Pompidou to do battle then and there. It might therefore be a good idea to prepare for the election during the coming months while he would be in semiretirement. Pompidou could travel, read, listen and meditate. He could get himself into good form.

That Wednesday, after a meeting of the cabinet, Pompidou said to Tricot: "As I told the general, I really would like to rest. I've had more than my fill of forming new cabinets, of having to face the fury of those who've been dismissed . . . I'd like to take advantage of this respite to visit countries I've never seen, and to meet their leaders."

The following day General and Madame de Gaulle entertained Georges and Claude Pompidou at a small, intimate dinner. The premier would be fifty-seven the next day. It was a somewhat premature birthday party. In the presence of the ladies all kinds of topics were discussed — everything but politics. But alone with de

Gaulle over coffee, Pompidou discreetly reminded the general of his desire to get some much needed rest to recover his strength after all these terrible weeks.

He then restated his attitude in a letter which he had delivered by hand to the Elysée.

A few days later, he admitted: "Often the general and I had talked about who would succeed him. It seemed to me that were I to take over his job, I would only be doing what he himself had envisioned. That's what I told the chief of state."

.   .

De Gaulle, meanwhile, jumped at the chance to get rid of Pompidou. But he did not immediately appoint a new premier. Rather, he allowed uncertainty to spread. That Friday morning, at the close of a conference held at the Matignon by several members of the cabinet, Couve said to Pompidou: "Do you know who the new premier will be? Neither you nor me. Probably Messmer."

The premier telephoned Foccart. It was true; the general was considering Messmer, for seven years his "perfect" Minister of the Army. But he had not yet made up his mind.

At the Matignon fresh consultations were held. Pompidou couldn't believe it. Messmer as premier!

"Since the general's visit to Massu," people began to say, "it looks as if Gaullism is being swallowed up by the military."

From then on the future of Gaullism became to some extent Pompidou's concern. Throughout the day he conferred with the majority leaders. He emerged from these consultations claiming that the "people begged him" to change his mind about resigning.

That evening, when Pompidou returned to his home in the Ile Saint-Louis, his wife and sister-in-law gave him the same advice. For the first time since he had been considering the matter, the two ladies ventured an opinion. "It may seem ridiculous," Pompidou later confessed, "but I was agitated all night long."

On the following morning, Saturday, he telephoned Bernard Tricot and asked him to give the general a message: having thought things over, he would be available if the chief of state wanted him; he was willing to resume his post if he could be useful.

Later that morning, Pierre Lazareff, the editor of *France-Soir,* came to see Pompidou. The premier invited him to lunch.

Lazareff arrived at the Matignon a little early. He immediately went into Pompidou's office. "Well, what will you do when you're no longer here?" he asked.

The premier paled. "Have you heard something?" he asked. Lazareff proceeded to give Pompidou the latest news. In the course of their conversation, the telephone rang. It was Tricot calling from the Elysée. "I gave the general your message," he told Pompidou. "But it was too late. Steps had already been taken. Couve was appointed premier yesterday, after dinner." In all sincerity, Tricot added: "It's really too bad!"

The entire political seraglio soon learned of Pompidou's humiliation. A few deputies shed genuine tears. Others began to wonder. The retired premier put a good face on it. Four days later, at a farewell luncheon he gave for his cabinet, he explained the situation. But the French public was informed only of André Malraux's toast. Malraux raised his glass to drink to the future of "the gentleman deputy from Cantal" — such was the only official title to which the former premier was now entitled.

Pompidou's response has not been recorded. How much distress and unavowed disappointment it would have revealed! "I have heard it said here and there that certain differences of opinion arose between the general and me," Pompidou later commented. "Actually, I don't remember that we ever differed during the past six years. In any case, not before May thirtieth."

And in a reverential tone, he added: "But if these rumors were true, I would be deeply distressed, please believe me."

. .

Pompidou often had seen de Gaulle behave cruelly or unfairly toward men who had served him unselfishly. This did not surprise him. But he never thought that one day he himself would be a victim of the monarch's ingratitude. Unusual ties had been formed between him and de Gaulle, or at least so he believed. He would never lend himself to the kind of humiliation that Debré, Giscard and others of lesser rank had experienced. He had taken quite literally the chief of state's indications of favor. To be sure, a premier could be replaced; but one did not part with a dauphin.

Tricot's telephone call and the impersonal manner in which Pompidou had been dismissed had taken him by surprise. Pompidou was very upset. He reviewed all his years of docility, unable to understand the general's coldness. "I've been tricked," he sighed in the presence of a few friends.

For a moment he forgot that he himself had wanted to leave, that he had weighed all the advantages of taking a rest. It was the way de Gaulle had proceeded that seemed so outrageous. Pompidou had been cashiered as if he were a complete failure. In his own heart and mind, he knew that he had been the most adroit, the most zealous, and the most vigilant of all the general's collaborators.

Naturally, there would be an exchange of letters to formalize the rupture. De Gaulle wrote long, flattering phrases as if nothing had been changed in Pompidou's destiny. The ex-premier, embittered, did not send the letter of resignation he had promised to Tricot. Instead, he wrote three laconic lines that alluded vaguely to the constitution.

The general felt no remorse whatsoever. "I never had any intention of keeping the same government for ten years," he said, alluding to the end of his presidential mandate. "There's no reason for Pompidou to be surprised. I had told him many times what I intended to do, and he himself had agreed."

Ten days after that painful Saturday, Pompidou said to a member of the cabinet: "Some people have thought of me for the presidency of the National Assembly. That's out of the question. I prefer to be an ordinary deputy."

Having held a high post, he could not think of a single position that would not represent a comedown. All that remained now was his legend, his undeniable influence within the Gaullist family

where almost every member owed him something. As just another
Gaullist deputy, he had to submit to the hard rule of loyalty and silence.

On Wednesday, July 10, after Pompidou's last cabinet meeting,
which proved quite a painful experience for him, he was surrounded
by a group of Gaullist deputies whose honorary president he had become. He calmed the ardor of his partisans: "If so many of us are
here," he declared, "it is thanks to General de Gaulle and his influence."

Pompidou, more than anyone else, commanded the obedience of
the deputies. It was now up to him to set the example. The general
would not tolerate a marshal in his midst. In spite of what his followers were saying or hoping for, he was only Georges Pompidou, a
deputy from Cantal, a man with no special honors or privileges.

.   .

In July Pompidou went to Carnac in Brittany, a town of 3700 in-
habitants whose number in the summer swelled to four times that.
For political reasons, the former premier had decided to give Saint-
Tropez a wide berth; the place was too much in the swim of things.
He settled down in a house screened by high bushes that smelled of
the sea.

With him was his wife, one or two brothers-in-law, one or two
nieces, books, cards and easy chairs in the sun. He was determined
to get some rest. But too many memories and plans were at work,
agitating him and preventing him from having a real vacation.

The few friends who came to see him — they seemed to be making a pilgrimage — noted that he was trying hard to forget the
month of May and all its consequences. He still felt keen resentment and sometimes he yielded to it. "One thing consoles me," he
said, his gray eyes lighting up, "and that is that Couve is my successor."

Couve was making his debut under trying circumstances. Pompidou enumerated the problems that were bound to arise as soon as
the summer was over. One day his niece complained that the price

she had paid for a pair of shoes in Carnac was twice as high as the one she would have had to pay in Paris. Pompidou commented: "You can be sure that the premier is not the man to straighten out economic affairs or settle the problem of prices."

He kept coming back to all he had lost. The idleness to which he was now reduced was dull and sickening. "I feel as if I have just emerged from Plato's cave and have to keep blinking," he said. "But I suppose this is only temporary."

He had looked forward to taking long walks against the wind, to buying his own newspapers and cigarettes on the boardwalk, to doing the simple things he used to do — resuming old habits acquired before 1962. But nothing of the kind! "I want to stay out of things," he nonetheless insisted.

Everything reminded him of de Gaulle, even this exile in the provinces which for twelve years de Gaulle had experienced, managing, however, to turn it into a work of art of sorts.

He tried to reassure himself: "Couve doesn't have a chance. He has no future with the voters." But then he remembered other examples: Debré, Mendès-France, Pinay — all of them hurriedly forgotten by the French people as soon as they were removed from office.

Georges Pompidou was a deputy from Cantal, one member of a parliamentary majority that consisted of 300 deputies. The general's promises, the Gaullists' oath of allegiance, the acclaim of his countrymen — these would not last forever.

.   .

Luck alone was left, but Pompidou felt that it would be kind to him. The thought that he might have a future consoled him a little for the blow he had just suffered.

Since the month of May, almost all the Gaullists had come to believe that the monarch's reign would soon be over. On May 29, Chaban-Delmas, chatting with a friend who visited him at nine in the evening, stated quite flatly: "Although the game has been won, the general is finished."

Even Debré was mystified by de Gaulle's confusion, his mental lapses. And the general himself never stopped saying that he wouldn't be there for long. Everything associated with his name and career — the solidity of the state, the stability of its institutions, the loyalty of his Gaullists, the value of the franc, respect for order — all these were again being called into question. De Gaulle knew that he was too old to reform his country in accordance with his plans, or to embark again upon epic undertakings in order to erase the memories of the shameful recent past.

Day after day, as he listened to the stories that people were telling him, he realized how close he had come to the very brink of ruin. And he was afraid that the abyss might open up again.

Pompidou was aware of the general's dark thoughts. "De Gaulle is a broken man," he kept saying.

He held that in a year or two at the most, the question of who would succeed to the presidency was bound to arise. He had no doubt that the succession belonged to him.

Part V

THE QUARREL

. . . O, how wretched
Is that poor man that hangs on princes' favours!
There is, betwixt that smile we would aspire to,
That sweet aspect of princes, and their ruin,
More pangs and fears than wars or women have:
And when he falls, he falls like Lucifer,·
Never to hope again.

Henry VIII, *act 3, scene 2*

CHAPTER 16

The Baneful Effects of May

As soon as Couve de Murville had put together a new cabinet, de Gaulle notified his minister that participation would be the order of the day. Everything that this word signified would be spelled out to them almost daily. That the general was now set on this course was demonstrated by the fact that at one out of every two cabinet meetings held between the summer of 1968 and of the spring of 1969, he brought up the question.

In mid-July, the general asked his minister in charge of reforms, Jeanneney, to get to work immediately. He himself drew up a blueprint for the way in which business, regions, institutions, and universities would participate.

Jeanneney, the son of a deceased President of the Senate, intended to proceed with these reforms in the usual way, through parliamentary channels. There was a large Gaullist majority in the Assembly. The minister sounded out the deputies, analyzed various constitutional texts, and pored over all kinds of studies on the subject. Then he took the results of his work to the Elysée.

The general turned a deaf ear to Jeanneney's explanations. "If we go about it this way," de Gaulle said, "if we try to please the deputies and senators, the results will be mediocre."

In acid tones, he reminded Jeanneney of the interminable parliamentary debates that had prevented the Third and Fourth Republics from enacting any profound or lasting reforms. "I want to do this quickly," he added. "In parliament, things can drag on for months or years. There will be a rash of motions, votes will be cast for one thing or another, and in the end nothing will be left of the reform."

In the general's view, participation was the kind of thing that ought to be determined by a referendum. "It's up to the French people, not to the deputies, to decide whether they will join us in our efforts. It's up to them to signify their desire for social renovation."

The general said that his referendum had been merely delayed by events, not canceled. He needed to recover the confidence of his countrymen, to be reassured about his legitimacy, which had been severely challenged in December 1965, and even more gravely last spring. "Only the consent of the people as a whole will enable us to achieve our ends and surmount all the obstacles that will surely arise as we go along," he told his associates.

Once again, de Gaulle wanted to put the question to the French people, by-passing all intermediaries. To his ministers, de Gaulle explained the matter as follows: "What we need is a very simple plan. One that will make the issues so clear that everyone will be able to understand them."

His first objective, then, was to win the approval of his countrymen. De Gaulle no longer alluded to something he had said in May, during his bleakest hours: "This referendum will serve as a good pretext for quitting with dignity." Besides, during the early part of the summer, it had not yet occurred to anyone, least of all to de Gaulle, that the answer might very well turn out to be negative. Having undertaken a task, he no longer spoke of quitting, neither to his intimates nor even to his family. His decision would be determined by statistics: if he obtained more than 60 per cent of the votes, he would stay — perhaps even to the end of his mandate. If he obtained less, he would resign.

.   .

"During this entire period," Jeanneney has recalled, "I spent several sessions working alone with him. He would discuss the texts I had prepared, going over them very carefully; at no time did I have the impression that he was thinking of withdrawing from the presidency before the expiration of his mandate."

In actual fact, the referendum represented his last challenge. De Gaulle was gambling his fate. What mattered most to him was to keep his historic image untarnished. The word "succession" displeased him as much as ever. Now, as before — indeed ever since his return to power in 1958 — he preferred the word "continuation."

In the beginning, during the sixties, the general had sought another historical personality as his successor. He had seriously considered the Comte de Paris, the heir of the kings of France, in whom he saw the repository of a legitimacy born of past centuries. He had even appointed the Comte de Paris to the presidency of the Red Cross, thinking that this might serve as a springboard for a career in public life. Then, having reluctantly given up the idea, the general considered one by one a number of men who already enjoyed a certain fame.

Since December 1965, de Gaulle had learned that universal suffrage was a hard test to pass. He had found this out himself. Characteristically, he remarked: "Of all the possible candidates for the presidency, Pompidou has the best chance of getting elected." The former premier was being kept "on ice"; the general had not changed his mind about this.

But now there was a new premier who as such became the president's natural heir. Couve had become a front runner simply because the general had chosen him. "I know of course that Frenchmen think he is boring and lugubrious . . ." de Gaulle said to one of his collaborators.

Then he went on to say the very same thing he had said about Pompidou in 1962: "He'll work into it. In any event, he won't play his own political game."

.   .

France was still suffering from the havoc wreaked in May. The scars and destruction were everywhere evident. Indelible memories had been seared into people's minds. The summer loomed as a brief intermission between that mad spring and an autumn that everyone dreaded. Couve de Murville had accepted without enthusiasm the uncertain role of successor. He would have preferred to see Pompidou saddled for a few months at least with the consequences of the crisis. Then, just as his predecessor had done six years before, he would have been able to step into a stable situation at the Matignon. He mentioned this to the general but refrained from stressing the point. The general did not listen. Allowing nothing of his true feelings to show, exhibiting only that fastidious ennui that all the capitals of Europe knew so well, Couve became the premier of the day. With his slim, unmuscular figure, his forehead lined with indecipherable cares, and his soft voice, he seemed to be the very epitome of disillusionment. His appointment displeased only Pompidou's partisans.

Couve had served for ten years as de Gaulle's official assistant in the battle waged by the general to force the world to accord France an honorable place. Seeing in Couve a discreet artisan, the chief of state credited him with having co-authored the vast plan.

Couve has acknowledged with imperceptible irony that fate did its work well. "It so happened that my point of view coincided with de Gaulle's," he said. "There's nothing mysterious about foreign policy. It's a matter of conviction. In the ten years I've spent at the Quai d'Orsay, only once have I disagreed with the chief of state. And the issue was merely a debate at the United Nations on a relatively secondary matter."

He was appointed foreign minister in 1958 because the general had requested his chief of staff, Pompidou, to find the most experienced and highest-ranking diplomat. The name of Couve de Murville, who was then posted to Bonn, was taken from the files of the Quai d'Orsay.

Taken by surprise, Ambassador de Murville learned of his promotion while he was playing a round of golf. At first he discharged his new functions as if he were a "diplomat on special duty." As time passed, self-confidence and ambition increased. After having en-

joyed a special status within the Gaullist family, he discovered his
political vocation. This occurred in 1967 at the Gaullist party con-
vention in Lille. Here he along with André Malraux were among
the most applauded heroes.

Couve displayed all the necessary obstinacy when de Gaulle pronounced anathemas — against the Americans, against the British,
against the champions of an integrated Europe, against the two
blocs created at Yalta, against the representatives of "totalitarian
communism," and against the "domineering" Israelis. His very silence served to reinforce the chief of state's diatribes. That was his
prime virtue.

Couve was born to an upper middle-class family. He was also un-
bending, like all Protestants from the Cévennes area, some of whose
ancestors were Camisards. Finally, he had always been a great servant of the state — before the war as Inspector of Finance, after the
war as a diplomat. He had never trafficked with the world of private interests. No one suspected him of itching for money; his comfortable standard of living had all the earmarks of being a boon from
the Almighty, a natural and abundant gift. He was the living coun-
terpart of Pompidou, the negative of a snapshot.

De Gaulle discovered in Couve the makings of a statesman. The
general believed that Couve had a national destiny. But once again
de Gaulle clashed head-on with reality. "Couve has no talent for
getting himself elected," he was forced to admit.

This lack perhaps represented an additional asset in the general's
eyes. But it was also a handicap. In appointing Couve to replace
Pompidou, de Gaulle had hoped that he would somehow manage to
win the favor of public opinion. In any case, he would be assuming
the post because of de Gaulle's confidence in him, not because of a
popularity that boded no good.

Couve gave himself four years, until the next presidential election, to accomplish all that the President of the Republic expected
of him.

. .

His first task was to form a government. It would be awkward to put new men in key positions. Those who lost their posts would be envious and resentful. Anxious to avoid having a group of embittered malcontents on his hands, Couve proceeded with tact and delicacy. He tried not to hurt anyone's feelings. A natural diplomat, he was loath by a stroke of the pen to relegate some incumbent minister to an obscure position. He therefore did his best to retain the team he had inherited, thus avoiding ill will.

Couve's strategy was one of prudence and patience; Pompidou had set the example. "I estimated that it would take me a year and a half or two years to settle the most urgent problems and to get the situation in hand," he said. Then he added: "Under the circumstances, I wondered about the most propitious moment for holding the referendum."

Once installed in the Matignon, the premier hoped he would have a short respite. "The French people need a period of calm. They are tired of having constantly to vote on issues."

But de Gaulle insisted. He was in a hurry. And so with much patience Couve went to work. Week after week he tried to appease the public anger that was still smoldering and might at any moment burst into flames. In his view, to hold a referendum now was to risk another holocaust. By gaining a few days here, a few more weeks there, Couve hoped to delay the referendum until the autumn of 1969, fifteen months from now.

But the general was adamant.

. .

After a gloomy summer at Carnac, Pompidou returned to Paris. Acquiescing to the request, included in de Gaulle's letter of thanks, that he should hold himself in readiness, Pompidou settled down at his listening post on the other side of the Seine, on the Boulevard de Latour-Maubourg. The Minister of the Interior had made an apartment available there. The offices were huge, the ceilings high. The former premier and the small group of associates he took with him found these quarters quite comfortable even though there were very few furnishings and almost no files. Pompidou selected the smallest office for himself. The windows opened onto a courtyard. He had a few modern paintings hung on the walls and placed flower vases on the tables. In an adjoining room, two secretaries handled his mail; nearby, a chauffeur and a bodyguard killed time working on crossword puzzles.

Pompidou was only a few yards away from the Palais-Bourbon and the cabinet. His offices were very conveniently situated for anyone who might wish to visit him. On his desk was a plain telephone, very different from the large instrument studded with red and green flashing lights he had used when issuing orders and conducting the affairs of state at the Matignon.

The rhythm of his life, he confessed, had been interrupted in a way he found most disconcerting. To allay a persistent feeling of nostalgia, Pompidou returned to his early literary pursuits. He started to write a book dealing with political ethics, a work of meditation inspired by his teacher, Alain.

His rise in politics had not cured him of the passion for writing that had possessed him for almost thirty years. The only area in which he had failed so far was literature. He had published only commonplace academic works, and this bothered him. He was jealous of Malraux's literary fame, to say nothing of de Gaulle's. He, too, thought of himself as a writer and dreamt of being read by people all over the world. Now that he had the leisure, he would prove himself. Unfortunately, however, an active political career and the harboring of sundry ambitions were not compatible with the solitary, ivory-tower life suitable for an author.

Faced with blank sheets of paper, Pompidou fought a new kind of battle. But, if the truth must be told, he was bored. It was quite a comedown, even pure misery, for a premier to be reduced to the thousand and one petty preoccupations of an ordinary deputy — attending lunches, answering mail, calling on ministers, and so on. Pompidou was fifty-eight — much too young for the routine of semiretirement. Even his evenings in town, the art exhibits and avant-garde movies he attended did not help him to fight off the political bug that had bitten him.

His protégés, including those who were still at their posts, reported all the gossip to him. Pompidou did not relish what de Gaulle was saying about him. Every Monday evening, he invited former collaborators, ministers and others, to have a drink of loyalty with him. At these gatherings, the goings-on of the government were discussed, along with the mood of the general. For more than ten years the state had been an open book to him.

Pompidou brooded over the real significance of his departure; no longer was he the general's confidant, the "great man's" *collaborator and friend forever* — as de Gaulle had pledged in an inscription on a photo. Well and good. But he could not resign himself to being criticized and even, it seemed, lampooned by the chief of state. He took great pride in his achievements and in the influence he had exerted.

He himself could see how he was being disgraced. De Gaulle had promised to maintain a "particularly close relationship" with him. But weeks went by and nothing happened. In moments of rancor, he began to wonder whether he would be condemned to cool his heels until December 1972, when de Gaulle's presidential mandate would expire.

Many things could of course happen in three years, not all of them favorable. And yet his title of Dauphin had not been taken from him. On the contrary, the general continued to say to anyone who would listen that Pompidou would probably succeed him.

De Gaulle spoke in this vein to ministers and even to deputies. This was likewise his refrain when he chatted with his own family. Everyone was thus given to understand that Pompidou's departure was part and parcel of a prearranged strategy. In private de Gaulle explained: "I wanted my former premier to become disengaged from everyday political and partisan doings." In the meantime, Pompidou would do well to forget his days as premier. He needed to broaden his horizons, to acquire greater stature. "All this is really in his own interest," de Gaulle said, "as well as in those of the nation."

But immersed in his sorrow, Pompidou was not moved by these remarks. How often had he heard de Gaulle say such things!

The deputy from Cantal had no intention of remaining on the sidelines. He had to be present and vigilant. He knew "better than anyone else," as he kept saying, that de Gaulle had broken down in May. He did not believe that the general would hang on to power. Rather, he thought that one fine morning he would leave — in his usual theatrical and unexpected way — just as he had done in January 1946, before the French people had time to realize what was happening.

This possibility was being whispered at all levels of the Gaullist hierarchy. Some even surmised that on June 18, 1970, thirty years to the day since the launching of his famous appeal, the general would resign.

As if de Gaulle needed anniversaries to pace himself! Eighteen months, two years, or three, what did it matter? Georges Pompidou could not afford to tarry on the long and uncertain road to power. But the path he would follow was dangerous, the door narrow. Never could he traffic with the opposition. Circumstances forced him to remain in the Gaullist camp. Should he speak out or express the slightest reservations, the general and the Gaullists would turn their backs on him. Yet if he remained silent and content to intone the oath of obedience, he would be forgotten.

By September Pompidou had worked out his strategy. He would rely on the parliamentary majority, on the Gaullist group in the Assembly. In a presidential campaign they would prove invaluable allies. As the leader of a large and powerful contingent, he would be able to keep an eye on the government and on Couve without displaying any distrust of the general.

This was not what de Gaulle had in mind for a future chief of state. Politics, parliament, unimportant interests were the very reverse of what he associated with the dignity of the presidency. Pompidou was foolishly espousing the views of a small cohort of grumblers who were hostile at heart to the referendum and to great social reforms. The general was worried.

In mid-September, the Gaullists met at La Baule where summer vacationers were still enjoying the beach. They launched a concerted offensive against the general's program of university reforms. There was lively discussion, even some shouting. Coolly observing the protagonists, Pompidou — who of course had been welcomed by the small turbulent court — issued a warning to his successor at the Matignon. "Our group," he declared, "expects to be called upon to participate."

This annoyed de Gaulle. He expressed his disappointment in no uncertain terms. First, there was Debré, a foreign minister who "secretly torpedoes our plans." And now Pompidou was lending himself to squabbles offstage. This, the general exclaimed, was "lamentable."

De Gaulle urged his followers to hold firm; reforms must be enacted. He summed up his position by stating — in Latin — "There is nothing like having principles."

.   .

Toward the close of September, four days before the parliamentary debate on university reforms, Pompidou, having already been invited to consultations at the Matignon, was asked to dine at the Elysée. The general was his most amiable self. When coffee was served, he alluded to more serious subjects: education, of course — a new academic year was beginning — the referendum, and social reform.

On the subject of the referendum, the former premier showed no eagerness to oppose de Gaulle. A few days before, he had remarked to one of the barons: "In any event, the general has made up his mind and nothing can induce him to change it. So let's hold this referendum — some other might be even worse."

Pompidou responded to the general's questions without betraying the slightest trace of annoyance. "The referendum should be held as soon as possible," he agreed. "Before February fifteenth, if possible. The longer we wait, the greater the risks. It seems to me that the first week of February or the latter part of January would be best."

De Gaulle concurred. He was determined not to allow the preparations to drag on. "By February the people will still remember May and the results will be all the more favorable, my general," Pompidou said.

Visibly satisfied, the general talked about the future, Pompidou's future. He again alluded to the premier's "national destiny." He encouraged and advised him. Pompidou must shun the corridors of the Palais-Bourbon and all such "shady political dealings." The atmosphere in the Assembly was not healthy. Pompidou ought to go abroad, talk to people, meet other chiefs of state. That was the only requisite he still lacked.

Paternally, de Gaulle planned an itinerary for Pompidou. It was to be systematic: first Italy, then Great Britain, finally the United States. But to begin with, as an hors d'oeuvre of sorts, he ought to go to Yugoslavia.

However, Pompidou had to give up this trip, which had been planned for the end of the year. He did so reluctantly as a consequence of events soon to be recounted which precipitated an estrangement between the two men.

CHAPTER 17

High Stakes

THE GENERAL ASKED EVERYONE the same question: "When are we going to hold the referendum?" And everyone counseled prudence. All the Gaullists, from the premier to the last of the old companions, were loath to engage in a new conflict so soon, when the drama of May was still fresh in the minds of many people. Solid arguments were marshaled in favor of delaying an operation that evoked such widespread alarm.

Couve, Tricot and most members of the cabinet took shelter behind the supposedly complicated problem of perfecting the wording of the proposition. "If we do this quickly, we'll pose the question in terms that are too simplistic and vague. Then we'll have to enact laws in order to implement the reforms."

But the general remained opposed to delay. "The parliament will sabotage everything," he grumbled. "I'm in a hurry. The referendum must settle a maximum number of questions in a minimum of time."

De Gaulle asked the Minister of the Interior for a memorandum on the amount of time needed; the answer was two months. Accepting the realities of the situation, the general reluctantly yielded.

Jeanneney told the general: "Taking into account every factor, we can schedule the referendum for the last week of November or the first part of December. We'll have to set up the debate in parliament around mid-October. We can sandwich it in between discussions of the budget."

Couve tempered Jeanneney's enthusiasm. For a week the pre-

mier kept the files on the referendum in his own desk. When Jeanneney wanted to place the matter on the agenda for the next cabinet meeting, Couve told him: "We can wait. Time is a gallant man,
Jeanneney."

Couve made no effort to disguise his reluctance. He would have
preferred to hold the referendum a year later, around Christmas of
1969. He was focusing his attention on more immediate affairs: the
start of the academic year and the burgeoning economic crisis.

But he could not convince de Gaulle, as Pompidou had managed
to do in May, to put off the moment of truth. "I feel, in any case,
that I haven't the right," Couve confided to a close associate. "This
referendum is bound up with the general's wish to test his destiny
and to secure popular confirmation of his mission."

Within the cabinet, the barons — Frey and Guichard — were
just as reluctant as Couve to proceed. Frey thought that the political climate was unfavorable. As for Guichard, he had long champi-
oned regional reform, but at no time had he favored a procedure as
dramatic as a referendum.

"In any case," Guichard said, "we must convince the general to
put two questions: one on regionalism, the other on the reform of
institutions."

It was also Guichard who suggested the idea of first consulting all
the important people in France on the question of regionalism.
Thus, thousands would be queried and their opinions would be recorded in huge files. The results of these soundings were eventually
to be formulated.

This would take several weeks. The general was worried about
the delay, but he admitted that "We must pave the way for a revolution as drastic as this."

The preliminary work was finally concluded. De Gaulle had
made his views clearly known. Everyone of importance had been
informed or consulted — the VIPs had expressed their wishes and
the senators had been appeased. The fears previously harbored no
longer seemed justified. The general was ready. Some of his loyal
followers did underscore the risk he was incurring. Was public

opinion capable of realizing how high were the stakes? Would the public take an interest in issues that in the last analysis concerned nothing more than the use of certain political techniques? With a shade of annoyance, the general answered: "We're not holding a 'phony' referendum with questions posed in such a way that Frenchmen will automatically answer yes. On the contrary, the referendum will subject the people to a difficult test. But this makes an expression of their confidence all the more important; it will enable us to institute really profound changes."

The challenge was a bold one. The referendum represented a great gamble. The general was resolved to bet all his remaining "poor" strength on it. And if, by some misfortune, the French people should close their eyes and ears, the venture would at least be an honorable one.

Rejecting the warnings of his anxious collaborators, de Gaulle laid down the lines of battle. The debate would take place in the Assembly in November. The texts would be published in the *Journal officiel* on December 20. The French people would vote in mid-January.

The premier succeeded in obtaining an additional delay of about a week. November 20 was the day fixed for the discussion in the Assembly. The referendum was to take place on January 26, 1969.

Having resolved and settled everything, the general returned to his solitude. In the park of the Elysée, the trees were shedding their leaves. Autumn was coming to an end. De Gaulle was sensitive to the rhythm of the changing seasons. His long career abounded in harsh winters and rich springtimes. How many more months or years would he have to endure before reaching the end?

CHAPTER 18

"Nothing will be forgiven"

POMPIDOU, TOO, was at the mercy of time. But the referendum was not expected to signal the end of his penitence. Not a single Gaullist ventured to imagine that the general would be defeated — Pompidou least of all.

Although many had deserted Pompidou, his office on the Boulevard de Latour-Maubourg remained nevertheless an important meeting place for various politicians. In this office files and archives were piled up, and Pompidou's closest associates, Pierre Juillet and Michel Jobert, were as busy as they had been at the Matignon.

In spite of de Gaulle's apparent benevolence, Pompidou was determined to maintain his hold on his followers. To no man would he yield a Gaullist party that continued to boast a goodly proportion of Pompidouists. It so happened that Couve de Murville had not succeeded in establishing himself as the majority leader. Pompidou was consequently able to maintain his position as the benign counselor and intimate confidant of a cohort of deputies who grumbled about the administration, the government, and even occasionally about de Gaulle himself. Pompidou had no official responsibility. He could therefore demand — he, who had so often reduced the Gaullist deputies to silence — a little consideration for his new colleagues.

Relations between Couve and Pompidou cooled — they had at no time been really cordial. The two men occasionally saw each other at meetings of the party's political bureau. They pretended to be friendly but no one was taken in.

"When Pompidou wasn't there," one member of the group has related, "his successor would suavely offer a few acid comments on the actions of the preceding cabinet. Once, he spoke rather harshly about the nationalized industries, saying he was surprised that for six years no attempt had been made to put them in order."

During the "after-May" period, which was embittered by certain memories and fears, many were the opportunities to place the blame on past mistakes. Couve took advantage of this, and Pompidou knew it. The former premier had loyal supporters at all levels of the government, within the Gaullist party and even at the Matignon, where four advisers of the new premier had worked with Pompidou.

Regularly but discreetly, Pompidou reminded the Gaullists of the mission with which de Gaulle had charged him: "To be prepared to assume the mandate that the nation might elect to confer upon me." He was quite prepared. Reviewing in his mind the topics he would dwell on when the time came to campaign, he boned up on problems that he had previously overlooked. He plotted his electoral strategy and maintained contact with the business leaders who would provide the necessary funds. He knew in detail the political situation in every district as well as the individuals he could count on.

"One day, when I was in the district of the Lot," a young deputy from Normandy has recounted, "I telephoned Pompidou, who was also spending a few days there. He immediately asked me to come over. I was ushered into the large low-ceilinged room of his house at Cajarc. In one corner, a few of his friends were playing cards. Pompidou took me aside. He seemed to be much more serene than he had been in July. 'During the past three months,' he told me, 'I have received many letters and met many people. I can see that since May many more Frenchmen have learned to appreciate me.' Then he proceeded to speak very severely about his successor, declaring that the general had made a poor choice. Finally, he questioned me at length about my own district. He wanted to know how many party members and how many cadres we had and if he was popular with them. He questioned me closely about the major concerns of the voters in my constituency.

"At the time, this interview surprised me. But as soon as I left Cajarc, as I drove off and began to think about it in the car, I remember that I was very struck by Pompidou's remarks. The former premier had spoken to me as if he were already a candidate, as if he were ready at any moment to launch his campaign. That was in October. There seemed then no reason to believe that the general would quit in a few weeks."

A Gaullist leader grumbled. "During his entire ordeal, Pompidou's main concern was to see to it that we did not demobilize. Every word and gesture was aimed at reminding us that after de Gaulle we would not be orphans."

Pompidou felt that he had every right to announce his candidature. He made no secret of the fact that he hoped to become the official heir and successor. However, only the general knew when the question of the succession would arise. In three months or three years? The general could alter the course of things at any moment. With a wave of the hand he could destroy Pompidou's fine strategy as easily as he could knock down a house of cards.

After twenty-three years of zealous devotion and constant observation, Pompidou knew that it was impossible to guess the general's secret.

.　.

On November 1, 1968, de Gaulle went to Colombey to think things over. His meditations, however, were interrupted by the unexpected arrival of Bernard Tricot, his discreet and invaluable confidant. The dossier that Tricot brought contained nothing tragic, nothing that endangered the future of France. It concerned an ordinary, sordid murder, that of a young Yugoslav named Stefan Markovic whose body had been discovered a month before.

This was obviously the general's first inkling of what the press was already calling "the Markovic affair." Tricot gave him a brief run-down. Markovic had been the friend and bodyguard of a famous actor, Alain Delon. The inquest so far had yielded no important clues, but the star's relations with various people were being investigated and all the newspapers were headlining the story.

With evident distaste, de Gaulle asked his collaborator to come to the point. Tricot showed him the large dossier which contained all the accounts of the inquest. "My general," he said, "the name of Pompidou appears in these accounts — or rather that of Madame Pompidou!"

Seated at the desk where he had written his war memoirs, de Gaulle gazed at Tricot and then stared at the dossier. By departing from custom and coming to Colombey on All Saints' Day, Tricot made it plain that he did not take the matter lightly. He apparently foresaw political repercussions. Friends of Pompidou later said angrily: "It was Tricot who sowed doubt and suspicion in de Gaulle's mind."

De Gaulle leafed through the dossier. One thing was plain: Pompidou's name appeared there in black and white. Georges Pompidou had been the general's premier, his friend. Today — if God and the French people were willing — he was also a chief of state in the making. The general could not be indifferent to this new development.

"Who knows about this?" de Gaulle asked.

"The Keeper of the Seals, René Capitant, and the Minister of Interior, Raymond Marcellin. And Couve de Murville, naturally."

"What about Pompidou?"

Tricot said that the former premier was at his place in Cajarc.

"All right. I'll think about it. I'll talk to Couve. Thanks."

Marcellin was worried. He did not hesitate to admit that he was entirely loyal to Pompidou. Besides, everyone knew it. He called up the premier. "Has the general come to a decision?"

"He'll see us on Wednesday when he returns from Colombey."

"And what about Georges?"

"He's in the Lot," Couve replied. "I'm not going to bother him about this story in the middle of his weekend. I'll warn him about it myself after our meeting at the Elysée."

Marcellin thought that was all right. He advised everyone to say nothing to the former premier for the moment. Couve said it was only right that he should be the one to break the unpleasant news to Pompidou.

On Wednesday, as soon as he returned to Paris, the general called Couve, Marcellin and Capitant into his office. The famous dossier occupied a prominent place on his desk, as if the chief of state wished to make a show of his interest in the matter.

De Gaulle consulted his ministers. Couve expressed his contempt for this kind of story, Marcellin said nothing. Then Capitant spoke up. The other two men knew that he was a ferocious enemy of Pompidou's and this fact had its importance.

"I frankly gave my opinion," Capitant has related. "I said that I thought we were confronted with an ugly case of blackmail. And I added that the Pompidous were perhaps somewhat imprudent in their choice of acquaintances, especially in artistic circles."

The people the Pompidous frequented constituted another chapter in the Pompidou legend. De Gaulle knew all about it. To the general, the world of actors and painters, of people "the journalists talk about," was alien territory. It had always surprised him that his premier had not severed all connections with such people. According to de Gaulle, it was wrong for a statesman to spend his time in society, in ladies' boudoirs, or in cafés. Not so very long ago, professional actors were socially taboo and actresses were regarded as women of ill repute. Middle-class folk never invited such people to their homes. They brought with them an aura all their own, something to be avoided at all costs.

To be sure, the general had adapted himself to changing times. He had entertained artists at the Elysée, thus showing his flexibility. But if one could believe the rumors that were floating about, Pompidou's friends were cosmopolitan people who belonged to a frivolous and bizarre circle. A future chief of state has no friends — especially not friends like these!

De Gaulle agreed with Capitant. Perhaps, too, he was not loath to use this opportunity to call Pompidou to order. For several days he had known that his former collaborator was stirring things up, agitating among the Gaullist majority and placing stumbling blocks in the way of the premier.

Capitant continued: "Justice will have to take its course. If there is the slightest doubt about the insinuations regarding the Pompidous, and if the government hushes the matter up, the opposition will not hesitate to use it against the government and against you yourself, my general."

De Gaulle again agreed and, speaking like a chief of state, declared: "Well, then, let justice take its course." He did not realize that he was dealing his former premier a terrible blow. He also had no idea how deeply wounded and outraged Pompidou would be. The full implications of the decision that had been reached never dawned on de Gaulle.

The discussion was over. But Raymond Marcellin suddenly asked: "Who will make sure that Pompidou is told about this?"

Obviously, this was the premier's job. The general always laid great stress on the requirements of protocol and hierarchy. It would be improper to send someone of secondary importance to the Boulevard de Latour-Maubourg.

During the four months since he had been installed at the Matignon, Couve de Murville had encountered his predecessor intermittently, and then only on official business. To a colleague he later remarked: "I couldn't go and visit him right after taking office. It wasn't customary. Pompidou himself had felt the same way toward his predecessor, Debré."

So he remained silent.

. .

Rumors spread. They crept into the editorial rooms of newspaper offices, drawing rooms and political corridors. Parisians, often amateur weavers of scabrous stories, whispered that Madame Pompidou had had imprudent friendships, and even that she had participated in rather special evenings. The young Yugoslavian, Markovic, had been killed after setting up a large-scale blackmailing operation. All told, it was a sordid and banal episode, including vice, blood, and not a little scandal.

But Pompidou still knew nothing — he had no inkling of what was going on.

In the political seraglio, friends of the former premier remained silent. Profoundly distressed, they hid their heads in the sand in order to shut out the alarming news.

Pompidou still heard nothing.

Civil servants, magistrates, ministers, police officers of every rank had all read the dossier.

But Pompidou was told nothing.

Finally, one of his oldest associates, Jean-Luc Javal, went to the Boulevard de Latour-Maubourg. A journalist had told him the story. Besides, he had heard the gossip. Arriving at a decision, he said to Juillet and Jobert: "It's our duty to draw the boss's attention to the scandal that is taking shape. It would be a great mistake to remain silent out of a sense of delicacy. I'm going to tell him the whole thing."

Pompidou was alone in his small office. Javal entered and sat down. Both men lit cigarettes. The former premier was relaxed, a thousand miles from suspecting anything.

"Then I told him," Javal said. "I tried to sum up all the lies, treacheries and calumnies. I shattered the silence with which he had been surrounded. He paled. Then he looked at his watch and excused himself. He had a date. He left his office without saying a word."

When Pompidou recounted what had followed to Jeanneney a few days later, he spoke with great feeling: "I was so ignorant of the whole affair that on November fourth, after All Saints' Day, I received several of my former colleagues, as I do every Monday. Among them was Somveille, the chief of Marcellin's staff. I remember asking him jokingly: 'Well, Somveille, tell us something amusing. Tell us the name of the VIP who is being mentioned in connection with the Markovic affair.' I don't remember that he even changed color. Then I learned all about the affair through the palace gossip. I waited two or three more days, hoping that a message would come from the government. Nothing. So Jobert called up Somveille and told him: 'You must come here and tell us all you know. I advise you to do so.' Somveille came. But first he went to Jobert's office. On the verge of tears, he tried to exculpate himself: 'I was sworn to secrecy.' 'In that case,' said Jobert, 'you committed a wrong. As Pompidou's former associate, you should not have allowed yourself to be bound by secrecy.' Finally, Somveille came to my office and told me the story. It was as painful for him as it was for me."

By the time Pompidou was finally informed, the dossier had been in the government's hands for an entire week. The former premier was deeply hurt. One of the most elementary rules of political life had been violated. Even had he been a sworn enemy of the government, he should have been warned. That was how such situations had always been handled.

The government had allowed him to step to the very edge of a precipice without issuing a single word of warning. Neither ministers, barons nor protégés had alerted him. The general too had failed him. Each of these men, by remaining silent, had made himself an accomplice in this nasty affair. Pompidou was seized with an icy rage. Never, never could he have imagined that he could be the victim of such wretched machinations! He recalled the case of the socialist minister, Salengro, who, thirty years before, had committed suicide as a consequence of a campaign to defame his good name. "This is ten times worse because my wife is involved," he murmured to himself lugubriously. Then, controlling himself, he vowed: "Nothing will be forgiven, nothing, nothing!"

Pompidou was convinced that people had plotted against him. "Someone is trying to break me. But who? The police? Which members of the police? Who extorted this so-called information? Who is the stool pigeon? Where is the evidence? And who are the false witnesses to whom the evidence was given? How is it that newspapermen were the first to be informed? Whose dirty work is this? I'll find the culprit. Someday, I swear, I'll find him."

He was told how de Gaulle learned of the affair. Pompidou shrugged his shoulders sadly. Over and over again he kept asking himself the same questions. He charged Jobert to find out anything he could and put the following question to the barons, Jacques, Roger and Olivier: "What would you do if such garbage were dumped on your doorstep?"

Even after he was elected to the presidency, for months Pompidou tried to find a clue to the mystery, to find one person, just one, on whom to lower the boom. But in vain.

The hardest blow was the discovery that de Gaulle had allowed it to happen. Pompidou would have found it easier to accept political disgrace. In any case, he was convinced that his national destiny had not been compromised by the affair. The truth, he felt sure, would eventually come out.

Suddenly his image of the general had become tarnished. After so many years of devotion and hard work . . . Every explanation he could think of seemed implausible: de Gaulle would never allow his collaborator — the man who had been associated with him longer than anyone else — to be trampled on this way. The general couldn't have permitted such conniving against a couple whom he counted among his friends, whom he had often received as dinner guests. The general could not lend himself to something that was worse than a crime — a sin.

Or else de Gaulle was no longer de Gaulle.

Alone in his office, Pompidou tried to uncover the mainspring of this tragedy. He thought of his six years at the Matignon and the innumerable marks of affection he had received from the general during the past quarter century. He mulled over all kinds of unanswerable questions and insoluble enigmas.

Something had been severed. Pompidou suddenly felt free — free to plan his retaliation.

. .

Pompidou had not realized that he was the object of so much hatred. He suddenly discovered the cruel truth: in the game of politics, power alone was a refuge. Here he was, exposed to the shabbiest of traps. And he had no defense. Alone, he faced invisible, pitiless enemies — and cowards.

The gossip found its way into the dossier. Packets of photographs, of so-called police reports, were sent to the newspapers by anonymous persons. Pompidou invited columnists, newspaper editors and reporters to lunch with him. He told them the truth. But he had to listen to repulsive bits of gossip that wounded him deeply. For twenty-four hours a day, he had to breathe this poisoned air. Yet whenever visitors appeared, he himself could not resist bringing the conversation around to the affair. He even forgot about politics.

The most intimate aspects of his life were examined under a microscope by malevolent eyes. Twenty-year-old stories were dug up and presented as accusations. Saint-Tropez, his band of friends, pleasurable evenings — all the things he had never made a secret of were brought up against him.

At times, when he felt very low, he would sigh: "I give up. I'll give up public life, if not for my own sake at least for my wife's."

One day a deputy, not one of his own adherents, came into his office and placed a large manila envelope on his desk. "I see," said the ex-premier. "Some more falsified photos. Three of your colleagues showed them to me a few days ago."

The deputy told him what he knew: "Two men brought me this dossier. They said with a nasty smile that the photographs might prove useful to me. I threw them out; I gave one of them a good kick in the rear which he's likely to remember."

Pompidou looked at the supposedly compromising photographs and said with a gesture of discouragement: "These are fakes. Take a look. Even an amateur can tell. I know the identity of your two visitors. I can show you their pictures; they're there, in my desk. I'm convinced that there's a plot against me, with ramifications that will lead all the way to some Gaullist leaders. You see what a mess I'm in."

Pompidou proceeded to describe a world of police connections, of renegade "barbouzes," members of a curious Gaullist network of spies, all sorts of officials or semiofficial agencies with which he had had to deal in the course of the Ben Barka affair. But these were merely underlings. Who was their chief? Who was protecting them?

"In spite of all my experience," Pompidou added, "I must confess I really don't know."

At the Elysée, rumors of this campaign reached the ears of the chief of state. Several times the general expressed his dissatisfaction to the Minister of Justice. "Well, Capitant, what about your magistrates? Are they asleep? It's high time to put an end to these insinuations. The press, naturally, is happy to lap it all up."

At the Elysée there were other matters of concern. The general had no inkling of Pompidou's resentment against him. He viewed the whole matter as something of secondary importance, since the state was in no way implicated. Couve and most of the ministers attached no more importance to it than he did.

Pompidou alone took it seriously.

From then on there was virtually no contact whatsoever between de Gaulle and the man who had been his most important collaborator. Pompidou couldn't forget the general's indifference — "a calculated indifference," he claimed. At times he spoke his mind and let off steam by confiding his resentment to his intimates. "De Gaulle," he charged, "is covering up for someone."

The former premier naturally thought that the Markovic affair should have been given top priority. It constituted a paramount political issue because it jeopardized the national destiny of the deputy from Cantal. Unfortunately for him, the general's concern was now focused on other individuals and on different kinds of dossiers.

Until 1968, thanks to the protection of the chief of state, Pompidou could have withstood any blows. He was the second in command, the favorite, the untouchable protégé. Now, having nothing more than his ambition to rely on, he was discovering what the political jungle was like. Without de Gaulle he was just another politician, dependent on chance. The luck that had always been with him was a gift from the general. But now the wheel had turned.

He lost friends, people presumably fond of him but whose real allegiance was apparently owed solely to the general. He guessed that even some of the barons were ready to desert him. Bitterly, he reproached Jacques Foccart, the oldest of his political friends, for a silence that in his eyes was tantamount to treachery.

But he also discovered unexpected allies; Michel Debré, his predecessor, was one of them. Another was his erstwhile rival, Giscard d'Estaing.

As early as October, Debré began to pity Pompidou for his bad luck. Reminded of his own humiliation, he sent the former premier long, warm letters. Reacting to the surprise which some of his friends expressed at this sudden volte-face, Debré said: "I know of course that Pompidou wasn't the perfect premier, but in May he proved to be an excellent interim chief of state."

To his unfortunate successor, Debré confided his own anxieties: the general was growing old; Couve did not make full use of his authority; and Edgar Faure, as Minister of National Education, was granting one disastrous concession after another. The letters Pompidou wrote in answer to Debré's expressed similar anxieties.

For Debré, the Markovic affair was the last straw. "I know," he said, "that you can't expect mercy in politics. I'm used to all kinds of double-dealing. But this is particularly shabby. Pompidou's honor, his private life, are in jeopardy. How he must suffer!"

One letter followed another in rapid succession. "And the general's eyes haven't been opened yet," Debré lamented.

As for Valéry Giscard d'Estaing, as early as July he had approached Pompidou. He forgave the affront he had suffered at Pompidou's hands in 1966, saying with some humor: "I know how it feels to be dismissed."

Before leaving for their summer vacations, the two men had agreed to meet upon their return to the capital. There was still some distrust that needed to be dissipated. But in November, when the Markovic affair erupted, Giscard seized upon it as a pretext for seeking a full reconciliation. He sent Pompidou a message, claiming he was very shocked at the way he was being treated. Then he went in person to the Boulevard de Latour-Maubourg. Several times during the winter he visited Pompidou in his office. The epithet "the cactus" — that's what Pompidou had called his former minister at the time of their quarrel — was now a thing of the past.

Another ally was Chaban-Delmas. President of the Assembly, the fifth baron, he was waiting for the end of Gaullism to leave the perch where, for the past ten years, he had found life thoroughly boring. With disarming self-assurance, he said to one of his old friends: "Sooner or later there will be a new cabinet. Either Georges or I will head it. If it is headed by me, I will be serving under President Pompidou."

Conscientiously, two evenings a week, Chaban-Delmas met with five or six technocrats. He was putting his papers in order. The Elysée knew about these meetings. "Shady business," de Gaulle remarked.

Overzealous informers gave de Gaulle hour-by-hour reports of Pompidou's daily routine. But the general, usually so attentive to such matters, refused to believe that treachery was involved. "Pompidou," he said. "I made that man. He will never forget it."

But the former premier felt he had been released from his bonds. To his loyal colleagues, Juillet and Jobert, he repeated: "Nothing will be forgotten."

The plot was obviously directed against the successor. Pompidou knew how to obtain his revenge: through his succession.

CHAPTER 19

The November Squall

NOVEMBER WAS A MONTH OF GREAT FINANCIAL TROUBLE, a legacy of the disastrous spring and of the "excessive concessions granted by the former minister on the Rue de Grenelle," according to de Gaulle.

When he had left for Baden toward the close of May, the general had thought that the national treasury was filled with gold — "so that Mitterand will be able to govern for a while," the departing chief of state had told himself somberly. Now that illusion was gone. Upon succeeding himself, after his few hours of retirement in the Black Forest, de Gaulle began to notice sinister cracks in one of the pillars of power — the exchequer. The figures spoke for themselves. The liquid reserves, which had been partly reconstituted after the stabilization of 1963, were not sufficient to pay the huge bills Pompidou had run up.

The problem began to plague the government as early as June. An expert who specialized in financial therapy had suggested that the franc should be devalued by about 7 per cent and that taxes on wages should be eliminated. "All in all," the expert had predicted, "this will leave us a margin of ten per cent."

Pompidou had been won over to the idea. But he had found it quite impossible to make drastic cuts in the money supply during an election campaign. The government would have to wait until the following month. And in July it was up to Couve to decide.

The new premier was not at all inclined to shoulder the blame for the policies of his predecessor. Upon arriving at the Matignon, he told his associates: "The principal object of any devaluation is to encourage exports. But the factories have not been in operation. There are no stockpiles. We've nothing to sell. The conclusion to be drawn is quite plain."

Nevertheless, Couve asked Pompidou's former chief of staff, François-Xavier Ortoli, to serve as Minister of Finance. Ortoli was an acolyte of the ill-reputed school of thought that called itself technocratic.

The summer — the season of rash spending — was over. In October the bad news was announced. The cabinet shunned extreme measures, fearing to provoke another explosion five months after the turbulent month of May. Couve de Murville punctuated each passing day with a sigh of relief. But the money would have to be found. One couldn't go on increasing taxes forever.

"It was at that time that we decided to increase the inheritance tax," one of the premier's collaborators later recounted. "The idea was suggested by a technocrat. The nineteen sixty-eight budget, a deficit budget to begin with, had been bled to death in May. We took money wherever we could find it. At the time, Couve did not foresee the full consequences of such a measure."

The tax on inheritance provoked a tempest in the Assembly and among the Gaullists. The storm centered on Ortoli who was accused of surrounding himself with left-wing technocrats. Even Couve was not spared by the spokesmen for the majority. In the eyes of the Pompidouists, he was the usurper. In private, de Gaulle reminded his ministers that when Pompidou succeeded Debré a similar outburst had come from Debré's loyal followers.

Faced with violent criticism, the premier was obliged to make concessions. When the inheritance tax bill came up for debate in the Assembly, the Gaullist majority was allowed to have its way.

This period also witnessed the start of large-scale speculation that eventually brought disaster to the nation. The politicians were not the only ones who lacked confidence in the cabinet. Bankers, industrialists, employers, capitalists, middle-class people — all gambled in the belief that devaluation was around the corner. Capital flowed out of the country. At first a small hemorrhage, the difficulties soon attained catastrophic proportions. Pompidou, who was kept posted on every aspect of the state's financial condition, saw the number of malcontents increase each day.

. .

De Gaulle was forced to tear himself away from his labors on constitutional reform in order to eye the mounting dangers. The date of the referendum was again changed; his rendezvous with the electors was once more delayed.

Since January 1959, monetary stability in France had been a source of great pride to the Gaullists. The franc was a precise barometer of the political climate. At first the general refused to consider an expedient employed so often by the Fourth Republic. On November 13, at a meeting of the cabinet, he solemnly declared: "To agree to a policy of devaluation would be to consent to the worst absurdity in the world."

He authorized his youthful secretary, Joël Le Theule, to communicate this statement to the ministry of information. But although he tried to convince the French people, he himself wasn't at all sure that he was right. He questioned associates and specialists. It did not occur to him to consult Pompidou, who for ten years had continuously advised him on financial matters.

Everything seemed to indicate that only a miracle could save the country from devaluation. Couve slowly resigned himself to the inevitable.

At the Elysée de Gaulle was now confronted with a harsh reality. Devaluation, now considered imperative, was in his opinion the result of mistakes committed in May. He did not actually name the principal culprit, but to his collaborators he talked without restraint about Pompidou's "treachery." Sadly, he admitted to a delegation of deputies: "The consequences of the spring crisis are more serious than we expected."

No matter what he said or how skillfully he argued, the truth was that de Gaulle would have to take back his words — something he regarded as less than honorable. In devaluing the franc he would be forced to abandon the strong position to which the Fifth Republic owed its good name. The experts had persuaded him that there was no other possible solution.

The ship of state was taking in water. Couve tried to plug the leaks by makeshift means. He announced that the deficit would be met by drastic cuts in the state's expenditures, knowing full well that such a step would not be enough to instill confidence in worried deputies, employers, or savings depositors. That day, as he strode down a corridor of the Palais-Bourbon, completely absorbed by these problems, he ran into Jeanneney. No one was there to overhear them. Couve sat down on a bench and, turning to Jeanneney, said: "We'll have to devalue. We've just lost seven hundred million dollars."

Jeanneney replied vehemently: "You can do better than that. Issue orders. Make drastic changes in key positions, even if it seems unfair. Let heads roll at the ministry of finance. Replace the director of the Bank of France — you've been wanting to do that anyway. If necessary, find a new minister. If you stand firm, you'll be listened to."

It was useless advice. All the important people of France, the experts, the most knowledgeable officials at the Elysée, at the Matignon and the ministry of finance were agreed about one thing only: devaluation was unavoidable. It was rumored that the Germans were about to revalue the mark. The moment seemed propitious for a change in the value of the franc.

At this juncture, Ortoli went to Bonn to confer with the finance ministers of Western Europe. The day before, the Paris bourse was closed for five days.

Ortoli's mission was a delicate one. First, he had to ascertain if he could what the Germans intended to do about the mark. Then he had to secure loans from his European partners — without any strings attached, if possible.

From Germany Ortoli telephoned the Matignon every two hours. The negotiations proved difficult. In exchange for a loan, some of

France's partners demanded the immediate devaluation of the franc. During the second day of the negotiations, the finance minister informed Couve that the Germans were unwilling to do anything about the mark prior to the forthcoming general elections.

.   .

In the evening of Friday, November 22, Ortoli returned to Paris. "I'm exhausted," he said. He was promptly received at the Elysée. The meeting was brief. The general listened, said not a word, and thanked Ortoli. "I was very hesitant," the finance minister confessed. "I didn't venture to express an opinion."

Couve, like most of the ministers, favored devaluation. Michel Debré went further. He advocated a drastic operation involving a cut of no less than 25 per cent — a veritable Walpurgis Night that would gravely affect most of the European currencies.

The German government's decision came as a bitter surprise to the Matignon. It meant that even a 12 per cent devaluation of the franc would probably not be enough.

The zero hour was approaching. A final decision would have to be arrived at on the following day at a special meeting of the cabinet. Jeanneney took the center of the stage. To be sure, his place in the Gaullist family was a modest one. He was not a member of the clan. In 1959, in response to a request from his childhood friend Michel Debré, he joined the government. But ever since 1968, he had been on tepid terms with his erstwhile patron. In late May, having been dismissed by Pompidou, he was reappointed by Couve.

In this final year of the general's reign, Jeanneney emerged from the shadows. Frenchmen were to become familiar with his staccato speech, his eternal bow tie, the smile that somewhat softened his intransigent manner.

On Friday, Jeanneney phoned the Elysée. He had to see the general in order to "relieve his conscience," he told Tricot. An appointment was made for the next morning, Saturday at eleven-thirty.

"I already knew that the decision to devalue the franc was for all purposes an accomplished fact," Jeanneney said. "That Friday evening I called a colleague of Couve's at the Matignon. 'I must see the premier before going to the Elysée,' I said to him. He told me to stop by early the next morning."

At nine-fifteen that Saturday morning, Jeanneney walked into Couve's office. "I'm going to beg the general not to devalue the franc," he said. "Politically, it would be a catastrophe, an admission of failure."

"Go ahead," the premier answered. "But you'll be wasting your time. The only question that's still not been settled is how much we should devalue."

In narrating these events, Jeanneney continued: "So I telephoned the French vice president of the European Commission in Brussels, Raymond Barre, and asked him this question: 'Should France decide not to devalue the franc, will the European banks be willing to grant her a loan anyway?' Barre said he thought they would but he would first have to check with the governor of the Bank of Belgium. 'I have to have an answer before eleven,' I told him. 'I'll do my best,' Barre said."

Upon leaving the Matignon, Jeanneney rushed back to his office and hurriedly called Raymond Barre. "Well, what's the answer? It's getting late."

"The governor is taking a bath. He can't talk to me right now. Give me another ten minutes or so."

"Impossible. I have to go to the Elysée. Listen, if you get an answer before noon, call Tricot directly. I'll alert him. That will help me a lot."

Jeanneney went to the Elysée. He had prepared his arguments carefully. But the general was in such bad humor that Jeanneney began to lose hope. In an adjoining room where an aide-de-camp was stationed, he saw one of the experts who had just left the general's office. "Did you talk to him about this madness?" Jeanneney asked.

"I played my hand as well as I could. I told him what I thought the consequences of devaluation would be. But I didn't give him any advice, it would have been useless."

"No, you were wrong," said Jeanneney.

. .

Jeanneney did not wait to be seated. He told the general point-blank: "Don't devalue, my general. You must not devalue."

The chief of state gazed at him with astonishment. "You're the only one who thinks it's possible to avoid it."

"Pardon me for saying so, my general, but sometimes a man who is right is alone in his opinion."

Then Jeanneney grew excited. This would be the end of Gaullism — yes, the end, just as a journalist had recently predicted; it would bring a devaluation of the regime. Courageously, he reminded the general that what was absurd yesterday should not be called reasonable today. "Anyone can contradict himself. But not General de Gaulle."

He added that it would be unfair to the working classes, that one couldn't take away what they had just been granted on the Rue de Grenelle. The chief of state only shrugged when reminded of the recent, unhappy past, then said softly: "Well, then, Jeanneney, explain to me how we can avoid devaluation."

"It's very simple," the minister answered. "You have only to make up your mind and issue the necessary orders. This flight of capital can't continue forever. When a barrel is empty, it can no longer be emptied.

"Why shouldn't capital flee the country," Jeanneney went on, "when the government lets it be known that it anticipates a reevaluation of the mark? And when the national banks shamelessly promote speculation? When our inspectors of finance declare that devaluation is an accomplished fact? Make up your mind, my general. And if some of these people drag their feet, well, it won't be difficult to replace them. If some of our high officials don't inspire confidence, let our ambassadors negotiate directly with the European banks."

During this financial and monetary crisis, the general clearly saw the end of his own adventure. To devalue or not to devalue — the question was really of secondary importance. Frenchmen wouldn't be cured of their apathy if the franc were pegged at a new level, nor would such a move cure de Gaulle of the fatigues of old age. But if the French currency were allowed to remain intact, one could at least avoid sounding the death knell.

After devaluation, the state would experience a series of disasters and shipwrecks. These would eventually culminate in dreadful things — massive unemployment, strikes, violence, the enslavement of France by foreign powers. Of course, the general would be forced to forsake his mission, to quit the Elysée in shame.

.   .

There was no need for Jeanneney to enumerate the bleak consequences. The general knew them all; he had been thinking about nothing else ever since the spring. Jeanneney's exhortations struck an answering chord in the general.

"Of course," said de Gaulle, "if it were possible to avoid devaluation . . ."

"My general, anyone who tells you that it can't be done is lying." And Jeanneney proceeded to prove it.

"In the midst of the interview," Jeanneney has related, "we were interrupted by the arrival of a footman. This was entirely contrary to well-established custom. For a moment the general looked surprised. I glanced at the note the man handed me. It was Barre's answer, transmitted by Tricot, as we had planned. And the answer was positive. 'What is it?' the general asked. I handed him the note."

De Gaulle stood up. "Well, Jeanneney, it's time to end our interview."

"With his usual courtesy, the President of the Republic escorted me to the door. As I was about to leave, he said: 'Naturally, you'll repeat what you've just told me to the cabinet at the meeting this afternoon.'

" 'No, my general. That's not up to me. Besides, your cabinet is a sieve,' I said."

Upon leaving the chief of state, Jeanneney joined Tricot in an adjacent office. Meanwhile, de Gaulle summoned Couve. The special cabinet meeting was due to begin in less than three hours.

Information circulates quickly in governmental circles. When the members of the cabinet reached the Elysée early that afternoon, they already knew that the general had arrived at a decision. The evening newspapers were announcing the devaluation of the franc: some even specified how much it had been devalued.

Before the cabinet meeting, the premier took Jeanneney aside. "I want you to speak up. I'm counting on you. I'll give you a signal."

On that Saturday afternoon, the cabinet placed on the stage actors who had learned their parts well. Jeanneney, contrary to the prescriptions of protocol, spoke first. With triumphant enthusiasm, he reiterated all the arguments he had already presented to the general. Then Ortoli launched into a brilliant technical explanation, but offered no opinion of his own. Only three ministers spoke in favor of devaluation.

The die was cast. The general thanked everyone and announced that the franc would not be devalued — "in accordance," he added unsmilingly, "with the desires expressed by a sizable majority of this group."

But he did not deceive himself. Appearances alone had been saved. Several of the cabinet members, including those who had given a convincing display of enthusiasm, remained uncertain and worried. De Gaulle had united his men — but for how long? At any moment, ministers, officials and deputies would desert him again and take the easy way out.

De Gaulle found himself as lonely as ever. The praise that had greeted his bold challenge was but a feeble musical accompaniment. France was gradually sliding toward the abyss that had so often drawn her. Foreign governments had not been fooled, especially Bonn, whose monetary policy loomed so large in the crisis of the franc.

The following morning the general received his secretary, Joël Le Theule, who came to settle the details of a televised speech de Gaulle was about to deliver. On this occasion, the general once again gave vent to his bitterness. France had been deserted by everyone, by its allies as well as by its servants. De Gaulle cited Germany, a country that he had "rehabilitated," as a case in point. "More than anyone else, I helped to restore Germany to her rightful place in international affairs. But see here, Le Theule, the Boches will always be Boches — humble when they are beaten and arrogant as soon as they feel strong again."

For the second time in less than six months, the state had suffered a shock. At the very last minute, the general had managed to reestablish a balance of sorts. But miracles do not occur indefinitely. To a few of his ministers and collaborators, de Gaulle bluntly admitted: "Regardless of how it is resolved, the monetary crisis signals the decline of the Fifth Republic."

CHAPTER 20

End of a Reign

THROUGHOUT THE ENTIRE MONTH of December 1968 and during the first half of January 1969, the general no longer professed an optimism, which would have been unfounded. In speaking to strangers he talked about the past and the present with a superbly philosophical air. But in the presence of his own people, he gave way to melancholy.

One of the ministers with whom de Gaulle often conversed expressed his surprise at the change in the general. He confided his impressions to Tricot. "I know," the man who was now de Gaulle's closest collaborator answered. "I've noticed the same thing, a kind of emptiness. It began during the month of May."

Wherever de Gaulle looked, he saw nothing but colossal blunders or treachery. He began to regret lost opportunities, especially his decision of last July not to devalue the franc.

"The whole world would have understood that France was being forced to pay the bill run up in May," he said. "We could have devalued the franc seven or eight per cent without impairing our credit."

He kept saying: "No one was foresighted, no one looked ahead. Everyone just lived from day to day. In the end, we had a knife at our throats. But I'm not here just to reassure a lot of frightened people."

His collaborators, especially Tricot, urged him to hold the referendum immediately. He could thus take advantage of the surprise effect produced by his decision not to devalue.

De Gaulle thought it over, weighing the question; assailed by misgivings, he was unable to reach a decision. During these unhappy December days, his great social reforms suddenly seemed idle and irrelevant. Besides, it was a battle lost in advance.

Disillusioned, the general chose instead to concentrate on more immediate matters. Every evening Tricot presented him with a daily balance sheet showing the amount of gold reserves and cash deposits. De Gaulle studied these figures at length, as if they heralded the coming storm, a storm that he perhaps desired. Everyone was telling him that the next month, January, would be plagued by a mountain of economic troubles. According to the latest forecasts, many small businesses would be forced to close, unemployment would increase, craftsmen and trades people would rebel. In addition, of course, it was obvious that fresh violence would break out in the schools and universities. Several lycées had already shut their doors. Pessimistic as always, the general now believed that explosions would occur more and more frequently and would lead inevitably to the final catastrophe. But his prognostications did not come true. After Christmas the flight of capital from the country ceased.

. .

In the midst of his own troubles, de Gaulle was reminded of Pompidou's. Toward the close of November, when the financial problems still remained to be solved, the general had received a letter from his former premier. De Gaulle answered it the same day, agreeing to a meeting that was to be kept secret. Pompidou would come to one of the side doors of the Elysée where an aide-de-camp would admit him. Tricot would fix the day and the time.

In the presence of de Gaulle, Pompidou gave free vent to his resentment. He told the general everything he had had to endure. "Nowhere did I find an honorable reaction, neither at the Matignon nor at the ministry of justice. Not even here, my general."

"No, not here, Pompidou. But I never doubted you."

"I was speaking of course of the members of your entourage."

De Gaulle promised to intervene personally. He seemed most understanding and even somewhat embarrassed, as if suddenly realizing that a barrier had arisen between Pompidou and himself.

After this visit, the general conveyed to his Minister of Justice, Capitant, his annoyance with the justice department. He ordered Capitant to summon the magistrates to the ministry and to tell them they must shed some light on the matter as quickly as possible. "They're making monkeys of us," he scolded.

He gave all the dossiers on the Markovic affair to those in charge. And he asked the faithful Tricot to find out what was going on and to keep him posted.

Early in December Capitant became gravely ill and sent the general a letter of resignation. Jean-Marcel Jeanneney was immediately summoned to the Elysée where the chief of state offered him the post.

Jeanneney turned it down. Magistrates and lawyers, he respectfully explained, were part of a world that was unfamiliar to him. Besides, he didn't want to occupy the armchair of one of his oldest friends. "Capitant is a healthy man, my general. He'll recover. In the meantime, you can of course count on me to serve on a temporary basis."

De Gaulle said nothing to Jeanneney about the Markovic affair or about the insinuations regarding Pompidou. Moreover, during the six ensuing weeks, he never once mentioned the affair to Jeanneney.

But that very day Tricot gave the interim Minister of Justice an extremely detailed account of all the judicial, police and political moves that had taken place in the wake of the assassination.

"I had trouble grasping it all," Jeanneney candidly admitted. "I'm no reader of whodunits. I confined myself to telling Tricot that I thought it only proper to contact Pompidou."

Jeanneney telephoned the former premier and requested a rendezvous. The two men, who were not close friends, outdid each other in exchanging civilities.

"I'll stop in at your office," Pompidou volunteered.

"Please, don't do anything of the kind. I'll come to see you at the Boulevard de Latour-Maubourg."

Pompidou opened his heart to Jeanneney. He told him the whole story, or at least that part of it that concerned him. And Jeanneney, a good family man quite unaccustomed to "la vie Parisienne," was touched by Pompidou's tale. During his service as interim minister, Jeanneney was to encounter the former premier two more times. He also telephoned the Boulevard de Latour-Maubourg quite regularly.

But all his kindness could not salve Pompidou's wounds.

.   .

In December Pompidou paid the general a second visit, as secret as the first. But this time he did not come empty-handed. He brought all the falsified documents that had been circulated in the guise of evidence, as well as details about all the pseudo-indiscretions hinted at in the newspapers.

Although filled with consternation, the general refused to ascribe this to some sort of political conspiracy. In his opinion, it was simply one of those scandals that newspapers fabricated out of whole cloth. During the past thirty years — in fact, ever since his return from London — de Gaulle had repeatedly charged that newspapers were capable of the worst kind of moral turpitude. He himself had been the victim of that sort of thing. When he had moved into an obscure cottage in a London suburb, reporters had spied on his house day and night. Hidden behind a wall, they had taken pictures of his ailing daughter. Thereafter, though declaring himself "delighted" or "happy" to receive journalists in the Salle des Fêtes at the Elysée, he had never admitted more than two or three of them into the intimacy of his private life.

The mud slung at Pompidou did not surprise the general. "You can see for yourself," he said to his press secretary, Le Theule, "newspapers are vile."

The general wanted Pompidou to understand that he was not

affected by such underhanded maneuvers. The deputy from Cantal was still his friend. "He's a valuable man," he said more precisely to a few visitors. "Someday the country will turn to him."

Little by little, the chief of state lost interest in the affair. The end of it appeared to be in sight. Scandals die down quickly.

But Pompidou was not disarmed. Though with fine consistency, he insisted that the conspiracy would not interfere with his destiny — Frenchmen would not be fooled — nonetheless, he felt that he had been deserted by the general, by the government, and by a good many Gaullists. It was a little as if his name had been placed on the Papal Index — as if people wanted to deprive him of the title of Dauphin which public opinion had bestowed upon him in May.

He would stay out of politics and calmly await his hour. He would act with discretion. He had to emerge from the shadows some day.

.   .

"Let's bury all the devils that have tormented us," the general declared on December 31, 1968. But the devils refused to die. Anger and discontent, gloom, sadness, disappointment and disillusionment possessed and permeated the French people. "World-weariness," de Gaulle called it, "soul-weariness." The people were bored; they grumbled, jeered, on occasion flew off the handle. Four years before its end, the seven-year rule still dragged on. Who could reawaken a vanished faith in people's hearts? The general, the government, the state and its servants, the employers, the trade unions, the politicians — all were disillusioned. A strike, an explosion at a street corner, an incident — any of these could and did revive the public's fears. France was curled up, fretfully waiting for something that might trigger a fresh outburst.

The premier, Maurice Couve de Murville, was a perfect reflection of the country's mood — a man devoid of hope or joy. He was waiting. Avoiding tempests and stormy controversies, he exercised his duties in diplomatic fashion.

Everything was allowed to continue in the same old way. The Matignon was no longer a command post. Power had been diluted.

One of the oldest cabinet members has pointedly noted: "During that entire winter I never once received instructions from Couve. Whereas Pompidou, and especially Debré, gave the ministers no rest."

The premier was trying to project his own image, but the memories left by his two predecessors seemed to paralyze him. He was satisfied to employ phrases that had always been part of a premier's daily manner of speaking: "Order will be maintained"; "Economic conditions are satisfactory"; "France is once again enjoying stability." Few paid any heed to what he was saying.

Yet de Gaulle retained confidence in the man. Hadn't he appointed Couve? He was aware of all the criticism, but he stubbornly repeated, as if to convince himself: "He'll work into it. Just give him eighteen months."

The cabinet meetings were rather gloomy affairs. The general scribbled on a pad of paper, his face troubled by a tic. The soft-voiced premier said very little. The other ministers settled their affairs in their own offices, among themselves. The team, quite disunited, comprised the general's marshals, Pompidou's protégés, Couve's friends, with even a minister who, as everyone knew, had been hoping ever since May that the general would quit. Cliques formed, almost openly.

The finance minister, François-Xavier Ortoli, was considered largely responsible for this French malaise. Jeanneney, always impatient, urged Couve to replace him. "Take someone else. Take a new face. You have to govern."

But de Gaulle would not consent to a reshuffling of ministers after only six months. That was how things had been done under the discredited, reviled Fourth Republic. At least he was well acquainted with all the men who now surrounded him; he knew their weaknesses as well as their strengths. He was leery of new faces.

. .

Fresh trouble was expected from the ministry of national education. The minister, Edgar Faure, was rumored to be too adroit and lacking in principle. To make matters worse, he had become an enthusiastic advocate of the general's theories on reform. During the first weeks of the Couve cabinet, he called de Gaulle "Mr. President of the Republic," thereby paying obeisance to a tradition that had prevailed long before 1958. Now, however, he said "my general," like everybody else.

The chief of state, at first intrigued, supported Faure against the skeptics. The lycées and universities were once again in a terrible uproar. But de Gaulle and Edgar Faure continued to preach university participation, although they did not underestimate these convulsions. "Those little agitators have no guts," the general sneered. "They want to dish it out, but if they get it back they can't take it."

Edgar Faure had enemies everywhere: at the Matignon, where most of Couve's colleagues opposed his policy; in the government; and even in the chief of state's entourage. To all his critics, Faure replied by invoking the name of the general, his "mastermind," his "boss." But de Gaulle, who once described Edgar Faure as "a man who doesn't bore you," soon began to think of replacing him. In January, he confided this to several of his intimates, all the while imperturbably emphasizing his confidence in Faure.

In the Assembly, the Gaullists' recriminations grew more and more insistent — against Couve, against Ortoli, against Edgar Faure, against the entire cabinet, whose actions were judged to be chaotic. The massive majority was rebellious. Invoking the name of the general, the premier tried to control the agitation. But his prestige, already diminished, was vanishing. Behind this quasi-public revolt, a graver crisis was brewing. Their voices lowered, the faithful were saying that de Gaulle was no longer the de Gaulle they had served. The era of triumphs was over.

From his post as foreign minister, that heroic apostle of Gaullism, Michel Debré, perceived all the signs of a decline he was loath to acknowledge. In May 1968, he had seen the general falter. What he saw as the "weakness" of Couve, the "follies" of Edgar Faure, the "troublesome" plan regarding regionalism — all these proved to him that de Gaulle had not recovered.

This was the end. The end of a reign — that of de Gaulle and perhaps of the Gaullists. The party began to feel the repercussions during the early part of 1969. Jacques Chaban-Delmas, who consulted his colleagues with increasing frequency, admitted: "This government can't last much longer. Nor, in all likelihood, can the general."

At their weekly luncheons, Frey, Debré and the barons were the first to say that the referendum — no matter when it took place — would be lost.

And Valéry Giscard d'Estaing, who had one foot in the opposition camp, declared without mercy that Frenchmen no longer had confidence in de Gaulle politically, although "he continues to retain their affection."

. .

Georges Pompidou heard all these rumors. Putting his personal cares aside, he tried to reunite a faltering majority. He invited the most influential deputies to have lunch with him. He reappeared at meetings of the Gaullist party, offering advice to its leaders. He displayed a solicitous interest in the party's financial problems.

Forgetting his resentment, he presided over meetings of the barons and renewed his contacts with them. Always prudent, he advocated no specific strategy. But he paraded his trumps: good health, vigor, availability.

As head of the Gaullist majority, he still held the privileged place that Couve had been unable to win for himself. Within de Gaulle's shadow, a silent battle was waged between the former premier and the current one. At meetings of the Gaullist group, the two men, seated a few feet apart, took each other's measure. They did not speak. Neither dared to fight openly. In November Pompidou had said: "We're willing to follow the government provided we know where it is going."

This sort of talk by someone speaking in the name of the Gaullists, and especially as their leader, irritated the general and his premier. Decidedly, Pompidou was refusing to remain silent, as he had been advised to do. De Gaulle was not slow to reach a conclusion. He said to one of his former ministers: "I'm told that my premier doesn't exist. I prefer him to his predecessor, who exists a bit too much."

Betrayal is something natural, true loyalty a miracle.

CHAPTER 21

A Good Whiff of Gunpowder

On December 28, in retaliation for an assault on an El Al plane in Athens, Israeli commandos attacked a Lebanese airport. Libya offered to protect the Palestinian guerrilla organizations. Libya, a former Italian colony, was now France's friend and ally. De Gaulle fulminated against this blow perpetrated by Israeli activists. Just as he had predicted, the conflict was spreading and would soon embrace the entire Middle East. France could not remain silent. Arab affairs were of greater concern to her than to any other country.

During the ensuing six days, the general's anger grew. He talked about a "criminal insult." A very secret council of war was held at the Elysée. Present were the premier, Pierre Messmer representing the army, Michel Debré from the foreign ministry, and François-Xavier Ortoli from finance. The general gave his orders: no military materiel whatsoever, not a single shell, bolt, or screw was to be delivered to Israel from now on. Since the Six-Day War, only the sale of Mirage had been embargoed. France had continued to provide Israel with all kinds of military supplies, including helicopters and gunboats, to say nothing of innumerable pieces of industrial machinery. "Well, that's all over," de Gaulle said. "As long as this conflict continues, the Israelis will get nothing from us."

There was no answer to this. A high official of the Israeli embassy, Admiral Limon, was officially informed of the government's decision. French customs officers were also apprised. But they reacted more slowly than did the Israelis. Late that same day, January 3, two gunboats under construction in Cherbourg and earmarked for the Israelis went to sea to engage in maneuvers. They disappeared.

Messmer appeared at the Elysée early the following morning. The general raged against this fresh affront. In the end, he reluctantly abandoned the idea of reprisals because it might prove dangerous, and accepted instead a statement to the effect that the boats had been lost. But this piracy by the Jewish people reawakened his instinctive aggressiveness, which had lain dormant ever since the crisis of the franc.

On January 8, at the close of a cabinet meeting during which nothing was said about this matter, de Gaulle motioned to Le Theule to follow him into his office. Then, pacing up and down with long strides, and punctuating each word with gestures of arms and hands, he said to his youthful press secretary: "You're going to issue a statement, Le Theule."

The secretary reached for his pen. The words came in such torrents that he could understand only the tail ends of sentences. "You're going to say that this operation against Libya is intolerable . . . inexcusable . . . You'll say that France does not want bloody chaos in the Middle East. You'll say that we hope the four big powers will accept the Soviet proposals . . . You'll say, Le Theule, that the French press is sectarian: of course everyone knows it has sold out to Jewish interests. So get going . . ."

Upon leaving the general, the minister reconstructed as best he could all the statements that had been issued pell-mell. Assailed by a few scruples, he toned down what the general had said about journalists. De Gaulle would not reproach him for this.

The embargo against Israel caused a tempest in Paris. This did not bother the general. "Café talk," he said. "Drawing room conversation."

De Gaulle shrugged off such petty obstacles. He had been brought back to life with a good whiff of gunpowder.*

---

* Incidentally, this first Franco-Israeli clash over gunboats remained a State secret for one year. In December 1969 after Georges Pompidou had replaced General de Gaulle, five more gunboats were also spirited away from France. As a result of the second incident, the French government invited Admiral Limon to return to Israel.

Once again de Gaulle was in a hurry to implement his ideas on participation. He wouldn't listen to the counsels of prudence he received from almost everyone. Timidly, his collaborators and ministers tried to hold him back. Order had not yet been completely restored at home nor had an economic balance been achieved. The social dangers were not over. The premier still hoped that the referendum would take place after the summer, if all went well.

But de Gaulle paid no attention to such arguments. The daily grind was the cabinet's concern. His role was to transform the present, to prepare for the future. Was the referendum a challenge? Was it unreasonable? Nothing great could be accomplished by prudence, by sparing oneself, by engaging in deals. June 18, 1940, was proof of this. Let others be guided by petty fears! "General de Gaulle was not born to reassure the masses," the chief of state grandly declared.

With inexhaustible patience, he resumed his explanations. One had to change society, "to alter the individual's existence within this society." The general was certain that this would be his great work, a genuinely original contribution that would live on after him. Earlier, decolonization had been a painful necessity to which other nations — England especially — had yielded. Institutions were only worth "what men are worth." God alone knew what would remain of the Fifth Republic after de Gaulle. The participation of workers in the management and profit sharing of businesses would be his unique legacy to future generations.

The university, the regions, parliament — they were only imperfect experiments. His revolution, on the other hand, would make a genuine contribution to the world of industry and labor.

However, de Gaulle did admit: "Participation in industry is something no one wants." A few months later, he stated more explicitly: "Everyone is against it, even Couve."

De Gaulle was resigned to this. Within the cabinet, opposition to his idea was unanimous, except of course for René Capitant and his

new disciple, Edgar Faure. In the Assembly and among the Gaullists, opposition was equally widespread.

Pompidou himself never concealed his reservations. On June 5,
after the terrible month of May, he remarked to a journalist: "Between us, the general is just dreaming."

Undismayed, de Gaulle pursued his chimera. One had to disrupt
the order of things — yes! One had to find some sort of intermediate solution between East and West, between a parliamentary republic and a monarchy, between "outmoded totalitarian Marxism"
and "inhuman capitalism." "Long after I'm dead," he said to a
counselor, "your children and their children will associate my name
with participation."

Capitant frantically exhorted de Gaulle: "My general, don't be
afraid of waging an open battle against the capitalists. Of course,
they'll fight you every inch of the way. So much the better! Their
very opposition will serve to thaw public opinion. You must rely on
the French left. Then genuine Gaullism will make its appearance!"

But de Gaulle's strategy was shrewder. The referendum on the
Senate and on the issue of regionalism was a door that could open
up broader perspectives. Let all Frenchmen vote yes, generously,
and in large numbers! Then, with their backing and his new-found
legitimacy, he would be able to impose his ideas on employers,
trade unions, deputies, Gaullists and Couve. And on Pompidou, of
course.

What was the point of totting up the misgivings of people like
Giscard, who once again had committed treachery by condemning
the idea of a referendum in 1969; or of people like Debré — that
loyal Debré — "nervous but reliable," according to de Gaulle, who
was furiously opposed to regionalism and a reform of the Senate.
And there were many such others . . . The general said: "Frenchmen will understand me."

The referendum was but one step. Already de Gaulle was envi-
sioning what would follow — participation in industrial enterprises.
He had no intention of merely seasoning capitalism with a more ap-

petizing sauce, of altering the present system by granting material advantages to the workers: he wanted to create nothing less than a different way of life.

His objectives were fixed. In mid-January, without further consultation, de Gaulle made up his mind: the referendum would take place in the spring, perhaps as early as March.

. .

Pompidou was making preparations for his first trip as the Dauphin. He gave up the idea of going to Yugoslavia, for fear of being ridiculed. But otherwise he followed the itinerary suggested by the general. He would first go to Rome, then to London and Washington. These visits would represent so many stages of his apprenticeship. Couve had been to these places many times.

All the sundry details of protocol had been minutely mapped out. From his office in the Elysée, which adjoined de Gaulle's, Tricot had issued the necessary orders. Michel Debré, henceforth the faithful friend, had put the services of the Quai d'Orsay at Pompidou's disposal. In Rome, both of France's ambassadors were ready to roll out the red carpet.

Late in the afternoon of Thursday, January 9, Pompidou went to the Elysée. De Gaulle once again alluded to Pompidou's "national destiny" and spoke of his trip as being of major importance. "I've been told that you're going to see the pope."

Between France and Italy, few problems existed. Those that did exist received attention in Brussels, capital of the Common Market. The general reminded Pompidou that his future eminence made such trips and meetings necessary. Pompidou was of course well known in France, but his name must now become better known in foreign capitals.

For three quarters of an hour de Gaulle was his most charming self, showering Pompidou with all sorts of good advice. He mentioned Israel and went on to analyze the situation in a way which his former premier was later to describe as "flawless." The general also alluded to Edgar Faure and national education — this matter worried him. But it was the referendum, his last battle, that he mainly underscored. He was coming to the end of his reign.

Six days later Pompidou arrived in Rome and immediately let it be known that he was not there as an ordinary tourist. "Upon my return, I will naturally report my impressions to the French government and to the President of the Republic."

The former premier's visit evoked no curiosity. Politicians generally received little attention in Rome.

Two days later, on the eve of his return, Pompidou played host to a group of French journalists. He was feeling relaxed. In all his encounters with the press when he was premier, he had always been prudent and guarded. Every word had been carefully weighed, every sigh, every smile.

Today he felt somewhat as if he were on vacation. He had few burdensome responsibilities. As the deputy from Cantal who knew he had an important political future, he was now free from any obligation to the general. The unfortunate Markovic affair had helped him to discover the meaning of independence.

One journalist asked him a question about the succession. During his last three years at the Matignon, Pompidou had been careful not to fall into that trap. "I'm the last person in the world to think about it," he had said then. Or: "Ask the general." This time he answered publicly in much the same way that he had spoken privately during the past few weeks. "I think it's no secret to anyone that I'll be a candidate."

A candidate . . . Perhaps there were others who were secretly preparing for a national destiny. What about Couve de Murville? Or Edgar Faure, in spite of his denials? And surely Giscard. At a recent meeting of Gaullist party leaders, Pompidou had protested against all the publicity featuring his former finance minister. "Even when you attack him, you bring his name before the public, and he likes nothing better."

Pompidou was but the first to sign up on a list that would certainly grow longer. His statement to the press revealed nothing. As

Pompidou said at that time, "None of the diplomats who happened to be present expressed surprise. And the journalists didn't rush to the phone to communicate my remarks to their editors."

No sooner had he spoken than his words reached the ears of the French people. But his remarks were not accurately reproduced. A thousand ideas on the subject were attributed to the former premier. The next day, as he was leaving the Vatican, he voiced his surprise at the way his remarks were interpreted. But he confirmed everything that had been written.

The Gaullists heard him, even those who were pleased by the Markovic affair and thought he would have to take a back seat because of the scandal. He had left Paris as someone standing on the sidelines, as someone who might even be on the verge of retirement, with a little mud still sticking to the soles of his shoes. The trip to Rome proved to be his baptism and his coronation.

A few days after his return, Pompidou again received journalists, but this time in private. Of course he had spoken to them often when the Markovic scandal was at its height.

He said indignantly to one of the newspaper editors present: "You have blown up out of all proportion the things I told you in confidence. Had you set out to harm me, you couldn't have done better." Then he added with a gleeful look: "Okay. I won't make a fuss about it."

. .

The news from Rome touched de Gaulle to the quick. That Friday evening, when the press report was placed on his desk, the general murmured: "It's altogether incredible."

For a quarter of a century Pompidou had been his confidant, his protégé. Here was a man whom he had invited to dinner, to whom he had confided his secrets. De Gaulle could not understand such outrageous behavior. Only eight days before, here in this very room, Pompidou had sat in the armchair facing him. The general had encouraged him in his aspirations, had treated him with great friendliness. And now he found himself reading such unwarranted remarks. They were improper. No statesman worthy of the name would express himself in such terms. How could Pompidou have changed in so short a time? How could he have gone so far as to employ such wounding language? De Gaulle kept repeating: "I just don't understand."

To Tricot he said: "All the same, this is a bit too much. If I should choose not to wait until the end of my mandate, it's up to me and to no one else to announce it."

The general summoned Couve. As the minutes passed, his anger mounted. In the presence of his premier, he gave free vent to his indignation: "To stoop so low, when you're in a foreign country, in a foreign capital, on a semiofficial trip! To make remarks like those you hear at the Assembly's refreshment bar! Oh, I didn't expect that from Pompidou!"

De Gaulle stood up. He said to Couve that his dignity as President of the Republic had been flouted — his authority as chief of state. And this, on the eve of a referendum! "I don't understand it. Tell me, what on earth was he was thinking of?"

To all the ministers he happened to see on that day, de Gaulle expressed his disappointment. Coming from anyone else, he said, a rebuff like the one administered him in Rome would have seemed merely contemptible. Then the general embarked on soliloquies about man's ingratitude and vanity. "And the press! Have you seen the newspapers? They think de Gaulle is already finished, dead and buried. When something rotten happens anywhere, the journalists naturally jump on it."

Not without some cruelty, the general was reminded that Pompidou's presidential aspirations did not date from yesterday. As early as 1965 . . .

"Oh, long before that," the general retorted. "Long before, please believe me."

But he refused to believe in what Capitant called a "political maneuver." Pompidou was not mad. He wouldn't go off and fight de Gaulle. "Besides," the general noted, "it wouldn't be to his advantage."

For four days de Gaulle gave himself up to his chagrin. He even forgot about other affairs of state. But he was fortified in his resolution to proceed with the referendum, in fact to hold it as soon as possible. All the rivalry and competition would thereby be rendered pointless.

Couve believed that Pompidou's remarks might have serious consequences. The voters were now likely to think that the question of what would happen after Gaullism had been settled and that chaos would be averted. This would rob de Gaulle of a weighty argument. The general answered with a shrug. If Frenchmen allowed themselves to be taken in by such a simple game, well then, de Gaulle would leave with no regrets.

"I'm an old man," he said again to one of his collaborators. "An old man who has witnessed too many shabby things." But then he added: "Look at me. I'm not dead. Even if Pompidou wishes I were. But you'll see. The French people will not forgive him for this. He's made a mistake. He will never be elected President of the Republic."

De Gaulle himself was not inclined to forget it. "I'll never see him again. Anyway, he'd just depress me."

. .

On the following Wednesday the general entered the cabinet meeting with a resolute tread. The ministers assumed that the episode had been forgotten. The agenda listed only routine questions: the Middle East, to be discussed by Debré, and university reform, by Edgar Faure.

The session began. Each minister spoke in turn. Couve punctuated the speeches with brief commentaries. The usual thing . . .

Suddenly de Gaulle seized a piece of paper and began to scribble, as he sometimes did, paying no attention to what was being said. He covered the sheet with his vertical, slanted writing, crossing out words here and there. One minister tried to get a glimpse of it. Finally, as members of the cabinet gathered up papers and briefcases, the general stood up. He said:

"Gentlemen, here is the text of a communiqué I propose to give to the ministry of information: 'To accomplish the national task that is incumbent upon me, I was reelected President of the Republic for seven years by the French people. I have the duty and the intention of completely discharging this mandate.' Gentlemen, I thank you."

Then the general went to his office. He was soon joined by Le Theule to whom he handed the text. The Minister of Information respectfully asked the chief of state: what about Pompidou's trips to foreign countries? Should they be canceled?

"Oh, he'll travel, Le Theule, he can travel. But nothing will ever be as it was before."

Part VI

FAREWELL

Why, now, blow wind, smell billow, and swim bark!
The storm is up, and all is on the hazard.

Julius Caesar, *act 5, scene 1*

CHAPTER 22

"Shall we hold the referendum?"

THE ELYSÉE WAS A HERMITAGE. Over a ten-year span, de Gaulle had paced it ten thousand times: from his office to the dining room, from the drawing room to his office. The witnesses of his solitude were forever the same: aides-de-camp, guards, footmen. Occasionally, in the middle of a sentence, the general's eye would wander toward the park where long before he used to promenade. Or he would listen to the rumble of Paris, of life, as it reached his windows with a dying sound. Once or twice the armchairs were switched or the moldings regilded, but de Gaulle took no interest in such details. In the large room where he spent nine hours a day, there was not a single object, nor a memory. A room of sumptuous austerity.

Here, around him no one was left save functionaries: Bernard Tricot, the highest-ranking official, or Xavier de la Chevalerie. All were diplomats or magistrates — devoted, stiff, silent men. The faithful of the old heroic times had been replaced by a younger generation. Those of his war comrades who were still alive had retired. Men like Fouchet and Joxe came only for brief visits to share his memories. On other days, de Gaulle's sole companions were deferential listeners. Even the ministers rarely came to the Elysée.

To Madame de Gaulle, who began to worry about his weariness and sadness, the general would say reassuringly: "I will manage to leave power before it leaves me."

And to prove to her that he was really thinking about the future, he made plans to travel, spoke of the next volume of his memoirs, of the art of writing.

Ever since May 1968, the general had been through with crowds. He ceased going on trips or tours to the provinces. Now the only crowds he encountered were those that gathered at various ceremonies like the one commemorating the victory of 1918.

De Gaulle read the newspapers, questioned his visitors and watched television. It was thus that he kept tabs on the changes occurring in the world. The spectacle of the violence and despair that plagued all nations grieved him. To those who directed the nation's television, he said: "Give us some good matches, with French victories, and some good books."

The general was seeking remedies for his country's melancholy. Everywhere — in the bureaucracy, among peasants, small businessmen, shopkeepers — he saw nothing but grayness and defeat. "For ten years, I have asked the country to make so many sacrifices," he admitted. "Frenchmen prefer just to get on with their own lives."

One more battle, one more victory, and then de Gaulle would yield to his wife's wishes. He had reached a decision: he would announce the referendum for the end of the month. The die was cast. January had not been as difficult as predicted. No economic crisis had materialized. Students at the lycées and universities had indulged in childish activities, that was all. The moment had come to appeal to Frenchmen, to their ardor, their aspirations, and their good common sense.

·   ·

In Brittany — Christian territory, beloved, valiant Brittany, where his mother had been laid to rest — the general announced his new battle.

He was hoping that here, at least, agitation would not create any problems. In the villages of Brittany, the peasants gave de Gaulle a warm welcome. The general swung into the ritual of these campaign junkets without any effort: rural rehabilitation, 250,000-ton oil tankers, four-way highways, schoolbooks — he omitted nothing. But things were different in the big cities. At Rennes, the chief of state spent the night in hermetically sealed quarters, guarded by the police. At Quimper, the "International" was sung along with the "Marseillaise." Disregarding the cacophony, de Gaulle appealed to history, to the memory of Duguay-Trouin, La Motte-Picquet, Surcouf, Châteaubriand, as well as to that of his Uncle Charles, a Breton bard of the previous century.

"Since this far-reaching reform," he declared, "involves many features of our governmental organization, including certain stipulations of our constitution, we must submit the plan to the people. They, as sovereign judges, will decide by means of a referendum. And since we are paving the way for fresh hope to flower, we will hold the referendum in the springtime." But the sovereign people of Brittany, who so often had given him their votes, responded with silence and disapproval. The general of course noticed this immediately. The deputy from Quimper, Edmond Michelet, the Michelet of old, his comrade in arms, told him quite frankly: "It's going to be a tough fight, my general. You'll have the Jews, the bosses and the trade unions against you . . . But you've been through many tough fights since June nineteen forty."

"In nineteen forty, Michelet? Well, I'll tell you something terrible: in nineteen forty, without the English, the jig would have been up."

.   .

With keen attention, Pompidou followed the country's moods. He had gone back to politics. Nothing that was being done, said or written escaped him, not even the risks the general was taking.

The referendum announced at Quimper had originally been scheduled for May 24, 1968. The former premier reminded all those who complained: "I tried to dissuade the general from holding it. Couve didn't even put up a fight."

With cruel precision, he enumerated all the dangers inherent in the undertaking. Couldn't the general see that after ten years, the French people were clamoring for him to quit? No one could remain in office in France beyond a certain length of time — seven years at the most, more probably five. If, as the general had solemnly stated, he intended to remain until the expiration of his second mandate, he wasn't choosing the best way of going about it. "Oh, that referendum!" he was to say in May 1969. "It was an egregious blunder!"

Later, he was more explicit: "There was really nothing at issue. You can have a referendum on Algeria, on the election of the President of the Republic by universal suffrage, or on the constitution, of course. But not on the functioning of regional assemblies. Just try to explain that sort of thing to voters. I've always thought it impossible." Ever since the start of the year, Pompidou had been predicting that a fresh crisis would occur in the spring. The skillful game played by Edgar Faure would only infuriate the students. The idea of participation in industry would anger the employers. Workers would be encouraged to make additional demands. All these were interdependent things. De Gaulle would be unable to repeat the miracle of May 1968. The only solution was his precipitate departure.

And a referendum today! Pompidou sharply reproached Couve, Tricot and Jeanneney for not performing their duty, for not halting de Gaulle on his catastrophic course.

Even Pompidou's warnings were not heeded by the general. Ever since his Roman escapade the former premier was ignored by the Elysée. Since he was now really free, Pompidou saw no further need to be cautious. Indeed, from now on he could be less and less discreet. To everyone, Gaullists and non-Gaullists alike, the former premier mournfully confided his prognostications: the general would be defeated, he would leave and perhaps there would be violence. France would need a man toughened by the May holocaust. Constantly he kept harking back to the May crisis, explaining and justifying his actions in an attempt to make it plain that he had emerged victorious. The general had bet on the wrong horse. Even Pompidou had thought that the chief of state would resign at that time. In May 1968 de Gaulle had fired his last guns. "The king is naked," a columnist wrote.

Smarting at the communiqué published by the chief of state in response to his Roman venture, Pompidou now played his game in the open. "I said nothing in Rome that wasn't altogether natural. The general couldn't have been surprised. He is no more master of my fate than I am myself. It's up to the voters to decide."

Among the Gaullists, there were many who were troubled by the exchange of petty remarks between de Gaulle and Pompidou. "Some of us, most of us," a leader of the majority party explained, "said at the time: 'Pompidou is finished.' Others felt that the post-Gaullist period had begun. We had arrived at the point where we had to make an unavoidable, painful choice between our historic leader and the leader of tomorrow."

Pompidou could no longer rely on the general's promises. The two men were on such bad terms that the rift became common knowledge. Pompidou admitted that his innate, legitimate pride had been hurt. "The general stood me in a corner as if I were a small boy," he said to one of his friends. "I simply had to react."

. .

On February 13, 1969, eleven days after the general's trip to Brittany, Pompidou again alluded to the remarks he had made in Rome. He did so in the course of a lecture delivered in Geneva. "The question of succession has not been raised," he said. But he added: "This being so, it must also be said that someday elections for the President of the Republic will have to be held."

He said the same thing on Swiss television.

This time, he had carefully gauged the impression he would make. But upon his return to the Boulevard de Latour-Maubourg, his collaborators said: "You should have warned us. In the future, whenever you do something like that, please let us know ahead of time."

There was nothing surprising about the way the reigning monarch received the "pretender's" statement. The government forbade the director of French television to use the tape made in Geneva. Pompidou was excluded from going on the air, just as Giscard d'Estaing had been since 1967. That was all. Approving the ban, the general said to Le Theule with marked sadness: "He's getting in deeper and deeper, that Pompidou."

That very evening de Gaulle dined with his family in the small dining room at the Elysée. He had invited his brother-in-law, his nephew, and his sister-in-law. Ordinarily, he refrained from discussing his preoccupations at the dinner table. One did not talk about affairs of state in the presence of ladies. But this time de Gaulle could not contain himself. Stiffly, he uttered the name of Pompidou. "What on earth has he been saying again, and in Switzerland, of all places!"

On this occasion, de Gaulle spoke quite plainly of "treachery." It was a word he had learned to use during the last thirty years. No longer de Gaulle's "Georges," Pompidou was now but one more name to be added to the long list of candidates, politicians and partisans. Even were he the best of them, or at any rate the least harmful, never again would he belong to an elite of privileged friends.

A confidant has stated, "Until this moment, the general had always refrained from revealing his feelings about Pompidou. It was as if the man whom de Gaulle had himself chosen and 'made' had to be cloaked in a certain mystery. After Geneva, everything changed. The general plainly displayed his indifference and at times his contempt for Pompidou. For him the former premier had become an ordinary man, like all the others."

The chief of state did not hesitate to make it plain that the bond that had linked him to Pompidou was severed forever. Whenever a collaborator or a minister showed him the results of a public opinion poll on the popularity of politicians (de Gaulle was very interested in this new form of political analysis) the general would examine the figures and grumble, clearing his throat: "All these Pompidou-type politicians . . ."

Spite, chagrin, fury . . . The cruel law of power leaves no room for sentiment.

A few weeks before the referendum, de Gaulle began to realize that Pompidou represented a serious political threat. No longer

could he frighten Frenchmen with the specter of chaos if they failed
to demonstrate their confidence in him. The strategy he liked best
— conjuring up a dark picture of what would come after de Gaulle
— was bound to backfire. He was well aware of this. Even the referendum was threatened.

· ·

Several days later, de Gaulle was ready to call off the "decisive
test." On February 15, he invited his old friend General Catroux to
lunch. Catroux was one of the few men alive — the only one perhaps, with the exception of Malraux — who inspired respect, affection and a feeling of fraternity in the chief of state. De Gaulle
seemed calm, detached from events. The talk reverted to old
memories — the war, Africa, the colonies, and that forgotten era
when the French army was "the most important thing in the
world." Perhaps he secretly pitied the embodiment of old age that
confronted him. General Catroux was ninety-one.

A few ministers were also invited to lunch. When coffee was
served, de Gaulle, a cup of coffee in his hand, went over to his minister in charge of reform and, without a trace of irony, said to him:
"Well, Jeanneney, what about this referendum? Shall we go ahead
with it?"

The minister almost choked. Two weeks before, the referendum
had been solemnly announced at Quimper. Ever since, de Gaulle
had constantly voiced impatience and determination about it.
Jeanneney remained silent for a long time, attempting to perceive
exactly what the general meant to convey. But de Gaulle was impassive.

"My general, you can't back out now. You have announced the
referendum. It's too late to give it up."

De Gaulle interrupted him. After all, he explained, his trip to
Brittany hadn't been a great success. Nor had the welcome of the
voters been warm. Yet he had always thought of them as loyal supporters. Besides, the sky was full of clouds . . .

"The only possible solution," said Jeanneney, "is for you to disengage yourself from the outcome. Let the French people answer yes or no, and whatever they decide should be of no consequence to you. All things considered, it will be a referendum on purely technical issues. And if the proposal is rejected, well, my own political career will be over, that's all."

The general raised his voice. "Oh come, Jeanneney, you can't believe that I would allow you to do battle all alone?"

The chief of state shook his head. The referendum was off to a bad start; he couldn't get into the swing of it. The French people couldn't either. The first bits of information from the prefects indicated that the voters were still undecided, with a slightly preponderant tendency to vote no.

As his guests were leaving, the general again asked Jeanneney to think it over. Upon leaving the Elysée, Jeanneney went to see Couve at the Matignon and reported the general's strange remarks. At first the premier refused to take them seriously. De Gaulle was probably depressed; he was often that way now. Jeanneney had been taken in by the general's somber prophecies. But Jeanneney stood firm. He insisted on going into the details of his conversation with de Gaulle.

"God is my witness," Couve said, raising his arms to heaven, "I was the last person to want this referendum. But it's too late now. In any case, even if the general decides not to gamble his fate in this affair, we still have to consult the voters on two issues: regionalism and reform of the Senate."

Roger Frey, the minister in charge of relations with the parliament, was completely bowled over when Jeanneney brought him up to date. "Two questions?" he said. "Oh, no! That would be crazy. You're giving Frenchmen two chances instead of one to vote no."

Two days later, Couve and Frey were summoned to the Elysée. The latest complication put the premier in a very embarrassing position. He explained that to postpone the referendum after having talked about it so much would completely denude the government of authority, of credibility. "We'd be placed in an untenable position," he contended.

In the presence of Roger Frey, the general was even more undecided and pessimistic. His minister took a firm line: "I was never enthusiastic about holding a referendum at this time," Frey said. "But to put it off now would be even worse. It would look like capitulation in the very midst of a campaign. Consequently, it would be unworthy of General de Gaulle."

Wednesday the 19th had been the day set aside for the cabinet to fix the date of the referendum. De Gaulle had expressed his wishes on several occasions to most of his ministers. He wanted the referendum to be held sometime before the Easter vacation, about a week before Palm Sunday, which would fall on March 23.

But when the cabinet met that Wednesday, the general seemed hesitant. Since the question had been placed on the agenda, he would have to make up his mind. But suddenly he no longer seemed to be in a hurry. Seated around the large circular table, he allowed the ministers to ramble on and listened with a bored air to the most trivial arguments. One minister mentioned the social meeting in March. Not much good would come of it. A conference with the trade unions was scheduled for March 4. Someone else spoke of the shopkeepers who were agitating (they went on strike March 5). Economic difficulties and the taxes that were soon due were also brought up. Then there was the Easter vacation that would take up most of April. Even spring showers and the Ides of March were mentioned.

A few days later, de Gaulle said to Marcellin glumly: "Of course, no matter what date we choose it will be an inconvenient one."

Finally, amid all the suggestions and counterproposals, the general hit upon a solution: he would schedule the referendum for April 27, more than two months hence.

The meeting came to an end.

. .

During the past ten years, wherever issues arose between the French people and himself, the general had always shown resolution. Once he arrived at a decision, he lost no time in carrying it out. But now he was still weighing the pros and cons, mindful of the Almighty's admonitions.

After further painful meditation, he summoned his ministers, Debré and Marcellin. He asked them how the referendum could be tabled without giving the impression that he was vacillating. Completely immersed in the affairs of the Middle East, Debré suggested that de Gaulle lean on this issue — on the fact that the big four were concentrating their forces there — to postpone the vote. The government could explain that at a time like this, when France had a vital peacemaking role to play, it was important to insure political stability at home. De Gaulle thanked Debré but concluded that all these excuses seemed implausible.

The Minister of the Interior had more complex tactics in mind. Turning to him, the general asked: "Well, Marcellin, what about the referendum?"

"It's risky, my general. This is the zero hour."

"But what do you think?"

"It would be best to give it up for the moment. That's my feeling. This referendum will bring all the malcontents together. Even the mothers won't vote for you. For the first time, my general, the women will not be on your side."

"What shall we do, Marcellin? We've already postponed the referendum once. How can we get out of it?"

The minister suggested that they should resort to legislation to effect the necessary reforms of the communes and cantons. Then, in the same way, the regional issue could be resolved. Finally, the question of overhauling the Senate, which would round things out, should be decided by a referendum. All in all, the entire undertaking would require three or four years. By then, his mandate would expire.

"Well, then," the general answered with obvious satisfaction, "you'll tell that to the ministers at the next cabinet meeting."

A few days later the ministers were summoned by the chief of state. He wanted to discuss the text of the proposal that was to be submitted to the voters. At the very outset, the general announced: *"Alea jacta est."* Marcellin had brought with him a sixteen-page report. He still believed that he had convinced the chief of state.

The meeting proved interminable. Every word was carefully weighed. At tea time, the general suggested an intermission. Marcellin used the break to talk to the general in his office. Should he speak up, as they had agreed? De Gaulle declared that there was no longer any point in his doing so. But Marcellin insisted: "My general," he said, "we're going to lose the referendum. I've gathered a lot of information and contacted several people during these last few days. I must warn you: we're going to lose."

Raising his hands toward the ceiling, the general retorted with sovereign eloquence: "Well, what a fine end that would be!"

He was obviously being carried along by the inexorable course of events. The drift had begun. Still, he hesitated.

"At the close of February," Jeanneney has recounted, "I answered a group of newspapermen very evasively about the consequences of a possible no. I said that it was not at all certain that the general was gambling his future. In any case, I for one did not think so. Something the chief of state had said gave me reason to believe that my surmise was correct. De Gaulle was really undecided. I still think that if the general had been able to hit upon a good excuse, he would have postponed the whole thing. Just as he'd done in May nineteen sixty-eight."

By the beginning of March de Gaulle was as skeptical as ever. He listened to the opening roll of the drums. He noted Alain Poher's impatience as well as Giscard's and Pompidou's. Neither the political parties nor their leaders gave him pause. What he really dreaded was the weariness, the "caving in" of the French people. "This country has never had a stiff spine," he observed.

He consulted the oracles. Opinion polls painted a black picture. He tried to detect in them a clue to his own fate. The figures were contradictory, changing from day to day, and the general's heartbeats fluctuated with them. Bernard Tricot was worried and tried to protect the chief from bad tidings. Attentive, with practiced eye, he followed the ups and downs of popular favor.

In seven times seven days, the die would be cast.

CHAPTER 23

Final Encounter

RECOVERED FROM HIS ILLNESS, René Capitant returned to the ministry of justice. The magistrates were mired in the Markovic affair. No light had been shed. But at least the stench of scandal had disappeared. The "plot" directed against Pompidou had failed.

Late in January, Alain Delon had been questioned at length. His activities as well as those of a dozen others had been carefully scrutinized. Having failed to discover the killer, the judge who was handling the case tried to ascertain the motives of the crime. The whole thing turned out to be a banal detective story, complete with blackmail, resprisals, and sudden assassination.

In his statement to the police, Delon claimed that Stefan Markovic had played no part whatsoever in his social life. He described Markovic as a person of secondary importance, a bodyguard, a mere employee.

Alexandre Markovic, the brother of the victim, instituted a civil suit. He denied Delon's statement, claiming that Stefan had been taken by the Delons to a party at the château of the Baron de Rothschild, and that he had dined at the home of the Delons with the Pompidous.

This was quite enough to start the whole affair up again. "Another Yugoslav novel," sighed one of the lawyers.

Alexandre Markovic's statement focused attention on someone by the name of Marcantoni, who was arrested. The lawyers for the defense, in an attempt to explain the discrepancies between Alexandre Markovic's statements and those of Alain Delon, asked for an audience with the Pompidous. Very embarrassed, Judge Patard immediately informed Capitant. A few days later, François Mitterand publicly excoriated "the methods being used to discredit and injure the former premier."

Once again Pompidou suspected a sordid plot in which members of the cabinet — he would swear to it — had participated. Maybe Couve was the main culprit, but more likely Capitant. This time Pompidou was determined to respond at once in order to prevent fresh gossip from spreading. He drafted a short statement, which was signed by his secretary and immediately dispatched to the press. It ran as follows: "General de Gaulle's former premier and Madame Pompidou know nothing about the causes or circumstances connected with this news item."

The general promptly heeded his former premier's appeal. He told Tricot to alert Couve. A new campaign of insinuations would be both "unpleasant" and "deplorable." Capitant drafted a communiqué. That very night the Elysée announced that General and Madame de Gaulle were expecting the Pompidous for dinner within a week. This was the first time that such an invitation assumed the importance of an affair of state. Actually, the dinner proved quite different from any other.

This was the end of the Markovic affair: the general's intervention had effectively terminated it. But Pompidou kept repeating that he would forgive nothing. "When the proper time comes, I will deal with this matter," he vowed.

That moment was approaching. The referendum heralded the end of a reign. The general's vacillations — the former premier chastely termed them the political mistakes of the government — were so many infallible signs.

.   .

Not long afterward, Georges Pompidou went to the Salle Colbert at the Palais-Bourbon to join the Gaullist deputies whom he had so often led to victory. Both Couve and Debré were present. But it was the deputy from Cantal, the fallen prince, the man who had lost his title, who took charge. Even those Gaullists who were not beholden to him, who were not his bootlickers — and there were a few — yielded to his sway. Hadn't the general publicly underscored the respect due Pompidou?

The deputies numbered over 300. Knowing them all, Pompidou called a good many of them by their first names. He had resolved their electoral, financial, and sometimes even their personal problems. In the beginning, seven years before, he had been apprehensive of this palace filled with secrets and conspiracies. His natural timidity, now dissipated, had gotten the best of him. He had given the impression that he lacked self-confidence.

"The Assembly scared me," he later admitted. "I was no orator. I had never spoken in public and was awkward and stiff. I knew nothing about parliamentary procedures."

Even as recently as the year before, when Pompidou's position obliged him to appear before the Gaullist deputies, he had seemed rather truculent. Now, on the contrary, he could afford to be considerate, to listen patiently and with an amused smile to all their complaints.

"Don't forget, I'm not the premier."

Better than the general, certainly, and better than Couve, Pompidou knew what troubled these grumblers, wavering between de Gaulle and the electorate. He realized how greatly they feared the referendum. As a deputy himself, he did not conceal from them his own apprehensions.

He advised them to follow the Coué formula, as he himself was doing. The referendum was a mistake: regional reform was unnecessary; reform of the Senate would prove nothing short of disastrous. The entire Assembly, even the Gaullists, even Pompidou, admitted all this. But let it remain a secret between the Gaullist majority and himself. One had to choose, however, between black and white, good and evil; for or against the general. For his part, the former premier stated quite plainly: "We must participate in this fight. It's a fight on behalf of regionalism and its tremendous possibilities. But it's also a fight between the yeas of confidence in the general and the cartel of nays."

This fine spirit of sacrifice did nothing to soften de Gaulle. The chief of state knew very well that over there, on the other side of the Seine — "at the chamber," as the veterans phrased it — "they" did not want participation. And he knew that Pompidou was with them. But as a good strategist de Gaulle wanted to exploit the fame and talents of his former premier. "You must get him to speak on television," the general said to Couve. "That's something he manages to do quite well."

He also advised his current premier to "warm up" his predecessor. Reverting to the Markovic affair, he said: "I don't like such stories."

At the cabinet meeting on Wednesday, March 12, Capitant took from his pocket a statement he had drafted in collaboration with the premier. It was a communiqué declaring that false rumors had been allowed to spread in connection with the latest phase of the Markovic affair and that "justice will not be misled by maneuvers whose object is manifestly alien to its mission." The general approved. "That's very fine as it stands," he said.

.   .

That very evening the Elysée was illuminated with candles to receive the Pompidous and another former premier, Michel Debré, who was accompanied by his wife. Only Couve was missing. He was to invite Pompidou to lunch with him at the Matignon on the following day.

This dinner for three men who had so often fought together had been prepared with minute care. There had been a long discussion at the Elysée over the seating arrangements. Which of the two women should sit at the general's right?

The evening began in a strange and heavy atmosphere. The general was distant; Madame de Gaulle was ill at ease. The foreign minister was suffering from the grippe — and not a diplomatic one.

Madame Pompidou didn't open her mouth. Never taking his eyes from his wife, Pompidou held her by the elbow. He seemed to fear an outburst.

The guests went in to dinner. Madame Debré alone appeared to be hungry. The courses were served rapidly. There were long silences marred only by the sound of cutlery. Then coffee and liqueurs were served. Michel Debré excused himself and went home to bed. The general took the former premier aside for a few minutes as the Pompidous were about to leave. Madame Pompidou plainly showed her impatience. Coats, footmen, car — it was over! In the courtyard, disappointed photographers put away their cameras.

Laconically, Pompidou told his entourage: "The dinner changed nothing. Nothing at all." He did not know that it was a farewell.

. .

The storms broke before they were expected. The currency, the economy, the state — all were threatened again. The fearful specter of May 1968 reappeared. No one could be certain that the explosion wouldn't occur before the referendum. All the symptoms were present. Financial experts predicted that there would be a new monetary crisis toward the end of March and that this time it would not be possible to avoid devaluation. Speculation started up again. The value of gold bars suddenly increased from 7300 to 7700 francs. Tradespeople fretted. On March 11 there was a general strike. Most of the country's workers participated.

To all visitors, de Gaulle insisted that there was but one remedy: "This country doesn't believe in anything. Everything's falling apart — the church, the family, and of course, society. So the French people must be 'recaptured,' their enthusiasm and hope must be renewed. Last May, five hundred thousand people marched down the Champs-Elysées. The next time there'll be two million. And I'll be marching with them."

Surrounded by "cry babies" and "nervous Nellies," as the general put it, he was as yet undismayed and continued to define his great task. To his minister, Capitant, he predicted three years of gigantic transformations that would leave their mark on the century forever. In attempting to recapture the nation's imagination and allay its misgivings, the general tended to exaggerate. He enumerated the missed opportunities for revolution that studded the history of France since Napoleon. Nor did he hesitate to claim that his revolution would overshadow all others. Yes, three years would suffice. The regional assemblies and the new Senate would be constituted by early 1970. One could then proceed without delay to introduce participation in industrial enterprises. "Quite possibly," de Gaulle added, "we'll have to hold another referendum when this great innovation gets under way."

Thus there was time for everything. For the moment, however, the first battle must be won. Although it was only six weeks away, de Gaulle had not made a firm decision about the tactics he would employ. He still seemed inclined to make a few concessions. From all sides he was advised to pose two separate questions. According to the latest indications, the French people appeared ready to accept regionalism but not reform of the Senate.

De Gaulle was disappointed. If he didn't have a new Senate, how could he inaugurate participation in industry? By another referendum? Jeanneney told him that this would be plainly unconstitutional.

On March 11, the evening of the general strike, he declared on television, after having done his best to stir up the demons of fear that had so often proved his allies: "It is clear that regionalism and reform of the Senate constitute an indivisible whole."

· ·

All the discussion, all the froth reached the general but made no impression. On March 17, the jurists on the Council of State expressed their opinion — which was unfavorable — in regard to the referendum and gave the press their conclusions. De Gaulle was furious. In the presence of Jeanneney and Tricot — the latter was himself a member of the Council of State — he denounced these "functionaries" who abused their prerogatives to interfere with the conduct of political affairs and to publicize dossiers that should have been kept secret. The "betrayal" of the Council of State elicited epithets he had not used since his army days.

Jeanneney, until now, had hesitated. This time he said: "If they vote no there'll be the devil to pay."

Faced with so much "prejudice," de Gaulle made up his mind. To begin with, he informed his ministers that there could be no equivocation. For reasons that had to do with his historic mission, he had decided to gamble his personal fate. As for the idea of two separate questions, he rejected it out of hand. "The answer must be clear and unambiguous on any issue that concerns France and General de Gaulle."

Realizing that the general had made up his mind once and for all, the ministers stood by him. At a special cabinet meeting on March 24, the definite text was drafted. No quarter was given. De Gaulle rejected everything that might have made the referendum more "appetizing," as one minister put it.

"If we begin by listening to everyone, by trying to please everyone, we might as well give up the referendum right now." The general talked like a gambler: "The die is cast. It's heads or tails."

He grew calm.

CHAPTER 24

Heads or Tails

LIKE THE GENERAL, Pompidou calmly envisaged the two possibilities, victory or defeat, but especially defeat. Like de Gaulle, he studied the opinion polls and the various prognostications. He looked at the prefects' reports.

At the Elysée, the general was already considering what he would do if the answer was no. Pompidou likewise. His conscience was clear. The referendum was none of his doing, his advice had not been asked. To be sure, he would participate in the battle wherever necessary. But he was also preparing for the aftermath in which he would play a major role.

Pompidou discussed this with Edgar Faure, one of his rivals. He talked about whom he would choose as his premier when he became President of the Republic. "You see," he said, "I will need someone who can quiet the Gaullists, at least during the first part of my seven-year term. A man with a less pronounced personality than yours."

Actually, Pompidou had already chosen his premier: Jacques Chaban-Delmas. The President of the National Assembly was one of those rare Gaullists, perhaps the only one, who resembled the accepted image of the general's disciples. He was already making preparations for his new position. Each day, at the Hôtel de Lassay, he lunched with influential people, non-Gaullists as well as Gaullists. Of all the members of the majority party, it was he who became Pompidou's spokesman. He pictured a seductive post-Gaullist era, part continuity, part change, but more realistic, more youthful, possessing more muscle. His was to be a calming influence.

Naturally, Chaban-Delmas talked confidentially to his friends. The referendum, he said, was lost. He too had not been heeded. The general was finished, but the succession was assured.

Despite their distress, the Gaullists did not despair. The faithful and also the tougher members turned toward Pompidou. From the foreign ministry, Michel Debré addressed long pathetic letters, with words scratched out and rewritten, to the man who had succeeded him as premier. "I'm with you," he wrote. Pompidou answered by return mail, promising to preserve and maintain Gaullism. He shed a few tears over the melancholy end of such a glorious epic. "Debré is the greatest government man we have," Pompidou said. "Unfortunately, he has been misunderstood and is not well liked. Besides, he's ineligible."

Every Monday and sometimes more often, the barons met at the table of their friend Chaban-Delmas. Pompidou presided. While they lunched, they formulated slogans for the future presidential campaign and speculated about the size of the hoped-for majority. They looked for allies and found them.

Whether at the Boulevard de Latour-Maubourg or on the Quai de Béthune, the former premier saw many people — military men, high officials, economists, and even a few trade unionists. He also saw employers, financiers and businessmen. One of them, a director of an oil company — and a former collaborator of the general's — assumed responsibility for raising the money Pompidou would need for his presidential battle.

In great secrecy Pompidou saw Giscard.

The former premier opened his heart to everyone. Yes, the referendum was a political mistake, participation a chimera; reform of the Senate would prove useless; regionalism could be achieved by other means. He talked about his duty.

"It's too early," he said. "I did not want the succession to be opened up now, under these circumstances. I would have preferred to see things take their normal course. But I believe I can spare the country the troubles that everyone is predicting."

Nine months had not been long enough to perfect his political personality. He constantly harked back to the May crisis, which he portrayed as a fine victory. He showed surprise when some of his former ministers spoke to him of his "mistakes." "In any case, we never would have capitulated," he said to Christian Fouchet. "We had reserves and we were prepared to fight."

"Oh come, Georges, you know that's not so!"

Since he had not completed his essay on political philosophy, he thought of publishing all his speeches. He welcomed journalists, granted interviews, showed himself to be generous.

At the Elysée, the general was irritated by the impatience of his former premier. Told about Pompidou's preparations, de Gaulle jeered: "All this shady business is a waste. If Frenchmen part with me, it will certainly not be to take Pompidou."

He too spoke of the May crisis but only to underscore the blame due Pompidou for the way he handled the situation. "Everything stemmed from that," he said. "The Sorbonne, the strike and all the rest."

But at other times the general recovered his superb serenity. "We'll see. If it's no, I will at least have attempted the impossible. History will do me justice. Perhaps even sooner than anyone thinks."

. .

Under Couve's guidance, the campaign for the referendum was methodically organized according to a prearranged plan. Millions of throwaways were printed, free publicity appeared in the newspapers, subsidies were granted to deputies and district leaders. The fine electoral machine perfected by Pompidou was once more working smoothly. But fervor was lacking.

On April 10, exhibiting a stoical attitude, the general offered a long disquisition to his television audience. Systematically, he refuted the arguments of his adversaries and addressed himself to issues which the voters had never quite grasped in the first place. He talked about legal clauses and discussed the organization of the government. Then, brushing aside what he himself called "these boring details," he alluded to "the adventure."

"Allow me to add," he said, "that during the past thirty years, confidence has been at the base of our history. The vicissitudes that France experienced during this period — the least one can say about them is that they were very grave — were such that in order to serve her, I had to take exceptional steps, risks, in those domains where our destiny was being threatened. But I never failed to submit such undertakings to the approval of the country, and it has always backed me. The extent of the pitfalls and abysses we have avoided because Frenchmen granted me their wholehearted support whenever I asked for it will someday be realized."

One week later, all the opinion polls prophesied victory. They showed that 52 per cent would vote yes. "That's pretty close," de Gaulle sighed. The figures compiled by the Minister of the Interior were even more encouraging. The general, however, predicted defeat. Everything was slipping from his hands, even post-Gaullism. But the future was a matter of indifference to him. For the first time in ten years, he no longer controlled the succession.

April 17 and 18 were endless; they dragged on unbearably. The general seemed detached. One of his old companions came to see him and told him that all "his" men were prepared to "go through fire" for him. De Gaulle depicted France's deterioration: she would give up one thing after another — until the final disaster. With moist eyes, the visitor objected: "There's still a chance, my general. How many times have we seen the voters respond to your appeal at the very last moment?"

"Not this time. The referendum will be lost. It's already lost. Then new presidential elections will be held. There'll be one round of balloting, then a second. Pompidou will probably be elected. But afterward . . ."

Lapsing into silence, the general raised his arms to the heavens.

. .

The closer de Gaulle came to the zero hour, the longer grew the list of men whom he accused of treachery. He saw all his work demolished by a vast and obscure conspiracy. He cited names haphazardly as his resentment mounted. The lukewarm, the reticent, the cautious — all were included in this army of adversaries. Pompidou was one of them. Throwing caution to the winds, de Gaulle told this to some of his visitors. He was being deserted, betrayed. Shady deals were being made. People were conspiring against him. Then suddenly emerging from his dark thoughts, the general began to think about his victory. After all, there was a small, precious chance that he would make it.

He totted up the number of faithful. He began to plan the composition of his next cabinet. "I'll take Couve," he said. "You'll see, the French people will get used to him." Then he added: "We'll have to work quickly to get participation rolling after the summer is over. Maybe we'll hold another referendum. We'll need men who are determined."

But a few minutes later he would succumb again to his familiar devils. "Heads or tails," said the general, "but probably tails."

.   .

Five days before the referendum, the general closeted himself with Bernard Tricot, who had become the man people listened to the most, the confidant of good and bad times. Tricot, Couve, Jeanneney — none of them engaged in politicking. They were solid, reliable men. Five more days . . . Maybe this referendum, with its complicated wording, was a mistake; perhaps this time there was no basis for hope.

The general brushed aside his regrets. "Sooner or later it had to end. I expected it. I expected it from the moment I arrived at the Elysée more than ten years ago."

CHAPTER 25

Everything Is in Order

THE REIGN WAS DRAWING TO A CLOSE. During the past ten years, the general, Pompidou, the Gaullists, their enemies, and the French people had been wondering about what the future held in store. Various guesses had been made, all sorts of possibilities considered. These included the solemn coronation of a dauphin selected by de Gaulle. But no one had imagined that the general would be defeated in a battle he himself had sought and whose rules he had determined. No one imagined such an ordinary retirement, stripped of drama, of the element of surprise.

But the reality would have to be faced. By their votes, Frenchmen might put an end to the sublime adventure — just like that, for no reason, merely because ten or eleven years was enough. And the succession, so long disputed, would proceed in accordance with the stipulations of the constitution. Presidential elections would be held. Candidates were already in the field. Georges Pompidou headed the list.

· ·

At his listening post on the Boulevard de Latour-Maubourg, Pompidou was caught up short by events. The battle of the referendum called for a subtle strategy. He couldn't join the champions of a no vote without jeopardizing the support of the Gaullist army which would soon be taking orders from him. Nor could he advocate regionalism and reform of the Senate, or alienate all those moderates who today were voting against de Gaulle but who tomorrow might support Pompidou. Above all, he could not remain silent.

He was extremely cautious in everything he said. He discussed his feelings but not his convictions. For twenty-five years he had served de Gaulle. He would vote yes out of loyalty, out of sentiment. He of course knew, as he remarked on several occasions, that "Frenchmen have no love for traitors." In the few speeches he delivered during this final week, he skipped over the issues of regionalism and Senate reform.

Pompidou's attitude surprised and alarmed the already worried Gaullists. On April 25, Louis Joxe, who had been an interim minister in May 1968, talked with Pompidou at Lyon. He was shocked by the former premier's silence. "After all," Joxe said later, "there were some interesting ideas in the proposals submitted to the French people."

Two days before, at the tricolor-bedecked Palais des Sports in Paris, Pompidou attended the final Gaullist celebration. Malraux, too, was there. "You have to be a Malraux," Pompidou was to say later, "to draw a straight line between June eighteenth, nineteen forty, and the referendum of April nineteen sixty-nine. To start with the Resistance and end with regional reform — even the genius of Malraux wasn't enough to explain that!"

Although Pompidou protested his loyalty and his attachment, he couldn't prevent others from occasionally using his name against de Gaulle.

Perfidiously, some who advocated a no vote wished to raise the question of succession immediately, pointing to the fact that the former premier was available. How many Frenchmen would refuse to grant confidence to de Gaulle in order to bring Pompidou to power? This was the question now being asked by government officials, by party leaders, by the premier, and even by de Gaulle himself.

The rupture, the quarrel, the rivalry — these had become incontestable realities for all Frenchmen. Although the secret had been carefully guarded in the corridors of the Elysée, it was finally disclosed. More or less consciously, Frenchmen were participating in the drama by slipping the dagger of Brutus into Pompidou's hands.

Most of the Gaullists witnessed the spectacle without rebelling. Tired after having fought so strenuously under the general, of having labored so hard and been listened to so little, they hoped for a younger, fresher, more flexible leader. Indeed many, grumbling their discontent already, were mounting the attack.

The others, the old centurions, hoped to force Pompidou into making a sacrifice. They asked him to declare that he was renouncing his candidature even if de Gaulle were defeated. Christian Fouchet gave him this message from Foccart, one of the barons. And twice, once in public, once in private, Malraux begged Pompidou to yield.

"It is high time to realize," Malraux warned at the Palais des Sports, "that there is no post-Gaullism against General de Gaulle. Post-Gaullism must be based on the victory of Gaullism; none can be founded on its defeat."

But it was too late. Pompidou was deaf to all the exhortations of the general's old companions at arms. *La Nation,* a Gaullist publication, launched a final appeal: "No Gaullist candidate with a high sense of responsibility will find himself in a good position if the nays prevail."

. .

Pompidou remained silent. Years ago, he had been beholden to the general for power and the fulfillment of his ambitions. Today his national destiny depended solely on the people of France. He explained his position to a group of deputies: "What can I possibly say? If the general is beaten, there will have to be a Gaullist candidate. Am I not capable of winning the election? Am I not in a position to preserve the Gaullist legacy? Who else is there? Debré? Couve? You know very well that the French people won't vote for either of them."

Then, with a passion that carried conviction, he added: "I never wanted this referendum. I never wanted the question of succession to be raised under such conditions. I was the first to come out in favor of postponing things for two or three years. I would have liked a smoother transition — less abrupt. It's too early, too early," he repeated.

With fine precision, Pompidou proceeded to enumerate the dangers to which the general's departure would give rise. "Malraux is right," he said. "A victory for the nays would jeopardize my own plans. But I have a duty to fulfill to Gaullism and to the French people." To a Gaullist leader, he declared with great emphasis: "Believe me, to succeed the general is a very dangerous undertaking for someone who is not himself an historical personality. I would have liked to prepare for it calmly; I wanted to work, to meditate and observe. I was in no hurry. Why should I be? I had visualized a normal transition, without clashes or complications. I knew perfectly well that the general's defeat would decrease my own chances. But I can't help it. If de Gaulle leaves, Gaullism must remain. And that's my responsibility."

He had already perfected a strategy based on patience, reconciliation and flexibility. The referendum upset his plans. Frenchmen would split into two camps. Before, Pompidou had hoped to have Giscard and many others like him on his side. Now they would join the nays. Pompidou had no way of knowing whether he could get them back.

"I had already announced," he stated on one occasion, "that I would be a candidate for the presidency of the republic. I have no reason to retract. But when I had hoped that the election would be delayed as long as possible, I was sincere."

He defended himself for being ready. No one could ever be completely prepared for such an overwhelming responsibility. But holding the premiership under General de Gaulle for a period of six years, especially during the May crisis, represented the kind of apprenticeship that no one else could boast. He did not seek refuge in false modesty.

Times had changed. Three or four years before, it was the general who called all the plays. In those days, he could have insured the election of any heir of his choice: "Even his horse," Pompidou remarked, "remember, even his horse." Now, should he be defeated, were he to be removed from power by popular edict, de Gaulle would no longer be able to determine the destiny of France according to his own wishes. He would be condemned to silence.

People appealed to Pompidou's generous instincts. But he was as hard as stone. The fate of France should not be affected by sentimentality. That was a lesson he had learned from the general. "Nothing that I say or do will alter the course of events," he insisted.

His kind heart? Pompidou had not forgotten all he owed the general. But his humiliation in July, his unpleasant comedown, the sordid maneuverings during the Markovic affair, the snubs — all these freed him from any obligation. The de Gaulle he had admired so much, whom he had served and loved, belonged to the past. "I will vote yes out of loyalty to my past and to my future."

He was a Gaullist, to be sure. But Gaullism, he believed, had been disfigured since May 1968. He had been a Gaullist in 1948, at the time of the R.P.F., in 1958 during the war in Algeria, in 1962 and in 1965. The referendum of today was no more than a paltry caricature of the great undertakings of the past.

Or else de Gaulle looked upon the referendum as a convenient pretext for withdrawing. "That's not entirely out of the question, after all . . ."

The end of a reign. For five, six, perhaps seven years, Georges Pompidou, the son of pedagogues, the grandson of peasants, had been waiting for this moment. But now he displayed no impatience, no fever, nor even any emotion. "Let's wait until Sunday," he advised his loyal followers.

Then he added, "If the referendum is lost, what follows will be difficult; our cause might even be compromised."

. .

It was Wednesday, April 23, 1969. On the first floor of the Elysée, the general presided over his six hundredth, maybe his six

hundred and twentieth, cabinet meeting. For a last time he allowed
his tired eyes to look about him, above the heads of his men, many
of whom had deserted him. What did it matter? Amid the church-
like quiet, each of the ministers discussed problems of state. Seated
opposite Couve, de Gaulle remained remote. From time to time he
leaned toward André Malraux to whisper something in his ear. The
two veterans nodded and shrugged, as if they were already reviewing the long road they had traveled.

All the items on the cabinet's agenda were taken care of. The
premier said a few words. All eyes were turned to de Gaulle. The
chief of state sat up in his armchair, unfolded his hands, and said in
a voice that betrayed no emotion: "Presumably, gentlemen, we will
meet here again Wednesday next. Unless between now and then
the vote of the French people should put an end to a chapter of our
history."

Then, after thanking his ministers once again, the general, looking
relieved, stood up and strode quickly to his office.

That day, at one o'clock, de Gaulle lunched with his family. The
meal was consumed in silence. No one dared to revive chagrins that
were all too obvious.

Then, as he drank his coffee, the general launched into another of
his recapitulations. Everything was clear: the majority would refuse
to vote yes. In a few bitter phrases, de Gaulle designated one of
those who would be responsible for his defeat: Georges Pompidou.
He now was certain of this: his former premier's display of impatience during the past few weeks would cost him anywhere from
three to four per cent of the votes. Someone whispered the word
"betrayal." De Gaulle acquiesced. But there were other renegades,
not only Giscard but even Gaullists, yes, even Gaullists. Why be
surprised at that? What politician could be expected to smother his
ambitions forever? The general briefly summarized past developments: it was he who had made Georges Pompidou into a statesman. It was he who had appointed Valéry Giscard d'Estaing Minister of Finance. And there were others: ministers, secretaries of

state . . . The honors and privileges he had distributed during the past ten years — they were simply legion.

"The soup, always the soup."

.   .

The next day, April 24, the publication of the latest statistics confirmed the general's sad prognostications. The *Figaro* gave much space to opinion polls showing that 53 per cent of the voters would vote no and that 47 per cent would answer in the affirmative. All the newspapers predicted defeat, some with vengeful overtones. De Gaulle tried to be philosophical. He read the declarations issued by various politicians, noting the spread of the conspiracy within the Gaullist clan. It was time to turn the page. The general received one of his former advisers and said to him with gentle resignation: "If it's yes, that will be fine. But if it's no, that too will be fine."

Now de Gaulle spoke of his imminent departure with a touching coldness. He would leave with dignity, as he had always intended to do. He would devote his remaining strength to his last task: the writing of his memoirs. Complacently, he mentioned all the things he would do when he retired. He made plans for the future. He instructed his collaborators to put some order into his latest files. Most of his papers had been sent to Colombey on May 29. He would leave nothing behind. And he would take his memories with him. These last ten years, at least, belonged to him; no one, no one could take credit for a single part of that period. De Gaulle had performed his duty. Alone. Alone, as he was today.

A few Gaullist shock troops were secretly advocating a fight. Their newspapers bluntly announced that the general's departure would not take place without disturbances and violence. At the Gaullist headquarters on the Rue de Solférino, a clandestine mobilization was planned for that Sunday evening. Informed of this, the general remained indifferent. At the age of eighty, he had no hope of returning to power.

"Sooner or later the old society of this country must embark upon a new road. When that happens, Frenchmen will understand me and will render me justice. But I am quitting power without any nostalgia, believe me; and without any thought of returning, at my age, to the disorders of a civil war. I will do nothing to promote any fresh upheavals. I leave it to others to have regrets, or remorse. I am leaving with a clear conscience."

Friday, April 25, was of course a somber day; the sky was heavy with storms and rain. At the Elysée, bags were being packed. Everything would be ready when the time for departure came. The general gave Tricot very explicit orders. As soon as his tenure of power ended, everything had to be cleaned out, the place had to be left in order. "Remove everything," he said. Nothing was to remain, not a file or a paper, nor an employee. The doleful task of dismissing everyone and thanking them for the general devolved upon Tricot. Between de Gaulle and the state, no bonds were to subsist. He would be an ordinary old man; he wanted no honors. And especially no income. Let the Minister of the Army find a small office for his secretary and his aide-de-camp, that was all.

De Gaulle repeated these instructions to his premier. He handed Couve a sealed envelope. This was the communiqué in which the general announced his resignation. Couve was to keep the envelope in the pocket of his jacket for two days. He was not to open it until he had been authorized to do so, Sunday evening or the following Monday.

The general was calm and very grave. He had one last sacrifice to make, one last rite to perform: the recording of a televised appeal that would be broadcast to the French people that night. Once again the large drawing room at the Elysée, with its tapestries and its crystal chandeliers, was transformed into a studio. Technicians were plugging in projectors and electronic cameras. The directors of national television and the Minister of Information was there. De Gaulle appeared, sat down at his place, greeted the various people present, and allowed the make-up men to prepare his face for the cameras. Photographs of these last historical moments were snapped. But they were veiled in a kind of mist.

Silence. The cameras were turning. Applause. The great voice was raised one last time. It already sounded distant. As one minister remarked, it was impossible to listen to him without "a bit of heartache." For thirty years, in his speeches, his messages, his appeals, de Gaulle had always been able to influence the course of events to suit his own purposes, whipping up energy, stirring people, unleashing passions. But today all that one heard was the poignant plea of an old hero, manifestly prostrate. As de Gaulle spoke, he revealed some of his bitterness.

"When the tape recording was over," Joël Le Theule later related, "we all remained silent. We hoped that the general would request a second recording. We feared that his message would prove ineffectual. But without a word, the general went to sit in front of the receiving set. I hesitated to take my usual place next to him. He said, 'Come here, Le Theule, come and sit down.' The tape was played back. The general gazed at the television screen. Then he stood up, still saying nothing. Finally he turned to me and said: 'Well, Le Theule, everything's gone down the drain. As for the future . . .' But he didn't finish his sentence. He shook hands, murmuring his thanks. I watched him go off to his office escorted by two of his collaborators."

.   .

Having acquitted himself of his final task, de Gaulle was in a hurry to leave the Elysée, his gilded cage, for good. He wanted to forget the troubled faces, the pitying looks that accompanied him wherever he went, that hovered over him, never allowing him a moment of peace.

Everything was in order. As he was to explain to two of his confidants before driving off, he left a legacy that the whole world could appreciate: solid institutions that made it possible to govern this turbulent country — provided one had the will to do so; a

France that was peaceful, free, respected throughout the world; a favorable balance sheet with credits as well as debits; in short, an exemplary situation that might inspire future statesmen if they too set their sights high.

"As for myself," de Gaulle added, "I intend to remain entirely aloof from whatever happens here — no matter what the future holds."

The general, followed by Madame de Gaulle and his aide-de-camp, descended the majestic Elysée stairway a last time, striding across the blue carpet without fanfare, just as if he were going to Colombey for his usual weekend.

At the bottom of the stairway he met General Lalande, the head of his military cabinet, who said in a cheerful voice: "See you Monday, my general."

"Certainly not, Lalande, certainly not."

CHAPTER 26

Fear Once Again

FEAR. FEAR, DISCREET AND UNACKNOWLEDGED, as the momentous evening of April 27 neared. No one ventured to believe that it would be a Sunday like other Sundays, with families strolling in the streets and couples dawdling at café tables. Policemen were patrolling the school buildings that served as polling places. Mysterious rumors circulated among members of Gaullist action groups. A demonstration of young people, faithful disciples of de Gaulle, was scheduled for late in the afternoon. People arranged to meet with one another on the Champs-Elysées or in the Latin Quarter. Reliable regiments had apparently been placed on a wartime footing. The two principal trade union organizations saw to it that their alarm bells were in good working order. On the Rue de Solférino, where the militant Gaullists of 1948, 1958 and 1968 were gathered, motorized policemen were on patrol duty. But nothing else met the eye.

All these preparations proved needless. The Parisians, and along with them the entire French people, were about to part from de Gaulle without a whimper. The much-talked-about rupture, feared for so long by some, feverishly awaited by others, suddenly turned out to be a mere formality, an inevitable epilogue.

. .

The polls closed at eight in the evening. Five minutes later the fact of the general's defeat became apparent as the computers announced preliminary figures. Between bites, the voters listened to the results and then returned to finish their dinners. The house in Colombey was lit up. A long night began at the Matignon.

The first current-event buffs were already arriving at the ground-floor and second-floor rooms of the Matignon. Closeted in his office with a few associates, Couve kept tabs by both radio and interministerial telephone on the piling up of the no votes. Brittany and Alsace were not flooded by nays. But in all the other provinces, and especially in all the large cities, confidence was denied de Gaulle. Nations, like gods, sometimes experience such short-lived revolts; they must be accepted stoically. In the face of disaster, the premier never lost his perennial air of boredom and nonchalance. He was not surprised, merely worried about the possibility of disorders here and there. He was eager to avoid scuffles. They would leave a bad taste. Any demonstration, even a Gaullist one, would not be appropriate on this day of mourning.

.　.

At first the premier refused to call Colombey. Even on election nights, the general did not like to be disturbed by the ringing of a telephone. In any case, he had made all his arrangements before leaving. At the Elysée, Tricot was mounting guard in de Gaulle's office, thus insuring the permanence of power that had virtually ceased to have any legitimacy.

In a drawer, within reach, Couve had placed the white envelope containing the general's communiqué. But no one knew exactly when it was to be opened. A long discussion about it ensued between the Elysée and the Matignon. For a number of reasons, the premier hoped that the chief of state's resignation would not be made public until around four in the morning. At that hour the shock would produce fewer repercussions.

Around eleven that night, Tricot decided to call the general. He told him about Couve's wishes. But the general was adamant. He refused to consent to any delay. His communiqué would be publicized at midnight.

The Matignon was lit up as if a party were in full swing. Plates and glasses were being handed around. Ministers, deputies, functionaries, society women — all were discussing the defeat. The television had been turned on, the radio was blaring, there was a great deal of noise.

"Shortly before midnight, the premier, after a last conversation with Tricot, opened the envelope," Le Theule later recounted. "He was obviously surprised by the coldness of the communiqué. There were only two typewritten lines: 'I am ceasing to exercise my functions as President of the Republic. This decision will take effect today at midnight.' Below was the long, slanted signature, *C. de Gaulle*. We lost no time. The communiqué was published by the Agence France-Presse at eleven minutes past midnight."

. .

All eyes were on Couve de Murville. Some Gaullists were demanding the resignation of the cabinet. "After all, we simply cannot collaborate with Poher, with the general's victor," they said.

Couve considered this for a few minutes. Then he went into his office, closed the door and called the general. The conversation was brief. For the last time the premier consulted his chief. The two men were not to meet again for three months.

. .

At the Quai d'Orsay, Michel Debré spent the sad evening surrounded by the handful of people who made up his little court. At midnight he read the general's communiqué. His head in his hands, Debré remained silent for a while. Then, recovering his composure, he looked up and said: "Now we'll start to fight for Pompidou — without any hesitation."

Duty called. There wasn't a day to lose. De Gaulle was gone, but the Gaullists remained. Debré, too, called Colombey. His voice calm, the general said: "Well, what's there to do, Debré? You can't win every battle. We defeated Vichy, we defeated the O.A.S., but we failed to make nationals of the bourgeoisie."

. .

That night a few blows were exchanged in the Latin Quarter, a few cries were emitted on the Champs-Elysées. Then Paris went to bed. Ministers who happened to be in the provinces returned to their offices, traversing the peaceful capital in their black limousines. Was this the sum and substance of the much dreaded "split," of the long feared "chaos"? Couve and Foccart sent the militant Gaullists off to bed. It was an ordinary, rather warm, cloudless spring night.

The Gaullists remained. Their dismay was not long-lived. Another battle was about to begin; this time it was their own.

Leaving behind his small weekend house in Orvilliers, his books, his billiards and his dog, Georges Pompidou returned to Paris.

The Gaullists were waiting for him.

CHAPTER 27

The Letter

THE GENERAL returned to his "desert." After eleven years of strident shouts and political bombshells, he would have to reacquaint himself with silence, solitude, the sounds of the birds — with country life. The change was sudden. On Monday, April 28, de Gaulle immured himself in this memory-filled house and severed his last links with power. Only one visitor — Jacques Vendroux, Madame de Gaulle's brother — crossed the police-guarded threshold of "La Boisserie."

The general faced his humiliation. France and the entire world were reacting to his defeat. The press, radio and television deluged readers and listeners with explanations and posthumous praise. De Gaulle aired his disappointment. Unconscionable acts of treachery had caused his downfall. Someday he would tell "the whole truth" about these last weeks, about the "conspiracy." Then Frenchmen would open their eyes, and perhaps the general would still have a chance to savor the sweet taste of revenge.

Meanwhile he remained silent, listening absent-mindedly to his brother-in-law's comments.

· ·

In Paris the Gaullists were learning to live without de Gaulle. There were no lamentations, no tears. The faithful, thrown back on their own resources, were at a loss to know which path to follow. The silence was stifling.

On the Boulevard de Latour-Maubourg, Pompidou was discovering a new kind of solitude, the solitude of power. Journalists, deputies, men of good will, all were crowding into his antechamber, waiting for a statement, for an order. Ever prudent, Pompidou continued to meditate. People everywhere were hoping that he would announce his candidature that very day. But the former premier said to his colleagues: "There's no hurry. First, I'll try to contact the general. Give me one more day."

Advice was heaped upon him. He was urged to go to Colombey or to send one of the barons, Olivier Guichard perhaps. Guichard had served as liaison once before, in 1958. Pompidou, however, rejected the idea. From a political point of view, a meeting with yesterday's defeated leader would not be helpful. On the contrary. One of Pompidou's lieutenants offered this explanation: "It's better for Pompidou to avoid giving the impression of being tied to the general. After all, Frenchmen have just voted to reject de Gaulle. They want a change."

After weighing the pros and cons, Pompidou telephoned Colombey. He did this purely as a matter of courtesy, for he harbored no illusions. He knew the general much too well to expect any encouragement. So he did not persist. The general of course had his pride, but Pompidou also had his. "The general will remain on the sidelines," Pompidou said. "He will do nothing either to help or hinder a Gaullist candidate."

.   .

Pompidou had no intention of waiting. He would announce his candidature as soon as possible in order to get the jump on his rivals, whose numbers were growing. He didn't want the impression to get around that the Gaullists were reluctant to bestow the title of Dauphin on him, a title that had been his for a long time. But in order to show proper deference for the "decencies," he took one day, only one, to do this. The mourning would last twenty-four hours, no more. Such had been customary during the period of the monarchy.

He was already plotting his strategy and planning his campaign. Like de Gaulle, he would not be the man of a single party, group or faction. He would not choose his allies; they would come to him. He would set up his own headquarters, staffed with men who were discreet and reliable — his own men. The page had been turned. He was embarking upon a new phase of his career, a difficult one, but with free hands and no debts.

The failure of the referendum would constitute a handicap. Logic demanded the election of someone who had been de Gaulle's adversary, or in any event a man who had voted no. There were Poher, Giscard, Pleven, Mollet — to mention only a few who qualified.

Pompidou was determined to be the first to take the stage. At nine-thirty on Tuesday morning, he announced his candidature in a laconic communiqué. Then, speaking to newspapermen, he justified his action by stressing the word "duty." It was scarcely twenty-four hours since the general officially quit the presidency. Pompidou had consulted no one, warned no one, not even the premier in power, the executor of the Gaullist will. Couve would learn of Pompidou's candidature by reading the communiqué. To be sure, it wouldn't take him by surprise.

Throughout that Tuesday Pompidou paid calls. In the morning he went to the Gaullist party's political headquarters where Chaban-Delmas, Frey and Debré welcomed him with open arms. In the afternoon, in the presence of 280 Gaullist deputies gathered in the Salle Colbert, he shouted: "Those who like me will follow me. As for the others, I have no desire to force them to do likewise."

. .

Memories are awkward things. The general had left behind an empty stage, the Elysée, upon which the interim president, Alain Poher, stepped timidly. The presidential palace had been stripped of all reminders of de Gaulle. But the general himself was not yet absent. Should he utter a word, even from afar, the ambitions and plans of others would be immediately affected. His army remained; it embraced 46.8 per cent of the voters who had said yes.

That Tuesday Bernard Tricot went to the Boulevard de Latour-

Maubourg on a mission which he himself described as "very delicate." Everyone knew that during the past year there had been a series of misunderstandings between Tricot and Pompidou. But Tricot could not forget that throughout a seven-year span, his career had been furthered by Pompidou. It was the former premier who had suggested to de Gaulle the appointment of Tricot as secretary general of the presidency.

The mission appeared to be a rather simple one: to forward to Colombey a letter from the Gaullist candidate. Tricot assured Pompidou that the message would be delivered to General Xavier de la Chevalerie, de Gaulle's former chief of staff and the most discreet of diplomats.

But Tricot could not promise that Pompidou would receive an answer. Pompidou didn't expect one. His letter was a corrective gesture, nothing more. It enumerated the reasons for Pompidou's candidature — his duty — and stated his desire to insure the survival of Gaullism or, as he put it, its "continuance."

"Some very fine, moving phrases," General de Boissieu, de Gaulle's son-in-law and Pompidou's friend, remarked confidentially.

.   .

His conscience at rest, the candidate went to work. On Wednesday he signed an agreement with Valéry Giscard d'Estaing, who had himself momentarily considered the idea of competing for the top job. Pompidou's alliance made with a man whom the general's faithful followers had dubbed "the traitor" produced dismay in the Gaullist camp. Some saw it as the first sign that Pompidou was turning his back on de Gaulle.

Capitant, naturally, was the standard-bearer for the diehard Gaullists. There had been no mention of Couve as a possible candidate. "And I myself never thought of it," said the premier.

Capitant, who had resigned as Minister of Justice on April 28, gained the allegiance of disappointed, faithful Gaullists. But at this point he hesitated. General de Boissieu came to see him and tried to dissuade him from becoming a candidate. He mentioned the letter Pompidou had sent to Colombey and stated quite positively that his father-in-law would not like to see the Gaullist army decimated so soon.

. .

One had to live and try to fructify the legacy. Pompidou claimed that his was a painful, trying and difficult task. De Gaulle, at the age of eighty, rejected by the people, had left. With dignity. The only possible way to avenge him was to give him a Gaullist successor. "I won't really be a successor," Pompidou protested. "No one succeeds General de Gaulle. But everyone knows that I have been a Gaullist for twenty-five years. That's enough."

The general, forgetting his chagrin for a moment, had answered Pompidou's note by return mail. The exchange of letters was a carefully kept secret. During the summer of 1969, de Gaulle made only a brief allusion to it. In the course of a conversation with a former minister who had gone to Colombey on a pilgrimage, he remarked: "Pompidou wrote me on the morrow of his candidature. I told him: 'You are free.'"

The general's answer, which Xavier de la Chevalerie brought back to Paris, was not limited to these three words. It was a sad but serene letter. De Gaulle said that he approved of his former premier's decision but indicated he would not intervene in any way in the forthcoming campaign. He mentioned casually that he "feared" that Pompidou might be reproached for statements he had made in Rome.

The general had forgotten nothing. The hour for pardon had not yet struck.

A few days later, to a journalist who questioned Pompidou about the public manifestation of the quarrel — his now famous outburst in Rome — the former premier admitted: "I feel somewhat remorseful about it, I must confess."

But actually he felt reassured. De Gaulle intended to say nothing. Later, perhaps . . .

Part VII

ABSENCE

Glory is like a circle in the water,
Which never ceaseth to enlarge itself
Till by broad spreading it disperse to nought.

Henry VI, *Part I, act 1, scene 2*

CHAPTER 28

Two Departures

CHARLES DE GAULLE was an exiled king. More than forty years before, when he taught at the Ecole de Guerre, his superiors reproached him for his lack of involvement in things and people. His life was one long voyage from garrison to garrison, from Trier to Paris, from London to Algiers, from the Rue de Solférino to the Elysée Palace.

Now, in May 1969, he was back in the house at Colombey which had been his home ever since the prewar years. It served as a refuge, a redoubt for his solitude. Here in the setting that had witnessed his "crossing of the wilderness," the general was reminded of old sorrows. One day a journalist asked him where he had ever felt free and more or less happy.

"At the Elysée?"

"Oh, surely not."

"At Colombey?"

"No. We bought this small property because it was not far from the military centers of eastern France. But mainly because it didn't cost very much."

The house is large, furnished haphazardly with pieces that were inherited or acquired, and where the furniture — Louis XIV, Napoleon III, English or rustic — does not look authentic, perhaps it isn't. It's a family house where grandchildren and great-nephews used to spend their holidays. God willing, de Gaulle would also end his days here. After the failure of the referendum and his resignation, there would be no more career nor any other home.

A long, high wall discourages indiscreet curiosity-seekers. The entrance way, guarded by a couple of policemen, would be opened only two or three times a day. As an aide-de-camp explained to one inquirer: "The general always wanted to separate his public from his private life. Today all that's left is his private life."

In the early days of his retirement, de Gaulle freed "his" men from his tutelage: Tricot, Foccart, La Chevalerie, General Lalande. All took turns coming to lunch at his home. They confided the latest news to him. His reaction was always the same: "The page has been turned. What happens next is no concern of mine."

Commander Flohic, the last aide-de-camp, was to stay for a few weeks before embarking on the *Jeanne d'Arc*. The general retained only a cook, a maid and a chauffeur. From the state, whose chief he no longer was, he wanted nothing. Couve, who still performed the functions of a premier, insisted that he accept at least his pension as former President of the Republic: "My general, this will in no way affect your freedom."

De Gaulle refused. He was not one of those who liked money. He wanted neither honors, privileges nor a pension. He would live on his own income, on the royalties from his books, and on the proceeds of a farm he owned in northern France. He consented to accept only one of his rights: the use of a small apartment on the Avenue de Breteuil which the Minister of the Army placed at his disposal. A small office hung with gray-beige cloth and furnished with a wooden desk was also set aside for him, but de Gaulle warned: "I won't be using it. I have nothing to do there."

He received voluminous mail. By letter or simple cards engraved with his name, he answered his old companions. His sentences, with their elegant classical cadence, expressed keen bitterness. Stagnation, he declared, compromised the future of a country. Frenchmen did not understand him today. But soon perhaps . . . He sincerely believed that his defeat was the result of a world movement that would continue throughout the current era. But this was of small comfort to him.

The dark days were still too close. Alain Poher was installed in the Elysée. Georges Pompidou was launching his campaign. The general decided not to witness the contest for the presidency because in the course of it his name was bound to be invoked. He therefore decided to go to Ireland, a neutral country (Switzerland was a refuge for speculators and fallen sovereigns) — insular, Christian, the land of some of his ancestors.

Often, as one of his intimates has related, he would allude with ironic tenderness to the Irish blood that coursed through his veins.

Preparations for his departure were made in great secrecy. Even the French ambassador in London, Geoffroy de Courcel, an old and faithful companion, was not informed. All the details were settled with Couve through the good offices of the veteran diplomat, Xavier de la Chevalerie. This was to be the latter's final assignment in the service of the general. De Gaulle allowed the government to place a special plane at his disposal.

Between himself and France — his beloved France — he put an ocean of sadness.

. .

The Gaullists had suffered a shock — especially the little, obscure Gaullists who were derisively dubbed "old army boots." The general was gone. They were orphaned, "traumatized," as one of them put it. They felt a certain remorse at still being alive and well, secure in their jobs, with all the satisfactions that went with their positions as deputies, senators, economic advisers or cabinet attachés. Was it possible to be a Gaullist without de Gaulle? This was the question they kept asking themselves. For years their adversaries had been predicting that the Gaullist party would fall apart, that members would quarrel with one another — in short, that the party would offer the French public the same sorry spectacle so often witnessed before — and that the Gaullist party would become "a political party like all the others."

The Gaullists were the symbols of a legacy. Family unity was the very thing that de Gaulle had repudiated, leaving behind a group of three hundred deputies as well as ministers, well-placed friends, an organization, a treasury, and a flag with the Cross of Lorraine. Should such a phalanx be thrown away? For ten years the general had been their guide, their source of pride. One of their leaders, who was subsequently to become a minister, said in a quivering voice: "We would have walked through fire for the 'great man.' It's true that he made our lives unbearable: he exacted impossible sacrifices from us. But he was our general."

Pompidou presented himself before them in all modesty. He would not "ape" de Gaulle, he promised. He knew that among Gaullists, at any rate, he had no rivals. For twenty years he had witnessed the family's dramas and joys. He knew its big and petty secrets. He even knew precisely how so many who were quite poor only twelve years before had become powerful and well-to-do.

A few hours after the referendum, Pompidou began to assemble several of these people. Old veterans like Michelet told him: "The country is grateful to you for having averted the worst in May nineteen sixty-eight; you can count on us." He could also count on young deputies who owed their seats to him. And naturally the barons were on his side.

"Since nineteen forty-eight," one of them said, "there's been no break in our friendship. We immediately rallied around Pompidou."

All in all, rare were those who refused to rally to the side of the former premier. A few Gaullists among the old-timers said nothing — men like Joxe, Fouchet, and Malraux, immersed in their sorrow. Pompidou refrained from appealing to them.

The Gaullist army was intact. There had been no massive defections. And Pompidou could lead these men into battle, ignoring the grumbling that was audible here and there. Without him they would be lost.

The Gaullists would try to survive with the aid of all the political machinery — some official, some not — that they themselves had set up.

The enemy had already made himself known: Alain Poher, the man who had saved the Senate. "I knew immediately that the interim president would be a candidate," Couve said after the battle. "Every time I met him he spoke to me of his 'problems.' He obviously seemed to be enjoying the Elysée."

Poher had caused de Gaulle to flee, and within a few weeks had taken his place. In opposing Poher, the Gaullists could feel that they were avenging the general. They mounted their attack with light hearts. Euphoric, even the ministers around Couve, who continued to handle the state's business, took advantage of this forced coexistence to proffer their insults. On the day that the cabinet fixed the schedule for the presidential elections, a deputy was heard to say in Poher's presence: "There's no need to talk about the second round of balloting. There won't be a second round."

Only Couve de Murville, the diplomat, remained aloof from the fray — like the general himself, and like Malraux. "I saw no reason to intervene in the campaign," Couve later explained. "That was not my job. Besides, Pompidou never asked me to help him."

But the French people caught echoes of the cold war that was being waged at the summit between Poher and the Gaullists. Public opinion polls indicated that the nation disapproved. On May 12, one poll gave Poher 56 per cent of the votes on the second round. Nine days later another poll confirmed this trend. The Gaullist camp was worried and so were the party chiefs at the U.N.R. headquarters on the Boulevard de Latour-Maubourg. Hope was receding; uncertainty increased. Suddenly, the general's defeat appeared as a dark omen. No one could win on a battlefield where de Gaulle himself had been defeated. Malraux had predicted this. So had the general.

For a while Pompidou himself was shaken by these cruel alarms. To several Gaullist leaders, he declared quite candidly: "On paper, I'm licked. The French are ungovernable. The general often said so. Poher has logic on his side, and the tides of history."

To his friends in the cabinet, he offered the following advice: "No polemics with the interim president. It would be bad for our side."

Then, recovering his optimism, Pompidou brushed aside all the gloomy prognostications. He counseled his lieutenants: "Don't watch the opinion polls, don't look at the figures, I beg you! If you keep taking your temperature, you're bound to end up with fever."

He sounded the call to arms in the hope of inspiriting the vacillators: "It's not just for me, it's our legacy that's at stake. We must continue the general's work. If we don't, we'll be swept away."

Pompidou raised his voice, speaking with the authority of a leader, as he had done in 1965 and again in 1968. The Gaullists crowded into his antechamber, eager to offer their services. He decided everything, gave orders, and went off about his business.

He modified his strategy. Loyalty was obviously not going to pay off. De Gaulle was far away, invisible and silent. Pompidou began to plead for change. Some of the touchier Gaullists suspected him of disavowing their leader. As one of them caustically remarked: "Our Pompidou is becoming 'Poherized.'"

. .

Over and done with was the era of heroes and gods. Pompidou was "a man like other men." After de Gaulle, France would come back to earth. "And even lie down on the ground," a former de Gaulle minister added unkindly.

Politics was no longer to be a dazzling vision, a sacred mission. It was to become once again what it had been under the previous republics: a game, with its own rules, tricks, booby traps. André Malraux was already predicting that the future chief of state would be no successor of Charles de Gaulle but instead a descendant — or cousin — of the good René Coty. With good grace, Pompidou showed his willingness to become just such a man. During his premiership he had suffered from the general's stiff mien. He was now free to admit it. To parry tragedies, sudden thrusts, or haughty rejections, he preferred what he called flexibility, a patient stance that left room for accommodation. Loath to make solitary decisions, he opted for compromise, for cordial ententes, for friendly lunches in the course of which, especially during dessert, understandings could be reached.

The former premier was deliberately reassuring. He depicted a provincial France that would be good for people with savings accounts, for small artisans and shopkeepers. He mentioned the month of May 1968 only in order to exorcise the specter of disturbances and violence. He listened to the ordinary fellow, who like him was born in a small village, molded by the parish church and the communal school. Pompidou saw every one of them as a "fine chap" — a notion rather different from the general's.

For the moment, Pompidou attempted to present himself as the one statesman who could dispel the demons of fear. Systematically, the leading figure in the Gaullist camp increased the number of his vassals. He became reconciled with some of the general's enemies. And when the Gaullists objected, he reminded them stiffly that in May 1958 de Gaulle too had opened his arms to former enemies.

With something of the monarch about him already, like de Gaulle, he waged battle — his battle — alone. The campaign was run from the Boulevard de Latour-Maubourg. U.N.R. members and Gaullist deputies were urged to avoid excessive displays of zeal. Pompidou went off alone to the four corners of France. He refused to be escorted by the barons or by any of the Gaullist princes — the Freys or the Debrés. He had no desire to become a marked man, to be a reminder to Frenchmen of the past they had rejected. "I'm the candidate, it's my business," he repeated. "You can all attend to your own jobs, but no more than that."

When he entered his headquarters, he would look at the crowd that filled the antechambers to his office. There were former or future ministers, officials, cabinet attachés — quite a little court — burning to be of service so that tomorrow they too would be served. Remembering the silence that had reigned here four months ago, Pompidou murmured: "What a lot of people, what a lot!"

Inexhaustible, he traveled to Lyon, to Bordeaux. He was on television, on the radio. He spoke of an enlarged Europe, of the need to maintain the Senate, of commerce and small businesses, of repatriates from Algeria, of law and order. He quieted the malcontents who, in France, always constituted a large majority. He received their delegations in his small office. Seated behind a screen of cigarette smoke, he listened to all of them.

This presidential election, the legacy of the general, was an exhausting and solitary quest. But power was there, waiting at the end of a rough road.

CHAPTER 29

The Commander

A LONG DARK COAT thrown over de Gaulle's shoulders grazed the Irish soil. The general was accompanied by his wife and an aide-de-camp. At a respectful distance, a squad of journalists and photographers followed. In random fashion, he contemplated a corner of the sky, a beach, an old church. He shook hands with a few people, mumbled a few words in English, then climbed back into his car. Traversing small towns, he occasionally gave the slight salute, at once regal and military, that had so often aroused the enthusiasm of his own people. But there were no bravos, no shouted acknowledgments here. This was no tourist trip. Nor was it a rest. De Gaulle had come to Ireland in search of refuge, to escape from France, from his state and his people. And from the fever of elections. Twice a week only, newspapers and letters from Paris were brought to him. He read them with affected indifference. The French were not fighting in the streets. They were listening to Poher and Pompidou, to Duclos, the communist, and Deferre, the man from Marseille, to Krivine, the revolutionary. Frenchmen had completely forgotten him.

Madame de Gaulle showered him with discreet attentions. The general was locked up in his sorrow, in the sun and fog of Ireland, amid flowers, beautiful scenery, and peaceful, winding roads. These were days of mourning. "The general is sad," Madame de Gaulle confided. "He needs time to recover. He has done his duty. Everything must come to an end."

From Ireland, de Gaulle sent his oldest companions brief letters that were posted in Paris. He immersed himself in his cruel thoughts. The French people had refused to make an effort, they had turned their backs on renewal, on change. An era was ending. A new period, one of administration, was about to begin. This was a pause in French history. Then some fine day, France would resume her advance. Despite his despair, the general preached hope. This old nation that had known glory and suffering would never cease to astonish. The epic was over. Succession was out of the question, regardless of who won the presidential elections. No "continuer" would follow General de Gaulle. He had been discharged from his historic mission by the vote of the people. He was leaving behind a fund of assets that the future President of the Republic would be free to utilize or to squander. He had taken with him his "personal equation" and his own legitimacy, which sprang from June 18, 1940, from London, Algiers, Free France, the Resistance — and from May 13, 1958, from all the battles waged with and on behalf of France.

What would follow? The general kept informed but remained silent, saying nothing even to his aide-de-camp. He forced himself to refrain from uttering a name lest the tone of his voice or a movement of his lips should betray his true feelings. His memories had stopped on April 27, 1969. He claimed to be ignorant of anything that might have happened since that day. His letters were addressed only to old intimates, men of discretion, his confidants, who had nothing more to do with the current scene. Or else to military men, who wouldn't dream of gossiping. To a few of the old grumblers who were still deputies, he sent a few lines, merely to tell them he had not forgotten them, that perhaps he would see them someday, when the proper time came. But in the meantime they must be patient, as he himself was.

Madame de Gaulle, however, was not held to a like reticence. She sent letters to the "ladies," to the wives of the Gaullist princes. She urged them to join Pompidou's ranks right away. Loyalty was a duty, particularly for women. In Madame de Gaulle's opinion, loyalty was a Christian virtue, acquired at birth. To members of her family, she wrote more simply: "Better 'Pompon' than Poher."

No one knew whether her conclusions were her own or those of the general.

.   .

On June 1, 1969, the first round of the balloting gave Georges Pompidou a total that exceeded his expectations: 43.95 per cent of the votes. On December 5, 1965, the general hadn't done as well. But de Gaulle did not yield to such comparisons or recollections. The outcome merely proved that the mass of the faithful — the "army" — came to about 45 per cent of the French electorate, re- gardless of whether the test took the form of a referendum, a presi- dential election, or a legislative one. Unfortunately, de Gaulle had often had the opportunity of verifying this fact.

Three days later, Bernard Tricot joined the general in Ireland. In one of the rooms of his inn, de Gaulle closeted himself with his last remaining confidential agent to study the figures. During the last ten years, this had been a ritual. Now, of course, the general was acting out of habit and instinct. He launched into a series of prog- nostications, just as he had always done. But he did so without pleasure or enthusiasm. He predicted Pompidou's victory, which wasn't difficult to do. He didn't admit that it was a consolation for him, but by an adjective or an allusion he nonetheless congratulated himself over the fact that the French people had not again fallen victim to the charms of someone like Poher.

On June 15, 1969, Georges Pompidou — the man whose career had been fashioned by the general — was of course elected Presi- dent of the Republic. In his hotel in Ireland, de Gaulle did not wait to hear the final results before going to bed. He showed neither pleasure nor resentment. According to one witness, he seemed quite detached. Perhaps he really had no strong feeling about the outcome. It wasn't until several weeks later that he made a few sar- castic remarks about his former premier, much to the amusement of his visitor.

For the moment, at any rate, Pompidou was the chief of state.

Charles de Gaulle, as an exemplary citizen, owed him respect. He sent Pompidou a message whose language he had carefully weighed. It was neither too short nor too long, neither warm nor frigid. He wanted the missive to be read by everyone; he also wanted to make sure that no one would read into it any oblique message. "For both national and personal reasons, I send you my cordial congratulations."

His disciple acknowledged the message in the same vein.

To his aide-de-camp, de Gaulle nonetheless admitted: "Once again, France has been lucky."

. .

For fifty-five days, the general's armchair at the Elysée had remained empty. Unlike the interim president, Pompidou was not at all timid about occupying it. The office where power was exercised, on the first floor of the Elysée, with its tapestries, its gilt, its three windows overlooking the park (rarely opened because of the noise), was a familiar setting. He had spent innumerable hours there. And not only as a visitor. "As early as nineteen sixty-two, yes, as soon as I came to the Matignon, I knew that one day I would be President of the Republic," he later admitted.

The new chief of state allowed three days to elapse before moving into the Elysée. One of the days was a historic one — June 18 — and it belonged to the general. Pompidou was willing to comply with the niceties of protocol, but he warned: "I want everything to be as simple as possible."

There would be no coronation, but merely something simple — de Gaulle's stipulation in 1966.

His first task was not a new one. A government had to be formed. How many ministers and secretaries of state had he appointed since May 1958! Jacques Chaban-Delmas was officially the leader of the team, the second in command within the hierarchy. During the winter and spring, he had been told at various times by Pompidou, very discreetly of course, that this would be his job. Of all the men in the Gaullist family, he boasted the greatest advantages. He was one of the barons, he was everyone's friend, and he had had a glorious record in the Resistance.

Esteeming Chaban-Delmas to be too weak, de Gaulle had given him only honorary tasks throughout his reign. His promotion would not cause a ripple, Pompidou predicted; no one would resent it.

One week after Pompidou's election, the government was ready for business. The chief of state had made many people happy; he had appointed many ministers, many secretaries of state. But neither Couve de Murville nor Malraux figured among the new members of the government.

A new reign was beginning. It was summer.

. .

The Gaullists had already forgotten not only their recent fears but also the victory to which they owed their jobs. Eight days after Pompidou was inaugurated, remorse set in. The family was not split, but it was divided between pride in having overcome a major threat to Gaullism and apprehension that all Gaullists would be taken to task by their hero. The prospect caused a tremor among the faithful. The general had become a legend. Henceforth he was their sacred symbol.

Everything done by the new regime served as a pretext for solemn admonitions. The Cassandras were only too delighted to predict that Pompidou's reign would be but a return to the old republic, to the one that existed before May 13, 1958. This would constitute the supreme repudiation.

Such suspicions irritated and worried Pompidou. After all, de Gaulle had had no hand in making him his heir. And he was neither the oldest nor the best known of the general's companions. He felt a constant pressure to protest the purity of his intentions.

"Can anyone believe that I would forget the twenty-five years of my life spent at de Gaulle's side? I know the meaning of loyalty better than any other Gaullist. No one has to preach to me."

It was whispered that de Gaulle would soon be in Paris, that he would intervene. An apartment in town, on the Avenue de Breteuil, was in readiness for him, and already a series of interviews had been scheduled — or at least so rumor had it.

Frigidly, Pompidou said: "Anyone who believes that doesn't know the general."

CHAPTER 30

The Rule of Silence

AFTER IRELAND, the general went back to Colombey, to his silent house. The flood of letters had not ceased during his absence. People wrote to him in remembrance of June 18, or to ask for an interview. He answered, or had someone answer for him, thanked the writers but encouraged no one. De Gaulle was trying to fill his solitude. From now on, each day would be like every other, until the last. His life as an old man would be divided between history and nature; it would also be spent in the companionship of Madame de Gaulle, for thirty years a discreet witness of his aspirations and disappointments. The general was regulating his life in military fashion so that no event would intervene to alter its course. One day a week was devoted to his Parisian collaborators, one or two afternoons a week to visitors or members of the family. On Sundays he would take a longer walk than usual; sometimes he would go on a picnic, far from curiosity-seekers, from outsiders. "Now I'm a country gentleman," de Gaulle would say, undaunted.

From his window he watched the changing seasons alter the earth's colors. How many cycles, how many years were left to him?

The press and television depicted a world that was changing. Violence and folly were gradually engulfing the five continents. What would be the fate of France amidst all these convulsions? And whose voice would she heed? From his retreat, de Gaulle cast an anguished glance at men, peoples, and leaders, who were blindly marching toward disaster. Gently, he yielded to the sadness of age, recapitulating all the stages he had gone through since the turn of the century.

Immediately after his return from Ireland, de Gaulle went to work, planning the book he was to write, calculating the time it would take to complete it. With touching humility, he confided his uncertainties and misgivings as an author: "I'm neither a Tacitus nor a journalist. I'm not one to scatter my commas haphazardly."

He had his work and his book, and he was eager to get on with them. He still had a good many things to say and do. He began to work in accordance with a rigid schedule.

Naturally, he remained keenly attentive to the news that was brought to him each day. The squabbles and everyday decisions associated with power did not interest him. But he did take some interest in the essentials: the institutions, the independence of France, the stability of the state. He watched for any telltale signs of deterioration. The future seemed gloomy: recourse to the referendum as a mechanism of government would be dropped, the idea of structural reforms abandoned. Thus, if compromise followed compromise, France would gradually decline.

The general confided his prophecies to his rare visitors — old companions of Free France, members of his family, military men, former ministers. In passing, he directed a few barbs against his favorite targets, politicians and "traitors"; nor could he always resist the temptation of mentioning names. But he would quickly right himself, insisting: "None of this concerns me. It's a new chapter. France will experience many other such periods which neither you nor I will live to witness."

The general was kept informed of the doings of his faithful adherents. Instead of disavowing them, he let it be known that "Anything you do will be fine."

They were all free to interpret such vague remarks as best they could. He spoke amiably of his adversaries and of Pompidou's ministers. His words were full of ambiguity, but that had always been his way.

His informants reported that some of his companions were hesitant. De Gaulle was not moved by this. The portfolio of a secretary of state or some other honor would do much to allay such anxieties. "After all, men are only human."

The general made plans for the future, spoke of the trips he would like to take before his life was over. Occasionally he even issued warnings: "If they go off on the wrong road," he said, "then, yes, I would intervene. I'm not dead yet."

His heirs owed him everything. But he owed them nothing and was enjoying his freedom. In any event, he firmly declared, he would not make his voice heard through intermediaries. He had no need of a spokesman. He had never needed one before, he had no need of one now.

．　．

A week after his election, Pompidou, now settled at the Elysée, confided to a friend: "Now I must find my own style. It won't be easy."

As the general's premier, or as the deputy from Cantal, he had merely needed to be natural, and cautious. The voice of Charles de Gaulle could be depended upon to drown out all the others. As a candidate, Pompidou had tried to project a certain image of himself. The making of a president was admittedly a science. But there were no preordained rules for the man who was fated to be the general's successor. The new chief of state had no example to follow. He had to find his own way. "We must not go from one extreme to another — from Louis Quatorze to Louis Philippe," he told the members of his entourage. "We want neither grandeur nor boiled cabbage."

The Fifth Republic boasted a setting worthy of the general. During ten eventful years, the President of the Republic had left his mark on the workings of the state. He had set his own pattern. Laws, custom, protocol, the selection of high officials — all these had been the work of de Gaulle. Pompidou inherited a France that was not really his own; and yet he could not change it suddenly, lest he be accused of betrayal.

He began by modifying the daily routine at the Elysée. The running of this huge establishment became more flexible, less military. Pompidou was not loath to express his nostalgia for the kind of life he had enjoyed for so long — evenings with friends, the small fashionable bistros, leisure. Sundays he spent at Orvilliers or at Cajarc. In the evening, he occasionally escaped from the presidential palace and sought refuge in his apartment on the Quai de Béthune. Or he would go out to dinner with his son, Alain. He told a minister: "I wish I could wear a sweater, like Giscard . . ."

In a thousand tiny details he showed himself to be exactly what he was: a Frenchman of modest origins who had reached the top with all its attendant honors and power, a man convinced of his good luck, a lover of the good things of life — fine paintings, good food, good friends. Plumpness in de Gaulle was the price he paid for aging, for fatigue and the responsibilities of power; in Pompidou, it was a sign of contentment.

But it was mainly in his speeches and official remarks that the new chief of state signaled the difference between his tenure of office and the ten memorable years that still obsessed the French people. On the eve of his first press conference, he said to a group of his associates: "I will try to be simple, clear, and precise. Above all, I will shun theatrical phrases."

He talked about the housewife's bread box and her washing machine — pretty soon he might even allude to her boiled cabbage. De Gaulle, on the contrary, had always been loath to appear before the public in his "bedroom slippers" or his "pajamas." This required no effort for Pompidou. On the other hand, the epic thrust, the historical allusions, were not his meat. When he spoke in praise of Napoleon, one immediately sensed the professor's copybook. After Châteaubriand, here was a populist prose that smacked of the peasants' soil. It was studded with carefully prepared bits of humor. De Gaulle spoke the language of the glorious past; Pompidou addressed himself to each of his children rather than to the people at large.

A bourgeois king, but still a king. From the outset he laid claim to all his prerogatives. He warned his listeners: "My conception of presidential power will be strictly patterned after that of the general."

And to Chaban-Delmas, he spoke his mind even more explicitly: "In our republic, the premier is constantly on the firing line, the man who steps into the breach. I know something about this from personal experience. The President of the Republic is elected for seven years; he must husband his energy; he may want to change the composition of his cabinet. He must therefore intervene only in emergencies or crises."

People told him about the state of mind of the parliamentary majority but he paid no attention. That was Chaban-Delmas's domain. Pompidou merely warned of one thing: no one had the right to challenge his presidential mandate save the sovereign people. When the leaders of the Gaullist party came to dinner at a time when the shadow of the general still hovered over the faithful, he declared in a threatening tone: "If any of you would like to see me quit, you will have to say so frankly."

He demanded to be kept informed of all the government dossiers; the interministerial council meetings at the Elysée increased in number, just as they had done during the war in Algeria. In the early weeks of his rule, he expressed annoyance at having been taken unawares by certain of "his" premier's decisions. He had no intention of arbitrating quarrels or inaugurating flower shows; instead, he intended to govern.

"I am well aware," he said, "that ever since May nineteen sixty-eight, demands and resentful outbursts have always been directed at the Elysée rather than at the Matignon. It's up to me to deal with them."

From the very beginning of his presidency, Pompidou devoted most of his attention to foreign affairs. This was a domain in which he was a neophyte. He knew he would be judged by de Gaulle if not by the French people. Diplomatic dispatches were brought to him at the close of each day. He took a certain pleasure in studying them and making notations. During the past thirty years, as everyone knew, he had enjoyed learning new trades. And diplomacy was certainly new to him. On his trip to the United States — responding to an invitation that de Gaulle had accepted — Pompidou hoped to appear a worthy "continuer." In Chicago he expressed indignation at an insult hurled at him but aimed at France. The general was watching him.

He was in no hurry. His apprenticeship was to last for months. Little by little and step by step, he intended to discover the secrets of power, the clue to success. As time passed he would correct his errors, depending on the nature of events.

"You mustn't be the prisoner of a given style or manner. Look at the painters. When they hit upon a certain style, they feel they have to keep at it forever. They end up by copying what they've already done, by imitating themselves, and then their paintings deteriorate."

He was settling down for a long stay. He could afford to take it easy. For ten years Frenchmen had worried about the future, about what would happen after de Gaulle. Georges Pompidou would be careful to avoid giving them cause for such anxiety. He had been elected for seven years, and he would remain for the entire duration of his mandate.

Moreover, he seemed pleased at the prospect.

.   .

What a fine leave-taking!

After weeks of understandable bitterness and disappointment, General de Gaulle at the age of seventy-nine, was discovering serenity. All he still had to do was to put the finishing touches to his epic in an equally noble manner. At Colombey, his visitors encountered a man both calm and "delighted," as the general himself insisted when alluding to his departure. His fine exit was irreproachable and in harmony with the rules of democracy. It also was a great compensation for the trauma of April 27, 1969. After so many storms successfully traversed, Charles de Gaulle had reached port, in a small French village identical with so many others.

Madame de Gaulle was quite dumfounded: "After the referendum, the general gave way to sadness, as he has so often done. Today he has turned the page. He is devoting himself completely to his writing."

De Gaulle had rid himself of other burdens. The present no longer weighed upon him. Every day he spent hours in his tower. He glanced through the newspapers rapidly. Visitors were becoming rare. To everyone the general offered the image of a man more stable and self-assured than ever, of a "new man," as one of his former ministers put it. This solitary life amid the quiet of his fields, in the shadow of a modest belfry, suited him better than the turmoil of the Elysée. At Colombey de Gaulle rediscovered the simple pleasures he had so long forgotten: the smell of leaves in the woods of Blinfeix or Clairvaux, the freshness of morning fogs, silence interrupted only by the sound of a door banging or footsteps in the hall, the surprise of finding himself still living, after so many deep wounds. The general no longer paid any attention to the rumors from Paris. His companions and ministers still wrote to him — perhaps a little less often. He now answered only briefly; sometimes he even "forgot" to answer, particularly if the letters were too insistent.

On November 21, 1968, on the eve of his birthday, he had his entourage issue a communiqué in which he promised never to break his silence unless "certain people, claiming to be his heirs, make statements of which I cannot approve."

By these words he put an end to the hopes of some of his companions. He even declared that he would never again go to Paris, unless he did so secretly in order to embrace his son or daughter. "Whatever I say or am presumed to have said, my actual or supposed words will pass into the public domain." He alone would be the author of any message to be left to future generations. But what could he say? And who could tell if his words would ever again have their magic effect? De Gaulle was determined to express no opinion about the France of today. This unshakable decision was communicated to everyone who came to see him. Thus, no matter what happened, his promise would not be broken. Were he to approve or criticize his successor's actions, he would be helping not only to undermine the prestige of the chief of state but also to weaken the state itself. In addition, he would be damaging his own past. The Fifth Republic continued to exist. It was his work.

When Pompidou's name was uttered in his presence de Gaulle would turn to the Champagne sky or glance at the tips of his trees as they were being shaken by the wind.

The general had retired. He would not return to public affairs indirectly because of some remark he might recklessly make or some secret he might casually divulge.

And, after all, what a fine leave-taking it was! At every moment, de Gaulle would pause to congratulate himself on having left power upright, intact, at the close of an adventure that had no precedent. So often he had feared a degrading flight, a shameful end. He couldn't help being pleased, and he said so. Providence had managed things well. He might have been defeated in 1961, at the time of the generals' putsch; or in 1962, at the time of the referendum; or again in December 1965, or in May 1968. Or even, and this would have been worse, he might have ended up in a hospital bed! The French nation had rejected him in a free election. The mission of Charles de Gaulle could be terminated only by a verdict that emanated from the people.

History still remained. Sooner or later, it would render him full justice; of this he was certain. It was to history, to posterity, that de Gaulle would entrust his image. It was for history, for posterity, that each day he covered blank sheets of paper in his long, slanting hand. The time had come to explain what had happened from May 13, 1958, to April 27, 1969. The events that had preceded these eleven years or those that would follow — well, they were not for him to judge.

Alone at last, de Gaulle could put his past in order, without hope, but also without regret. A few months after his departure, in a letter to that prince without power, the Comte de Paris, he remarked that men will never know what they bequeath after they are no more.

Only after death would each individual know his own destiny. For the great ones as well as for the little people, the truth was until then out of reach.

CHAPTER 31

The Time of the Orphans

EVERYTHING WAS IN ORDER. Ever since his return to Colombey, the general had been awaiting death — his old enemy, his old comrade. It was against death, against time that he waged his last battle. He would soon be eighty.

Far from the sumptuous "house of sorrows," the Elysée, de Gaulle could reign peacefully over a village of 391 inhabitants. He affected to live as they did, to interest himself as they did in the condition of the roads, the inclemency of the weather, the change of the seasons. On Thursday, October 22, 1970, the general discussed mushrooms with the barber who had come to cut his hair: "There are quite a lot of them this year. But right now, the chanterelles are all that's left."

"That's true. But we still have a lot of field mushrooms, my general. And soon the giant puffballs will be coming."

"Oh, the puffballs! They'll show up later. And if they're going to be good, we'll have to have a lot of rain."

At Colombey, affairs of state consist of such things as water, electricity, and the condition of the soil. As a landowner, the general shared all these concerns. On Monday, November 9, the day he died, he dispatched his chauffeur to a village farmhouse to fetch René Piot, to whom he had written a note the week before. De Gaulle wanted to go over the lease of his farmlands with Piot. He wanted to settle the question immediately; for a man of his age, every day counted — this was now his constant refrain. Nothing should be put off until the following day.

At two-thirty that afternoon, de Gaulle ushered René Piot into his study. In this small, austere, book-filled room, at his desk facing the window, he was writing history after having made it. He asked his young neighbor to be seated in an armchair to the left of his desk. He offered him a cigarette, lit it himself with a small pocket lighter, then came directly to the point.

"Well, Piot, this is the time for the renewal of leases. As I mentioned in my letter, I don't want to farm out my lands anymore."

Intimidated, René Piot assented. The general continued: "But if you would like to do so, you may take care of the plot in the middle, the land that belonged to you and that became mine when it was reallocated. You could make money there and keep your harvest. In exchange, you would keep up my fields for me. Do you agree?"

"Yes, my general. Thank you. In other words, you're giving me a gift."

"Oh, remember, if you will, to remove the old fences. They're falling down."

"I'll do it at the end of this month, my general."

The matter was settled. De Gaulle questioned the young peasant, just as he used to do when he toured the provinces. Approximately 300 yards from La Boisserie, Piot was building a metal enclosure. You could catch a glimpse of it behind the trees of the park.

"What about all that work?" the general asked. "Is it moving along?"

"It's slow going. I'm behind schedule. I won't be able to put the animals there next winter."

"It must cost a lot of money, all that."

"Yes, my general." Suddenly cautious, Piot added: "It's very expensive."

The interview was over. De Gaulle accompanied his neighbor to the door, as he used to do with his ministers. Nodding his head, then gazing at the somber sky, he said: "This year, autumn came all of a sudden . . ."

Piot ended the sentence: "And winter will soon be here."

The general sighed and shrugged his shoulders: autumn, winter, falling leaves and the first frost were henceforth the only things he could be sure of.

. .

"All is calm here," de Gaulle wrote that day to a cousin of his.

Calm. When the summer of 1969 had begun, the silence of La Boisserie had been hard to bear.

Visitors still came, but more and more infrequently. They included his publisher, one or two former ministers, André Malraux, an industrialist friend, a few retired generals.

The family was far away. Commander Philippe de Gaulle, who was in charge of the naval aeronautics of the tenth maritime region, was stationed in an office of the maritime prefecture in the fortified enclosure of a château at Brest. His wife, Henriette, divided her time between Brittany and Paris, where three of her four children were in school. Philippe de Gaulle, forty-nine, the image of his father, in no way owed his career to the general. He had joined the Free French naval forces at the age of nineteen. Leading an artillery company, he had participated in all the campaigns — Normandy, the Vosges and Alsace. He had served in Indochina and Algeria, like all the men in his profession. At Brest he commanded 6200 military personnel and 611 civilians.

The Boissieu family, daughter and son-in-law of General de Gaulle, came to Colombey more often, usually about twice a month. Elisabeth de Boissieu, closeted in her room on the second floor of La Boisserie, had typed her father's manuscript. For the hundredth time, General de Boissieu, trailing his father-in-law, explored the forests of Blinfeix and Dhuits. Their daughter Anne, small and blond, was named after the child the general had loved so much.

The family observed certain traditions: the intimate *tu* was not used; rarely were personal confidences exchanged; each kept to himself his pleasures or sorrows. They communed with one another in an atmosphere of Christian peace and devoted themselves to the service of their country. During meals the conversation was humdrum. At no time was politics — as habitués of Parisian cafés understood the term — discussed.

In the hermetically sealed domain of La Boisserie, Madame de Gaulle held undivided sway. At Colombey she was at home, among her own people and her memories. She ran a very reduced household and was attentive all day long to the wishes of her husband. She was silent and amiable. She planned the menus, supervised the cooking from the corner of her eye, sent the chauffeur to pick up the half week's supply of meat from Renard, the butcher in Bar-sur-Aube. Renard would ready the package in advance and place it in a willow basket. The rest of the time, save for walks in the forest, Madame de Gaulle knitted and wrote letters to her cousins and nephews.

Monday, November 9, was a cool, gray day. In Paris the wind was blowing. In Colombey there were intermittent showers. The world was beginning to read the memoirs of one of the century's great men, Nikita Khrushchev. In France, elements of the noncommunist left were again planning to unite, following an appeal launched the day before by François Mitterand at Château-Chinon. A group of Gaullist deputies, stirred to action by two of the general's former ministers, had decided to review the contemplated regional reforms to which the April 27 referendum had suddenly called a halt.

Yes, everything was calm. At ten o'clock the premier, Chaban-Delmas, assembled his four closest collaborators in his small office on the first floor of the Hôtel de Matignon, as he did every day. Once again, the current problem was decentralization, or at any rate communal reform. The government was gradually coming to grips with an undertaking that de Gaulle had once hoped would prove revolutionary.

At the same hour, on the other side of the Seine, Georges Pompidou had already arrived at his office. He had read the morning newspapers, annotated a few dossiers, and read the most urgent letters. Afterward, he would work alone. At twelve-fifteen he would receive the premier, as he did every Monday; and at lunch he would entertain the President of Gabon.

. .

Having arisen an hour earlier, General de Gaulle descended the wooden staircase of his house at Colombey and entered his study at the foot of the tower he had built before the war. Before sitting down, he glanced at the miners' lamps on the tables near the bookshelves and gazed through his window at the rain-filled sky, grazed by tree tops. He was wearing a dark gray suit and a dark tie, as he did every day. The morning was spent drafting letters which he would dictate the next day to his secretary. He thanked authors who had sent him their books, adding a personal note to each; then he settled a few business matters, like the one pertaining to his land which he discussed with his young neighbor, Piot. Next de Gaulle reread what he had written the week before. He had just finished another chapter of his *Memoirs.*

It was lunchtime. He had his coffee. Today the general had little to say. But Madame de Gaulle was accustomed to his silences. She kept quiet. The house felt somewhat chilly, partly because of the humidity that is so difficult to dispel in the houses of this region.

Winter would not be long in coming. The last dead leaves had fallen.

At three o'clock, after René Piot's visit, the general was once more seated at his desk. A methodical writer, he was not one to wait for an inspiration, which at best is capricious. Rather, he worked with military punctuality and "knocked out" the two or three pages he had set for himself. His long slanted handwriting covered the pages, leaving almost no margins. There were many deletions. De Gaulle had reached the year 1963. He had come to that gloomy period of history so troubled by economic and social difficulties. It was the year of strikes. His government was still young.

. .

A little later the general interrupted his work to take a short walk around the park. How often had he done this — two or three thousand times? Then he returned to his desk. Around five o'clock he left his study to have a cup of tea with Madame de Gaulle. For thirty years he had never failed to observe this ritual, no matter how urgent the affairs demanding his attention. At the Elysée his collaborators had always managed to arrange for a twenty-minute break in the middle of the afternoon so that he could have his cup of tea. The general often appeared without any advance notice in the midst of a group of ladies whom his wife was entertaining. Madame de Gaulle was always amused by their looks of surprise. The general would enter easily into their conversation as if he hadn't noticed their astonishment. He would then proceed to drink his tea, nibble on a biscuit or a piece of cake, make a few pleasant remarks, and finally return to his "sorrows," as he called official business.

But on this particular day, the tea was an unusually brief intermission, like the short walk around the house. De Gaulle was immersed in historical meditation, which more than anything else kept him clinging to life.

Only one change occurred that day to make him deviate from his customary routine. A direct line to Paris had been installed in his study. He called the Avenue de Breteuil where he had his offices, directly behind the Invalides. A secretary answered and stuttered a little when she recognized the "great man's" voice. However, it was to her that he wished to talk. He wanted to change the wording in one of the letters he had dictated before it was presented to him for his signature. Then he spoke to his personal secretary. He said that he would expect her the next day at eleven forty-five and asked her to bring along some notes that he needed for the next chapter of his memoirs, especially those pertaining to Christian Fouchet, the man he had named Minister of National Education in 1963.

The conversations were brief. The general, as everyone knew, did not like to use the telephone. His voice betrayed no sign of fatigue. But some residents of Colombey later claimed that the day before, at mass, de Gaulle had looked tired. One lady in particular, who happened to be seated directly behind the general in church, noted that he had remained seated when the other parishioners stood up.

. .

In the country, the day ends when the sun sets. Seven o'clock is the time for soup in the small Colombey world. The chauffeur, a former policeman by the name of Maroux, was on duty that week at La Boisserie. Having just entered the servants' dining quarters behind the kitchen, he hung his blue gabardine coat on the rack and sat down. In all probability there would be nothing more for him to do until the following day.

Evening set in. The lights went on in the village. At La Boisserie, behind its dark screen of trees, half of the windows showed lights. The chill dampness of the air was uncomfortably penetrating. On the second floor, Charlotte, the maid, was turning down the general's bed. Below, in the dining room, the cook, Honorine, was silently setting the table for two. A little earlier, Madame de Gaulle had gone to the kitchen for a quick look around. A blanquette de veau was to be the evening's menu. The general was very fond of these simple dishes. He also liked duck, which, he at times complained, the chef at the Elysée had never served. Since his retirement he had been rediscovering the pleasures of eating "tripes á la mode de Caen," stewed rabbit, cabbage, baked potatoes, and all those other homely dishes that unfortunately had been deemed unworthy of a chief of state.

The general was putting away his work. At the Elysée he had never "pulled out the plugs" until eight in the evening. Here he adopted country hours. At six-thirty he turned out the light on his desk and went into the library. His wife was already there. She had put her knitting needles aside and was writing a letter at her small Empire desk.

In one corner of the room the color television flickered but the sound was turned off. De Gaulle was still a voracious television spectator. Like his preferences in food, his tastes here tended to be simple and homely. And he never missed a news broadcast. These were the last echoes to reach him from the outside world, that world of unreason and madness from which he had retired forever.

. .

Before the evening meal, while playing a game of patience, he would sometimes listen absent-mindedly to the regional news that came on at seven. Games of solitaire helped him to shed the cares or sorrows of the day. "The general is creating a void," his aide-de-camp would say, as he watched him shuffle the cards.

It began to rain again, an almost invisible drizzle. La Boisserie, especially the library where two large logs were burning in the fire-place, was now almost too warm. The library was a rather large room almost in the center of the house. Bound volumes were on wall shelves, separated at midheight by portraits of Popes John XXIII and Paul VI. Fifteen or so photographs, standing side by side, were on a high table. Various replicas of the Cross of Lorraine rested on the mantelpiece. Family and historical mementos formed a separate jumble. There were gifts from foreign sovereigns — like the beautiful Isfahan rugs presented by the Shah of Iran — together with earlier acquisitions that Captain Charles de Gaulle had collected here and there as he moved from garrison to garrison.

Seated in a small, scarlet velvet armchair, the general was about to lay out his cards. Suddenly, he sat up straight, gripped his waist, and emitted a hoarse cry: "Oh, it hurts, it hurts, there, in my back!"

The time was three minutes past seven. In circulatory seizures, the pain is intense, like a sword piercing the body. De Gaulle immediately lost consciousness, fell sideways, his knees bent, his arms caught in the armchair. His glasses slid to the floor. Madame de Gaulle rushed over to him as soon as she heard his cry. She called for help. Charlotte, who was closing the shutters in the next room, ran into the library. "A doctor!" The maid went to the vestibule and picked up the phone. The young doctor of Bar-sur-Aube, the nearest town, was away on consultation, but his wife managed to get in touch with him. By then it was probably no more than seven minutes past seven. But of course no one thought to check the time. It is difficult to reconstruct the precise instant of the tragedy, given the many clues and the contradictory nature of the information.

While Charlotte was still on the telephone, Honorine, followed by Maroux, the chauffeur, came running into the library. Now time would have to be computed by seconds.

Madame de Gaulle proved amazingly calm. She knew exactly what was to be done. The general had told her often enough. She merely had to repeat automatically each of the things she had done twenty-two years earlier when her daughter Anne died. To the maid, who had come back into the library, Madame de Gaulle said: "You must fetch a mattress."

Charlotte went up to the second floor and stripped the grandson's bed. Meanwhile, Maroux loosened the general's tie and unbuttoned his collar. Less than three minutes later they were able to lay de Gaulle down on a mattress in the center of the room. The general had been unconscious for more than ten minutes. His breath, a light whisper, was barely audible.

Madame de Gaulle asked that the village priest be sent for. At La Boisserie no one knew that five weeks before, a telephone had been installed in the presbytery. Maroux jumped into the car and was off. An opaque fog enveloped the village. At the gate of the presbytery, the chauffeur rang the bell twice. A light was turned on in the kitchen, on the ground floor. Shivering with cold, the priest walked across the garden and saw the chauffeur standing there in the gathering dusk. "The general isn't feeling well," Maroux said. "Your presence is requested at La Boisserie."

The doctor, who had driven up in his own car, and the priest entered La Boisserie at the same time — between seven-twenty and seven twenty-three. The priest was asked to wait a few minutes in the large drawing room, where he quickly slipped on his violet shawl. The doctor went into the library, extracted his stethoscope from his emergency kit, and kneeled beside the general. De Gaulle was very pale. His pulse was all but gone, his breathing weak, his abdomen distended — all the symptoms of a ruptured aorta. The doctor of course knew that an attack such as this produced death within half an hour. Internal hemorrhages had obviously occurred. To leave no stone unturned, the doctor gave the general a shot. It was plain to him, however, that de Gaulle no longer felt anything.

It was the priest's turn to enter the library. Only a few minutes had elapsed since his arrival at La Boisserie. He too knelt beside the general, opposite the doctor. From his black bag he took a prayer book and a bottle of holy oil. Then he administered the last sacrament: "My son Charles, by this holy oil may the Lord forgive you for all the sins that you have committed. Amen."

General de Gaulle was no longer among the living. The doctor removed the stethoscope from his ears and looked up. Madame de Gaulle, completely immobile, stood near the fireplace. A moment later, Maroux pushed an armchair toward her, but with a movement of the head she indicated that she did not want it. "No one," the priest later recounted, "no one said a word." It was seven-thirty.

For fifteen minutes these six people did not move. Praying silently in the library, they remained close to the prostrate hero. The general's glasses had been picked up and placed on the bridge table. The cook, Honorine, had rolled her handkerchief into a ball and kept it pressed to her lips to stifle her sobs. "Only God is left," as de Gaulle used to say.

Madame de Gaulle broke the pious silence. In a voice that was remarkably steady, she gave her orders. "The general will be laid out in the drawing room where we put our daughter Anne."

Pushing aside the drawing room furniture, the cook set up a camp bed. Stretched out on the mattress, the general's body was carried to the drawing room.

Madame de Gaulle sent Charlotte to the second floor to fetch the general's uniform and the old faded flag that the family hoisted each year on the fourteenth of July. Rolled in its cover, the flag lay in a chest that stood near the foot of the stairs. Clutching her pearl necklace, Madame de Gaulle supervised the five people who were awkwardly dressing the general in his uniform — a simple khaki tunic with but a single decoration: the Cross of Lorraine. Charlotte removed the watch from the general's wrist and placed it reverently next to his glasses. Stoically, Madame de Gaulle watched her husband being clothed in the burial garb that rendered all men equal in the face of death. A true soldier's wife, she had steeled herself for this moment.

.   .

The general's body was wrapped in the folds of the flag. Madame de Gaulle herself went to fetch from her room a white rosary that was a gift from the pope. She fastened it around the general's folded hands. On a table, two candles burned in their copper holders. A silence that nothing would interrupt ever again reigned in the room. The still body, the pale, peaceful countenance, the hands joined around the rosary, the boxwood log in the fireplace, the two copper candlesticks — such was the scene. It did not belong to history. Rather, it portrayed the ordinary death of an old man in a small French village — the kind of death Charles de Gaulle had wanted. Now Madame de Gaulle could be alone with the man who, long before becoming the majestic spokesman for his country, had been her husband. The man wrapped in a tricolor shroud had belonged to her first; only later did he become a part of history, with its fame and glory. She asked the doctor and priest to say nothing to anyone for a few hours.

Alone, Madame de Gaulle prayed. In a few hours, she would have decisions to make; she would wait until her children arrived.

The village slept, unaware of the tragedy. Four kilometers away, at Rizocourt, a farmer, Monsieur Plique, had just died after seventy-seven years of hard work and tribulations. Madame de Gaulle was praying. General and Madame de Boissieu, accompanied by their daughter Anne, were on their way to Colombey. Philippe de Gaulle, who had been dining at the navy base in Brest, was alerted by his wife, Henriette. At first he considered requisitioning a military transport, but decided he would make almost as good time by train. He climbed into his compartment at nine-forty. The train was scheduled to arrive in Paris at six-eighteen the next morning. Everything was done in accordance with the general's wishes. As yet the death of Charles de Gaulle was exclusively a family affair, and so it would remain until sunrise. Arriving at Colombey at twelve-forty in the morning, the Boissieus joined their prayers with those of Madame de Gaulle. A little later, General de Boissieu, now head of the family, made the first telephone calls.

. .

In Paris the night has been an ordinary one. Around seven the next morning, Pompidou got the news from de Gaulle's son-in-law. Later, the French people could not quite understand why twelve hours had been allowed to elapse before the country was informed that the general was dead. They suspected political intrigue or foul play. All kinds of rumors circulated around the general's coffin. Actually, nothing of the kind was true. Living or dead, de Gaulle belonged to no one but his family, a family that for thirty long years had remained in the background. To be sure, he also belonged to France. But the private mourning had lasted throughout only one autumn night. At seven in the morning, when Pompidou was informed, the public and political mourning began.

Telephones began to buzz, people assembled to discuss the news. The Elysée and other government buildings now occupied the center of the stage.

Arriving at his Paris apartment on the edge of the Bois de Boulogne, Philippe de Gaulle tried to put some order into all the confusion. Who had informed the premier? Where was the general's will? Who was the heir? To whom, from his grave, had the general granted his blessing?

At seven o'clock Philippe de Gaulle telephoned his boss, Michel Debré, the Minister of the Army. At seven o'clock Pompidou broke the news to Chaban-Delmas and to a few other Gaullist leaders. At nine thirty-two, Mr. Watson, the United States ambassador, informed the White House. He spoke to Mr. Kissinger, the president's adviser. Twenty minutes later, President Nixon, from Flor-

ida, where he had gone for a rest, called Mr. Watson. "I will attend
the funeral," he said.

. .

Unaware of all the hubbub and emotion, Madame de Gaulle continued to pray on the ground floor of La Boisserie. Gazing at her
husband's closed eyes the night before, she had uttered a heart-
rending cry in the presence of the doctor: "He suffered so much
during these last two years!"

The members of the family had to resign themselves to opening
the doors of La Boisserie. That Tuesday morning, people began to
arrive. A veritable sea of human faces was to surge into the village
during the next few days. The first to enter the old house, now a sacred shrine, was Merger, the nice old village carpenter, his tape
measure in his pocket, fully aware of what was expected of him. He
had all the self-assurance of a skilled craftsman, an experienced artisan who had seen many men, women and children on their
deathbeds. Madame de Gaulle said: "I want oak, very good oak,
and a very simple casket."

In his wake came the mayor of Colombey, escorted by ten alder-
men, the prefect and the bishop. They were followed by the general's sister and his brother-in-law, and General Massu, "the scrapper"
— de Gaulle had fondly described him as "a simple man and a pa-
triot." Then came Michel Debré, the only incumbent minister.

In the presence of all these people, Madame de Gaulle exhibited
great calm. She alone knew whom the general would have welcomed and whom he would have forbidden entry to his house. It
was to her that the general had confided his last secrets. But at
lunch time, when she entered the dining room and saw the empty
chair, she could no longer contain her sorrow in front of her children. She asked her daughter, Elisabeth de Boissieu, to take her father's chair at the table.

Philippe de Gaulle and his three children finally arrived at La
Boisserie at three that afternoon. He had spent the entire morning
gathering information about plans for the official ceremony.

Now at last Madame de Gaulle could respect her husband's last wishes. All the members of the family were together. The time had come to close the coffin, to protect Charles de Gaulle from the eyes of the curious, to shield him from idle tears. Merger had done his work quickly, as was the custom in Colombey. By eight that evening, the carpenter's truck was parked in front of La Boisserie. With the help of Louis Mouton, a friend from a neighboring village, Merger carried the casket in. Made of oak, it had four handles and bore an aluminum crucifix. For the last time, the family gathered around the patriarch's body and kissed the forehead which had been anointed with holy oil.

Charles de Gaulle was stretched out in the coffin on a white sheet, a small horsehair pillow under his head. Madame de Gaulle asked Mouton to remove the wedding ring from her husband's finger. Then the coffin was placed on two footstools.

In a few minutes, the two carpenters would go to the house of the peasant, Plique, and do the same thing for him. They would close a coffin exactly like de Gaulle's. This was the way the general had wanted it. Perhaps he too would have preferred to be buried with no outsiders present, without flowers, speeches or tears — like this unknown seventy-seven-year-old peasant — and like his daughter Anne, twenty-two years before.

.   .

The French people were in mourning. Men, women, children, even de Gaulle's political enemies succumbed to sorrow. For six weeks, long lines of people made pilgrimages to Colombey. By bus, by car, even on foot, crowds of anonymous people made their way to the small country cemetery where the heart of the nation was still beating. Why did Frenchmen gather around Charles de Gaulle so belatedly, too belatedly?

Pompidou kept his feelings to himself. To the French people he exhibited a grave, dignified, solemn mien. "France has been widowed," he declared eighteen hours after the general's death. Then he publicized a document de Gaulle had entrusted to him sixteen

years before: the last wishes of Charles de Gaulle in regard to funeral arrangements. It was neither a testament nor a political message. Two other copies of the text written in the general's hand had
been given to the de Gaulle family. But it was Pompidou's copy
that Frenchmen read. In this way, the chief of state erased unpleasant memories and malicious rumors. He projected the image of a
man in whom de Gaulle had placed his trust long ago. The rupture,
Pompidou's humiliation, the anger of both men, were quickly in-
terred. Georges Pompidou now ceased to be the Dauphin, the successor, the heir; he became the president. It did not take him long
to make this known.

Bibliography

Bibliography

General de Gaulle

d'Astier, Emmanuel. *Les Grands.* Paris: Gallimard, 1961.

de Gaulle, Charles. *Complete War Memoirs of Charles de Gaulle.* New York: Simon & Schuster, 1964.

de Gaulle, Charles. *Documents.* Vols. II and III. New York: Simon & Schuster, 1960.

de Gaulle, Charles. *The Edge of the Sword.* New York: Criterion, 1960.

Lacouture, Jean. *De Gaulle.* New York: New American Library, 1966.

Malraux, André. *Anti-Memoirs.* New York: Holt, Rinehart & Winston, Inc., 1968.

Mauriac, François. *De Gaulle.* Garden City, N.Y.: Doubleday, 1966.

Georges Pompidou

Bromberger, Merry. *Le Destin secret de Georges Pompidou.* Paris: Fayard, 1965.

Rouanet, Pierre. *Pompidou.* Paris: Grasset, 1969.

Vallon, Louis. *L'anti–de Gaulle.* Paris: Le Seuil, 1969.

The Crossing of the Desert (1946–1958)

Elgey, Georgette. *La République des Contradictions.* Paris: Fayard, 1968.

Elgey, Georgette. *La République des Illusions.* Paris: Fayard, 1965.

Fauvet, Jacques. *La IVe République.* Paris: Fayard, 1965.

Soustelle, Jacques. *Vingt-huit ans de gaullisme*. Paris: La Table Ronde, 1968.

Tournoux, Jean-Raymond. *La Tragédie du Général*. Paris: Plon, 1967.

THE RETURN TO POWER (May 1968)

Ferniot, Jean. *De Gaulle et le 13 mai*. Paris: Plon, 1965.

de La Gorce, Paul-Marie. *De Gaulle entre deux mondes*. Paris: Fayard, 1964.

THE 1962 REFERENDUM

Goguel, François. *Le Référendum d'octobre et les élections*. Paris: Armand Colin, 1965.

THE 1965 PRESIDENTIAL ELECTION

Sainderichin, Pierre, and Poli, J. *Histoire secrète d'une élection*. Paris: Plon, 1966.

THE CRISIS OF MAY 1968

Alexandre, Philippe. *L'Élysée en péril*. Paris: Fayard, 1969.

Paillat, Claude. *Archives secrètes 1968–1969*. Paris: Denoël, 1969.

Tournoux, Jean-Raymond. *Le Mois de mai du Général*. Paris: Plon, 1969.

THE 1969 REFERENDUM AND PRESIDENTIAL ELECTION

Burnier, Michel-Antoine. *La Chute du Général*. Paris: Édition Spéciale, 1969.

Pado, Dominique. *Les 50 jours d'Alain Poher*. Paris: Denoël, 1969.

Schwartzenberg, Roger-Gérard. *La Guerre de succession*. Paris: Presses Universitaires de France, 1969.

THE GAULLISTS

Charlot, Jean. *Le Phénomene gaulliste*. Paris: Fayard, 1970.

Viansson-Ponté, Pierre. *The King and His Court*. Boston: Houghton Mifflin Co., 1965.